In the Beginning

MYSTERIES OF ANCIENT CIVILIZATIONS

The Sacred Science Chronicles • Volume I

ROBERT SIBLERUD

Sacred Science Publications
9435 Olsen Court
Wellington, Colorado 80549
(970) 568-7323
E-mail address: SacScience@aol.com

Other Sacred Science Chronicles
Keepers of the Secrets: Unveiling the Mystical Societies
The Sacred Science Chronicles • Volume II

Printed and bound in the United States of America.

Published by
Sacred Science Publications
9435 Olsen Court
Wellington, Colorado 80549
(970) 568-7323
E-mail address: SacScience@aol.com

First Edition

ISBN: 0-9666856-0-1

Library of Congress Catalog Card Number: 98-090685

Acknowledgements
Cover Art: Ron Russell (Copyright ©1998, Ron Russell)
Editing: Shirley Parrish
Copy Editing: Betty Taylor
Typesetting and Layout: Pat Alles
Support and Encouragement: Patricia Barnard
A Shared Vision: Maury Albertson, Ph.D.
Libraries: Colorado State University, University of Colorado

TABLE OF CONTENTS

1ST Written Language Identified

FOREWORD

Maury Albertson, Ph.D.*

My entire adult life has centered around the academic world both as a college professor and director of research at Colorado State University. I know firsthand the scientific conservatism that permeates the universities. While director of research at Colorado State University, I encouraged the faculty to involve themselves in research concerning new paradigms such as the paranormal or the mind-body relationship, ideas that were outside mainstream thinking. During my tenure, not one faculty member pursued my suggestions. Perhaps there was a lack of money, perhaps a fear of ridicule, and perhaps a lack of interest. I am sure their belief systems already were established by the time they reached the university, and to venture beyond was considered dangerous territory. My tenure as director of research saw great developments at Colorado State University, making it one of the most successful research universities west of the Mississippi River. However, my dream to do new paradigm research in the university setting had been unfulfilled.

In the mid 1980s my path crossed with Dr. Robert Siblerud, a health care professional who was doing research on alternative health at Colorado State University. We shared the same vision about scientific research in the area of the spiritual, paranormal, and related areas. Dr. Brian O'Leary, a former professor of astronomy at Cornell and Princeton Universities, shared this philosophy as well. Brian had been an Apollo astronaut, chosen to be the first astronaut to journey to Mars before NASA canceled the program. Brian had also become frustrated by the narrow belief system within the academic world.

The three of us wanted to do something about our academic frustrations, and we formed the International Association for New Science. It was our philosophy to embrace new areas of study in science and to be open to new approaches in the scientific field. We encouraged scientists to research the relationship between mind, body, and spirit and to understand the connection between the physical world and nonphysical world. New science was to look at the whole of a subject, incorporating both physical and nonphysical influences.

For ten years the association has sponsored international con-

Maury is co-founder of the Peace Corps.

ferences, such as the annual International Forum on New Science, to provide a platform for the new scientists and their new paradigm research. Hundreds of researchers have presented papers, published in the proceedings that accompany each conference. The International Association for New Science has sponsored specialty conferences on new energy, UFOs, and new agriculture. Its local society, the Society for Psi Research and Education, has presented countless lectures and workshops on spirituality, new science, and alternative healing. These educational programs have provided insight to the science of the future, both in the physical and non-physical worlds.

Bob Siblerud has been the executive director of the International Association for New Science for most of its existence and, therefore, privileged to the knowledge revealed over the past decade. With his background in new science, Bob has commenced his ambitious project of writing the *Sacred Science Chronicles*. His goal is to record this sacred knowledge of new science into a series of books that will be easy to understand for those on the path to enlightenment. The books examine both the physical and nonphysical worlds of reality.

In the Beginning is the first of the *Sacred Science Chronicles* and looks at the heritage of our past. With their limited belief system, today's scientists cannot answer many questions of ancient times. If one expands the paradigm, our ancient past can better be understood. *In the Beginning* does this very successfully by incorporating conventional science, spiritual knowledge, and knowledge from the ancients to help explain humanity's mysterious past.

PREFACE

In the Beginning is the first book of *The Sacred Science Chronicles*. The Chronicles summarize the important information gathered over the centuries regarding the areas of sacred science and provide an overview of selected topics. The goal is to help explain the relationship between the physical and spiritual worlds. Much of this is accomplished by chronicling historical and spiritual aspects of the ancient civilizations that help explain the mysteries. What is sacred science? Webster's dictionary defines sacred as worthy of deep respect that is inviolable. Sacred, according to Webster, implies something extremely dear to God or the gods. Science is defined as knowledge acquired by study.

I begin with the premise that traditional science does not understand all the laws of the universe. Modern science, based entirely on the physical realm, depends on results that can be replicated by using the current scientific method. It does not consider the nonphysical influence. For example, psychology originated as the study of the soul but changed to the study of human behavior. However, the advent of quantum physics scientifically shows that the mind can influence subatomic particles that influence our reality. Traditional science does not take into consideration a spiritual world: whereas, an underlying axiom of sacred science is that a spiritual world does exist. Because the spiritual world operates on a different frequency, one cannot apply physical laws to this realm.

Modern science has accomplished wonderful things within the physical laws of the universe. However, with the limited belief system of physical science, it is very difficult to explain paranormal phenomena. Today's science cannot explain mental telepathy, psychokinesis, UFOs, clairvoyance, the spiritual, astrology, and apparitions such as ghosts, only a few examples. Modern science choses to ignore these phenomena and investigates only a limited segment of universal law. What it can not explain, it ignores. Granted, contemporary science is still evolving, but it is time for scienctists to expand their limited paradigm of reality.

Sacred science, on the other hand, looks at the totality of universal law. All phenomena that occur must operate under some universal law. Mental telepathy, proven to exist, suggests an energy that can travel faster than the speed of light. If true, we now have a new paradigm beyond traditional science. One cannot ignore the sound principles upon which orthodox science is based. Researchers should try to incorporate the rigor established by traditional science when exploring the new paradigms. However, if there is an unknown set of laws that govern this new paradigm, the techniques, beliefs, and criteria established by modern science need to expand or change to accommodate for this new paradigm.

In the Beginning looks at unexplained mysteries of ancient civilizations, which apparently operated on a paradigm much broader than our present one. The ancients spoke about the reality of the gods. This book explains who the gods were and gives evidence they may have been of extraterrestrial origin. Megalithic architecture was a hallmark characteristic of their ancient civilization. Modern science would have a difficult time, and perhaps an impossible time reconstructing these cyclopean structures. How did the ancients fit these gigantic polygonal megalithic blocks so precisely together? How were the great pyramids constructed? Some of these mysteries suggest the ancients possessed technology far ahead of ours in many respects. They used the principles of sacred geometry such as pi and phi, a secret known by mystical societies such as the Freemasons.

Sacred science does not ignore indigenous people's legends of their ancient past. Often these legends answer the questions that modern science cannot. The spiritual world was very important to the ancients. Their lives, vocations, and architecture often centered around the spiritual. Orthodox science does not accept anecdotal evidence as science. Personal experiences, an important part of reality that should be studied with vigor by the scientific community, are largely ignored. Are UFOs and ghosts a fabrication of a person's imagination? Modern science would have one believe so. A doctoral dissertation at the University of Wyoming found that individuals who claimed contact with UFOs were psychologically normal but had psychological scars, much like those of rape victims.

There is much evidence of large continents that existed in the Atlantic and Pacific Oceans. Modern scientists have done their best to ignore this evidence because they cannot conceive, in their limited belief system, of earth changes causing so much destruction in a short time. Historians have also suppressed important knowledge, as they too are confined by a limited belief system. As I shall show in chapter eleven, America was inhabited by Europeans long before Columbus. Too much evidence can no longer be ignored.

Over centuries, the state and church have often suppressed knowledge They are often more concerned with preserving the status quo than seeking the truth. To protect truth and perhaps their own lives, those who knew the world was not ready for such truth formed secret societies. These mystical societies are discussed in Volume II of *The Sacred Science Chronicles,* titled *Keepers of the Secrets.*

I dedicate this book to the pioneer researchers. Many suffer the ridicule of the scientific establishment when their ideas have not conformed to the current belief system. Most of these researchers used traditional scientific methods in their investigations. Even playing by the rules of traditional science does not guarantee their findings will be accepted. They have sacrificed their reputations, careers, and financial status to investigate a nontraditional hypothesis. These are the true scientists, not those who are dedicated to preserving the status quo. The world needs these pioneers to plant the seeds, making it easier for future researchers to become accepted. It often takes generations for modern science to catch up to the pioneers.

One should not believe everything in this book at face value, but use it as a stimulus for future research. Much information in the book is based on other people's research and their attempts to explain the mysteries of the planet. Hypotheses by the researchers are often presented throughout the book but much of the information presented needs furthur research. For some, the book may be contradictory to their belief systems, and perhaps those people are not ready for it. We are all on the path to God, and sacred science examines this path and acknowledges that we are all at different stages on this godly path. For others, the book may plant a seed that will open doors to this marvelous universe.

As the ancients were aware, we live in an evolving universe. At the same time, our soul evolves and hungers for the truth of the many universal mysteries on its path to perfection. Knowledge is one key to evolvement, and I hope *The Sacred Science Chronicles* will help provide answers to the relationship between the spiritual world and the physical world.

Robert Siblerud

Chapter One

LEMURIA
Mother of Civilization

The ancients considered a lost continent called Mu to be the mother of all civilizations. Few people, including scientists and archaeologists, have heard of this ancient land in the heart of the Pacific Ocean. Before its breakup, Mu's borders ranged from the west coast of North America to the east coast of Africa. Archaic records found in China, Tibet, and India suggest that this was the location of the Garden of Eden, where humanity as we know it originated more than 200,000 years ago.

Lemuria, another name for Mu, left a legacy of clues to its existence. This continent seeded all the world civilizations, according to ancient records. Because science and religion cannot fit this prehistoric civilization into its current paradigm, proper research into this continent's rich heritage has been avoided. Geologists have a difficult time believing that major earth changes in Lemuria and Atlantis could happen so quickly. They are taught to believe such changes occur over millions of years. To properly research this ancient civilization, one needs to incorporate a holistic approach based on geology, archaeology, ancient writings, and native legends. What one discipline cannot provide may be answered by another. Each has left its clue, and the wise scholar will incorporate all to facilitate the research.

The geology of South America, archaeological research on Easter Island, the ancient writings of India and Tibet, and the legends of North American natives give evidence of a great civilization that existed west of North America and east of Asia. Incorporating all these disciplines gives us a picture of what probably happened to the lost civilization of Mu.

ANCIENT WRITINGS

Few researchers have dedicated their lives to the investigation of a lost continent in the Pacific Ocean. James Churchward, a rare example, has written three books from his fifty years of researching Mu, the lost continent. His interest began in India during the 19th century while assisting a high priest of a Rishi temple. The priest was highly knowledgeable in archaeology and language of the ancients. Churchward asserted that the priest had "greater knowledge of those subjects than any other living man."

The priest possessed writings in an ancient language. He and two other priests in India understood this dead language, called Naya-Maya, believed to be the original tongue of humanity. All the ancient writings regarding Mu were written in Naya-Maya. Many of the simple inscriptions hid meanings designed especially for the Naacals, a priestly brotherhood. The motherland Mu had sent them to the colonies to teach the sacred writings, religion, and science. For two years the priest taught Churchward this language in order to decipher bas-relief inscriptions found in the temple.

The priest told Churchward additional tablets were stored in the secret archives of the temple, and he had not examined these ancient tablets because they were sacred records not to be touched by anyone. The tablets were written by the Naacals while they were in either Burma or Mu. These writings were part of a vast collection taken from one of the seven sacred cities of India. The other writings were lost. After great persuasion, the priest allowed Churchward to examine the tablets. Many of them were broken, and Churchward repaired the damaged artifacts with cement. He spent months translating the tablets, which gave great detail about the creation of Earth and man, and about Mu, the land where man first appeared. Churchward pursued other Indian priests in search of the missing tablets and even traveled to Burma to look for them, but without success. The Naacal writings are thought to be 50,000 years old. Two of the tablets, one in India and another in Tibet, state that man appeared on Earth in the land of Mu about 200,000 years ago. Religious teachings followed closely behind the advent of man, according to the writings. The classic Hindu epic *Ramayana*, written by the sage and historian Valmiki, mentions the Naacals as "coming to Burma from the land of their birth in the east." The

Naacal tablets provided the foundation for Churchward's relentless passion to uncover the secrets of the lost continent of Mu.

Writings from a later date, written in Mayak, Egypt, and India, describe the destruction of Mu. According to the writings, earthquakes broke up the Earth's crust and it sank into a fiery abyss, allowing the water of the Pacific Ocean to roll in.

The *Troano Manuscript*, now found in the British Museum, was written in Yucatan and estimated to be fifteen hundred to five thousand years old. It speaks of the Land of Mu, which existed up to the edge of times and places its destruction 12,500 years ago. Extract I states, "In the year 6 *Kan*, on the 11 *Mulac*, in the month of *Iac*, there occurred terrific earthquakes which continued until the 13 *Chuen* without interruption. The country of the hills of Earth, the land of Mu, was sacrificed. Twice upheaved, it disappeared during the night, having been constantly shaken by the fires of the underneath. Being confined, these caused the land to rise and sink several times in various places. At last the surface gave way and the ten countries were torn asunder and scattered. They sank with them 64,000,000 inhabitants, 8,060 years before the writing of this book."

Extract II states, "The birthplace of the sacred, Mu, the land of the west. That land of Kui (departed souls), the motherhood of the gods." According to the Maya language, Kui-land is the land of Kui, the birthplace of the goddess Maya, the mother of the gods and man.

Another old Mayan book, the *Codex Cortsesians,* found in the National Museum of Madrid and about the same age as the *Troano Manuscript* states, "By his strong arm, Homen caused the earth to tremble after sunset, and during the night Mu, the country of the hills of earth, was submerged . . . Twice Mu jumped from her foundation; it was then sacrificed by fire."

Mineralogist William Niven unearthed twenty-six hundred stone tablets near Mexico City. Believed to be more than twelve thousand years old, they contain direct references to Mu. Churchward deciphered the tablets, which were similar in language to the Naacal writings.

Ancient manuscripts preserved in secret archives of Tibet and China came into the hands of the Rosicrucians, a worldwide mystical society who has tried to reconcile spirituality with science.

These archaic writings revealed the ancient records and traditions of Lemuria. Rosicrucian Wishar S. Cerve was chosen to incorporate the manuscript information, along with recorded facts about Lemuria and its people, into a book entitled The *Lost Continent of the Pacific*.

THE LAND OF MU

The ancient Naacal records researched by Churchward and the Tibetan manuscripts analyzed by Cerve related similar stories about the continent of Mu. Legends of indigenous people corroborate these findings, as do archaeological and geological evidence. However, today's scientists refute the evidence and refuse to believe major earth changes could have happened so rapidly.

Churchward placed Lemuria in the middle of the Pacific Ocean. Evidence shows it extended north beyond Hawaii, to the south as far as Fiji and the South Sea Islands, and to the east slightly beyond Easter Island. It ranged from five thousand miles east to west, and three thousand miles north to south. Mu was composed of three land masses separated by narrow channels or seas.

The writings describe Mu as beautiful, mostly tropical, and with low rolling hills shaded by lush vegetation. Vast plains covered Lemuria with rich grazing lands and tilled fields. No mountain ranges were found on Mu until the latter part of its existence. Both the *Troano Manuscript* and *Codex Cortesian*us refer to Mu as the land of ridges of earth. Many broad, slow-flowing rivers meandered through the rolling hills and plains. Palm trees intermingled with numerous ferns and lined shores of both rivers and ocean. Many of the shallow lakes were surrounded by sacred lotus flowers. Butterflies, hummingbirds, crickets, and locusts inhabited this beautiful paradise, as did mastodons and elephants.

Cerve gives evidence that early Lemuria was quite large, comparable to North America. His ancient manuscripts describe it as spreading from the east coast of Africa to the west coast of North America. This was 200,000 years ago. New Zealand and thousands of Pacific islands were all remnants of Mu. The east shoreline permitted migration to North America. Large portions of North and South America, Asia, and Africa, either submerged at that time or became swampland, and were not fit for habitation. Cerve describes the central part of Lemuria as somewhat level with occasional volcanic peaks, measuring four thousand feet high. Mountain ridges formed in both the western and eastern regions. Large insects inhabited all of Mu, and birds proliferated. Bald eagles were thought to have originated in Lemuria. Many creatures of various size lived here, with the lemur being one of the most common animals. Both Churchward and Cerve believed the Land of Mu was the Garden of Eden.

Destruction of Lemuria came quite quickly. At the peak of its civilization, earthquakes and volcanic activity destroyed the southern part. Gigantic ocean waves rolled in over the land, destroying many of the cities. Since the land was so flat, lava built up, forming many of today's South Pacific islands. After the first cataclysm, many cities were rebuilt and commerce returned. Generations later the cataclysms returned. Earthquakes caused the continent to heave and roll. Temples and palaces were destroyed while great monuments were toppled. The cities were again in ruin.

The ancient writings describe the land as rising and falling. Fires burst forth from underneath and enveloped the land in roaring flames. Thick black smoke blanketed the land, while huge waves engulfed the terrain, destroying cities and life in its hellish path. The Lhasa records discovered in an old Tibetan temple, describe the holocaust: "Agonizing cries of the multitude filled the air. The people sought refuge in their temples and citadels only to be driven away by fire and smoke, and the women and men in their shining garments and precious stones cried, 'Mu save us.' During the night Lemuria was torn apart. The doomed land sank and fell into a great abyss of fire. Flames shot up and engulfed her, and the fires claimed their victim."

Geology provides evidence that floods destroyed much of the planet at one time, and most native tribes around the world have a story about the Great Flood, similar to the one found in *Genesis*. Such evidence comes from gravel deposits in Frederick, Oklahoma, and Raton, New Mexico. Both sites revealed artifacts buried in association with camels, elephants and mastodons. Some digs have revealed human-made relics, such as spearheads, lodged in the bone of animals. At least fifty locations in North America have revealed similar evidence. Geological and archaeological evidence show that another continent, thought to be Atlantis, may have existed between Europe and North America. It, too, suffered a similar fate.

According to ancient records, about 100,000 years ago, cyclic changes began to take place below and on the Earth's surface. Volcanoes, gas belts, earthquakes, and magnetic waves from east to west began to upset the Earth's equilibrium. At that time there were very few high places in the world, and no mountains in Europe. Likewise, Lemuria had hills but no mountains. In their early stages, all the continents were somewhat level.

Approximately 82,000 years ago, according to Cerve, the first recorded magnetic waves moved around the earth from east to west. The magnetic and electronic heat often reduced the hardest materials to molten lava. Dramatic changes occurred in the civilized lands. The part of Lemuria connected to Asia and Africa began to sink slightly and broke into swampy islands. Other portions of Lemuria were submerged, resulting in a smaller continent located entirely in the Pacific Ocean. Europe rose and ceased to be a swampland. It became a high and dry desert with a few inland seas. Several thousand years later the motherland began to colonize both to the east and west.

Land engulfed by vast internal spaces of the Earth resulted in lowering the ocean surface. The continents of North and South America began to drift westward, separating from Europe, Africa, and Greenland. Mountains began to grow. The western shore of North America reached the eastern shore of Lemuria, and the area Alaska now occupies touched eastern Asia. A new continent, Atlantis, began to arise in the Atlantic Ocean between Europe and North America. Both North and South America rose to a considerable height.

A sea formed in South America in the valley of the Amazon. Ancient records describe boats departing from Lemuria and sailing into this sea and out again into the Atlantic Ocean. Tiahuanaco, 13,500 feet above sea level, is an ancient prehistoric Bolivian city on the shores of Lake Titicaca. Here a monolith covered with symbolic figures describes the lost continent of Mu. The remnants of canals on the shores of Lake Titicaca are believed to have been built 16,000 to 18,000 years before the time of the Incas. An ancient map of South America, discovered in Tibet, shows canals connecting the Pacific Ocean to an inland sea, which occupied the whole of what is now the Amazon swamp. The canals on the map are located in the same place as the Lake Titicaca canals. On the eastern side of the

Amazon Sea, a strait connected the sea to the Atlantic Ocean. E. B. Enock, the great South American geologist, believed Tiahunaco had been built before the mountains were formed. When the Andes rose, the city was carried up with it. Originally the city occupied a plain several feet above the Pacific Ocean. Many sea shells unearthed west of Tiahuanaco support this hypothesis. When Atlantis was submerged, the Amazon basin became a swamp. The Tibetan map shows a point of land, believed to be Atlantis, beyond the outlet of the Amazon Sea straits. Churchward asserts that South America was once flat, and 15,000 years ago, mountains rose and protected man from constant destruction by cataclysms and submersions.

As North America moved westward, it joined the high eastern coast of Lemuria. As this happened, the hills of Mu rose higher and became mountains. When Mu was submerged, this higher portion of the continent joined the western portion of North America. It remained above water to form the Pacific Coast and coastal ranges, including the Sierra Nevada and Cascade Mountains. The Great Salt Lake is a remnant of a large inland sea that filled the valley between the Rocky Mountains and the Sierra Nevada foothills. The land east of the Sierra Nevada foothills and the Cascade foothills is entirely different from the western shoreline of the Pacific Ocean. The Grand Canyon of the Colorado River formed after Lemuria was submerged, drained the water between the Rocky Mountains and the Sierra Nevadas into the Pacific Ocean. According to Cerve's research, the western United States is a remnant of Mu.

For several hundred years, strange happenings around Mount Shasta in northern California near the Oregon border have been reported. Strange-looking people have appeared in local communities dressed in peculiar attire, paying for goods with gold. They are described as tall and graceful, old and virile. Covered with a headdress, their heads are large with much larger foreheads than today's humanity. The locals have reported seeing hundreds of people at midnight ceremonies around mysterious fires. Many people have testified to strangely shaped boats flying out of the region and landing in the Pacific Ocean. Legends tell of a tunnel at Mount Shasta's eastern base that leads to an underground city of unusual homes. According to legend, these people are the direct descendants of the people of Mu.

The ancients claim the mountain ranges were formed by gas belts after the earth went into final magnetic balance. No mountain ranges existed before these gas belts appeared and were organized. The subterranean continents were undermined by the volcanic gases. The granite foundation of the continents was honeycombed with large chambers filled with highly explosive gases. When the chambers were emptied of their gases, the supporting roofs collapsed, resulting in the submersion of the land. None of the gas belts ran deeper than twenty miles, and most were at depths from several miles to fifteen miles. Shortly after Mu repopulated following the earlier cataclysms, great gas belts formed along the western part of North America, resulting in the formation of new mountain ranges. Ancient records, according to Churchward, claim that mountain ranges were quite rare prior to 15,000 years ago. Gas belts permeated the Earth's crust throughout the world forming mountains all over the planet. As old gas chambers were blown out, the land above sank.

Whether these ancient geological hypotheses and dates are correct remains to be seen. However, ancient manuscripts and unexplained archaeological ruins strongly suggest a highly civilized people existed somewhere between North America and Asia. These archaic records also give us a glimpse of who these prehistoric people were and how they lived.

THE PEOPLE

During the height of its highly evolved civilization, 64,000,000 people lived in Lemuria. At that time, 50,000 years ago, the ten tribes of Mu came under one government. The people selected a king and added the prefix Ra to his name. The people called him Ra Mu. Lemuria was known as the "Empire of the Sun," and the ancient writings referred to it as the "Motherland."

Lemurians were about six feet tall and weighed 160 to 200 pounds, according to some records, while others assert they reached a height of seven feet. By today's standard, their appearance might be described as strange. Compared to today's human, their heads were much larger in proportion to their bodies. They had large foreheads thought to be six to seven inches high. A large protrusion, about the size and shape of a walnut, lay in the center of the forehead, approximately one and one-half inches above the bridge of the nose. It was soft and delicate with an outer cuticle. Their arms were longer and larger than ours with well-developed muscles, and their legs were shorter in proportion but not well developed. They grew their dark hair long and frequently braided it or arranged it in fancy hairdos across their shoulders or down their backs. Necks were long and slender and commonly adorned with a decorative collar made of beads and stones. Women were shorter than men, with more refined features. Often they wore veils to protect them- selves from the sun. Lemurians had large brown eyes, small ears, small teeth, and broad flattened noses. The dominant race was white. Other races included yellow, brown, and black. Lemurians were considered a handsome people.

The protrusion from the forehead was an organ of sense, much like an eye, ear, or nose. It received impressions from both long and short distances, today called mental telepathy. With this sixth sense, Lemurians could communicate with animals in their own language. They were also able to sense things in the fourth dimension. Lemurians believed this faculty needed development and growth, and that the salvation of their race depended on per- sonal mastership of this extra sense. The forehead organ was con- nected to the pineal gland and is known today as the third eye. As humanity developed, this sixth sense would be lost through lack of use and development.

Ancient writings reveal that community life was well estab- lished among Lemurians. Seven great cities in Mu were seats of reli- gion, science, and learning. There were other large cities, towns, and villages throughout the land.

Great architects designed buildings for permanency–some structures have withstood 30,000 years of cataclysmic challenges. Magnificent temples and palaces were built of stone, and the land was graced with great monoliths and monuments inscribed with intricate carvings. The temples, without roofs, allowed the rays of Ra, the sun, to fall upon worshiping heads as a signal of acknowl- edgment by the deity. Two crescent curves on top of a sacred curve, shaped the portal to the main entrance of the temple, symbolizing the religio-scientific doctrine. Covered hallways connected large buildings. Homes, usually large and airy, had rectangular walls made of stone or wood, ten to eleven feet high. Wood, leaves, and a coating of mud comprised the roof. Sleeping quarters contained raised platforms with netting to protect against insects. The wealthy lived in great palaces attended by many servants.

Nearly all the communities lay along the shores of rivers or ocean bays. Small boats provided the principal transportation on the many rivers. Roads were smooth highways, covered by a thick layer of powdered stone, much like the concrete of today. Animals pulled sleighlike vehicles on these smooth roads. Airships similar to blimps were used for transportation and mapping.

Lemurians wore loose flowing outer garments much like the Arab's garb. The people valued rare brilliantly colored feathers, and the wealthy frequently wore jewels and precious stones.

The people of Mu did not hunt and seldom ventured into the wilderness of the land. Most were vegetarians, living principally on fruits and vegetables. They rarely ate large and wild animals, but occasionally consumed small animals and fish. They cooked food with fire or heat from the sun.

Agriculture was the main industry of the populace. They farmed in early morning or late afternoon. Pottery and ornament production were the main manufacturing industries of Mu.

A variety of energy sources advanced the lifestyle of the Lemurians. Wind propelled ships, as did certain volcanic stones that affected water. Such a stone, when placed in water, repelled the water, causing the raft to flow away in one direction. It was attached to the rear part of a raft, between two extended arms lying beneath the water's surface. As a result, the raft was pushed in a forward direction. Another stone that radiated magnetic energy created repulsion, which enabled it to turn large iron wheels. Windmills provided energy to manufacturing plants. A stone or mineral that radiated brilliant light produced light in homes. Pockets of boiling lava provided steam energy throughout the country.

Lemuria had schools and centers of scientific learning. Lemurians taught only knowledge proven to be true. They believed the cosmic mind was the only dependable source of knowledge, tapped into it with their sixth sense. By concentration and meditation they could search for new knowledge or eliminate doubts of existing knowledge. Believing the cosmic mind to be in all space, they taught that the human personality was an ethereal, spiritual, and invisible essence of consciousness that would occupy the fourth dimension of the spiritual world. Their sixth sense allowed them to sense and contact disincarnate personalities. Lemurians considered scientific knowledge their religion. They believed the creator God revealed to man all knowledge, a fundamental principle of their understanding. Knowledge helped man evolve to the same degree of understanding as possesed by God. Acquisition of this knowledge was considered spiritual attunement and looked upon reverently.

Before a young man and woman married, they appeared before a spiritual advisor, judge, or leader of the community. Relatives came in for consultation. Prior to setting a date for the marriage ceremony, the couple had to complete a difficult test of commitment. The couple was denuded of all clothing and escorted to the city's edge bordering the wilderness. They traveled fifty miles inland into the unsettled land for two moon cycles. Upon return they were to be clothed from animals, well fed, and show proof they could provide and care for each other. If they passed initiation, a date for the marriage was set. The wedding included an elaborate ceremony and ritual, and once married, they never divorced or separated.

No elaborate ceremony took place after one's death. There were no graveyards. Three days after death, they covered the body with a chemical or mineral, which would decompose it. Two people, one being the future occupant, dug the grave. The graves ran east to west with the deceased's head placed toward the east. Several days prior to death, an individual announced to loved ones that he or she was going to die. On the day of transition, the person would lie down in the grave and close his or her eyes. Within several hours, the person reached an eternal sleep. Most died between the ages of sixty and seventy, and occasionally some became centernarian. It was considered a violation of the highest level if individuals passed on before fulfilling their obligations and life purposes. Those considering the transition needed to demonstrate their missions were complete with no unfulfilled obligations.

Seldom did Lemurians suffer from unexpected diseases. In the latter days of Lemuria, disease became more prevalent and many became blind. The Atlanteans called them the blind race. Attacks by wild animals were their greatest fear and problem. Those who developed great knowledge and skills in healing, herbs, and surgery became physicians in the community.

Lemurians issued no coin or money. They received no remuneration for their efforts, except the honor of serving the communities' interest. They divided all crops accordingly. Lemurians gave a certain percentage to the government, another percentage to the temple, and a certain percentage to each person. Any surplus was placed in a community warehouse and given to people in need so that poverty was unknown to them. They traded agricultural products and minerals with other communities. Storehouses and warehouses belonged to the community. There was no incentive to accumulate personal possessions. Crime remained minimal, and social distinction was without power. Because individual's developed their talents, the arts and sciences also developed to a high degree.

SPIRITUAL PHILOSOPHY

The Naacal writings shed light on both the cosmogony of Earth and man, and Lemuria's spiritual heritage. As in the Bible, Mu's story of creation describes seven time periods involved with creation. In the beginning, the universe was only a soul or spirit that was calm and silent without life. Only the Creator, symbolized by a seven-headed serpent, moved within the abyss of darkness. He desired to create worlds, including the Earth, with living inhabitants. He did so with seven commands.

First, he brought together the gases without form, from which the Earth was to be formed. Second, he let the gases solidify to form the Earth. The third command allowed the gases to separate and form the atmosphere and waters. The gases within the Earth raised the Earth above the water on the fourth command. Life came forth in the water with the fifth command, and the sixth gave life upon land. The final command made humans in the image of the Creator and gave them power to rule the Earth. The Creator, the seven-headed intellect, placed within humanity an imperishable spirit and intellectual power, similar to the one he possessed. Creation was then complete through these seven periods of time.

An important teaching throughout the ancient Naacal writings related to the Four Great Primary Forces, called the Sacred Four. The Creator used these forces to create the universe by establishing law and order. These Sacred Four powers carried out the commands and desires of the Absolute. The Sacred Four were symbolized by a cross, a swastika, a cross similar to the Maltese cross, and a feathered winged circle. The latter is still found in the ruins of Mesopotamia, Egypt and Mexico. A wheeled cross symbolized these four primary forces in the Americas and Pacific Islands. This comprised a circle drawn outside the symbol of the Sacred Four and became the first symbol of the mystical Rosicrucian Order, which claims many of its mystical teachings came from Lemuria. The Four Sacred Principles began their work of creation within a cosmic egg, representing the process of germination symbolized by the wheeled cross. These forces created order out of chaos, created all things, and were in charge of the physical throughout the universe. These first four gods executed the seven commands of the Creator.

According to Churchward, the *Cosmogonic Diagram* was the first book discovered. Traced back to more than 35,000 years ago, the *Cosmogonic Diagram* was copied by all the ancients of Mexico, India, Egypt, Babylonia, and the natives of America. But only the Yucatan Mayas of Mexico retained its characters and meaning. The central circle represented Ra. Twelve divisions, formed by interlaced triangles, symbolized the twelve gates of heaven, each representing a virtue. Each soul must possess the twelve virtues to enter the gates of heaven. The diagram also symbolized the twelve temptations that the soul must overcome to enter the twelve gates. A falling ribbon in the diagram symbolized the need for the soul to ascend to reach heaven. An individual attained ascension after perfecting oneself.

The monotheistic religion of Mu acknowledged only one Supreme Being through a collective symbol, the sun, which was called Ra. All Lemurians followed the same religion and worshiped their deity through symbols. Lemurians believed in the immortality of the soul, which eventually returned to the Source. They never spoke his name because of their great reverence for him. A high priest named Ra Mu represented the deity in religious teachings. He was not to be worshiped because he was only Ra's representative. The deity had many attributes assigned to him, with each attribute having a symbol.

The people of Lemuria were highly civilized and enlightened. At that time, there had been no "savagery" on the face of the Earth. Ancients believed all the Earth's people were the children of Mu. They also believed in reincarnation and that the soul of man was incarnated in Lemuria. The greatest force connected with the Earth, except for that of the Creator, was the soul of man. When man died, the body decomposed, but the soul did not die with the body. It returned to the place of incarnation, the land of Mu, to await reincarnation.

The religion of Lemuria contained no doctrinal beliefs and had no false gods. Each community had at least one temple. Temples were equivalent to present-day universities and schools. There were two types of religious services. One gave adoration to God through prayer, while the other disseminated knowledge. Science was the twin sister of religion. It taught that humanity was a high and grand creator, while religion taught humans how to become better people.

REMNANTS OF LEMURIA

If a highly civilized people once lived on a continent that had been submerged, logically there should be traces of that civilization to corroborate the ancient writings. Such is the case.

Easter Island, once considered part of Lemuria, is twenty-one hundred miles off the coast of South America, located in the southeast extreme of Polynesia. It measures thirteen miles by seven miles and contains a wealth of prehistoric ruins. There are 555 carved stones, colossal statues, and prehistoric ruins. The largest artifact is seventy feet high, and the smallest is three feet long. Statues carved from red igneous rock represent distinct personages believed to be memorialized in these large monuments. Near a distinct volcano sits a large stone temple, measuring twenty feet by one hundred feet, with standing walls that are five feet thick and five feet high. Seven tablets are all that remain of a vast number that told the story of Easter Island. Tablet one tells us that when Easter Island was discovered by our forefathers, the roads were beautifully paved with flat stones so that no rough edges were exposed.

The Cook Islands lay halfway between Tahiti and Fiji and contain ruins similar to those found on Easter Island. No quarries have been found, so the stone is thought to have been imported. Tonga-Tabu, a Pacific atoll, has a stone monument in the form of an arch. The two upright stones weigh seventy tons each, and the top stone weighs twenty-five tons. The nearest available stone quarry is located two hundred miles away. Both the Gilbert and Marshall Islands have tall slender pyramids. On Panope, a South Sea island, stands a temple, three hundred feet by sixty feet at its base, with walls thirty feet tall and five feet thick. Churchward believes Panope may be the ruin of one of the seven sacred cities of Mu. Natives do not go near the ruins, believing them to be haunted.

The Maoris of New Zealand possess many of the Lemurian sacred symbols. In Samoa and most of the Polynesian islands, there are legends of a Great Flood from which but a few escaped. In 1878, natives on the Caroline Islands of the Pacific are quoted as saying, "The people who occupied these islands when the islands were not islands, but a great land, had very large boats in which they sailed all over the world and were sometimes gone for more than a year before they returned."

The author knew a deep-sea diver, John Kennedy (no relation to JFK), who came across a coliseum on the ocean floor three hundred miles west of India. He discovered it in the 1970s while repairing telephone cables on the ocean floor. He only reported his observation on an audiotape which he gave to his supervisors. Elsewhere, underwater ruins off the coast of Peru, at a depth of six hundred feet, were found in 1966.

COLONIZATION

The ancients considered Mu the mother of all civilizations, believing most of the prehistoric civilizations around the world were originally colonized by Lemuria. Evidence suggests that Lemuria colonized in North America, Mexico, South America, Egypt, Greece, India, Uigher (Asia), and Atlantis. Naacal writings found in the Orient suggest colonization began at least 70,000 years before the sinking of Mu. One of the colonies was reported to have had a population of 35 million people. In all likelihood this was Atlantis. Colonization took place in lands both east and west of Lemuria. The sun rising on the horizon without rays symbolized the colony. Once a colony advanced far enough under the rulership of Mu, it turned into a colonial empire. The motherland bestowed the title "Son of the Sun" upon its ruler, meaning he was a subject of Mu, the "Empire of the Sun."

The Lemurians followed two principal routes to the east. One route went from Mu to the Yucatan and Central America, then to Atlantis. From Atlantis they traveled through the Mediterranean Sea to Asia Minor and through the Dardanelles to the southwest corner of the Black Sea. Another route started in southeast Mu and led to South America. Canals connected the Pacific Ocean to the Amazon Sea (located where the Amazon jungle is today). They sailed through straits linking the Amazon Sea to the Atlantic Ocean, then on to Atlantis or to eastern Africa. Other eastern routes went to present-day Nevada and the Mexican Valley.

Hindu records show that central parts of India, known as Deccan, were first colonized by a white race called the Mayas who came to India by way of Burma. The motherland was a moon's journey toward the rising sun, east of Burma. The term Maya referred to colonizers from Mu. The Nagas in India were Mayans who came from the motherland and settled in the Deccan region. They turned this settlement into a colonial empire known as the Naga Empire, thousands of years before the Aryans were known in India. It is well known that the Brahmins obtained their cosmogony, science, and arts from the Nagas. Both the Brahmins and Nagas used the seven-headed serpent to symbolize the Creator, as did the people of Mu. The Naacal tablets were written in the motherland with Nagaan symbols and characters. They were first brought to Burma and later to India. Valmika, the Hindu sage historian, states in the *Ramayana,* "The Maya adepts, the Naacals, starting from their birth in the east, went first to Burma and there taught the Nagas. From Burma they went to the Deccan in India, whence they carried their religion and learning to Babylonia and to Egypt." It continues, "The Mayas were mighty navigators, whose ships traveled from the western to the eastern oceans and from the southern to the northern seas in ages so remote the sun had not risen above the horizon." Valmiki said that, "More than 30,000 years ago, India was turned from a colony into a colonial empire."

From India, the Naacals went to Egypt as missionaries to teach the seven sacred inspired writings, religions, and sciences. The *Egyptian Book of the Dead* contains many references to Mu as the motherland of man. The book is a sacred memorial dedicated to those who lost their lives during the destruction of Mu. A close relationship exists between the ancient teachings of India and Egypt. Evidence suggests that Lower Egypt was settled from Mu via Atlantis and Mayax, while Upper Egypt was colonized by way of India and

Burma. Thoth, who started the first Lower Egyptian colony 16,000 years ago at Sais, taught the religion of Osiris. Osiris lived in Atlantis 18,000 to 20,000 years ago and was an ancient deified king.

Uighur was another principal colonial empire belonging to Mu and located in Asia in present-day Russia and China. Chinese legends tell that Uighur was at the height of her civilization about 17,000 years ago, which agrees with archaeological and geological evidence. The empire reached from the Pacific Ocean to Eastern Europe. India, Burma, and Persia bordered Uighur on the south. The Urighur people were highly civilized, and their culture included astrology, mining, textiles, math, reading, and medicine. Their artisans were known for decorative art on silk, metal, and wood. They made statues of gold, silver, bronze, and clay. The history of the Uighurs is the history of the Aryans. Their capital sat where the ruins of Khara Khota now exist in the Gobi Desert. A tomb unearthed fifty feet below the surface contained valuable treasures, showing a link to Mu. When Lemuria was submerged, about half the Uighur Empire was destroyed. The Aryans, who migrated to northern India, brought with them many of the Uighur symbols. These symbols are also found in Babylonia and Egypt.

Archaeological digs in Mexico by William Niven suggest a highly civilized race existed thousands of years before the glacial period and the European ape-man. In a two hundred square mile valley near Mexico City, Niven unearthed thousands of clay pits. He found traces of three civilizations that had three well-preserved concrete floors or pavements on top of one another. These at some time underlaid a large city. The pavements ranged in depth from four to twenty-five feet. Well-defined layers of volcanic ash lay over remnants of large buildings. Niven uncovered a tomb with many artifacts and human bones, including bones of a man five feet tall with long arms reaching to his knees and a Mongolian-type skull. Above the tomb was evidence that a great flood had raged and destroyed the city.

Yucatan and Central America were some of the first colonies established by Mu. Yucatan is filled with relics and ruins of ancient civilizations. Legends among the Aztecs of Mexico declare that the first settlers in Mexico were a white race conquered by a race of darker skin people. The white people sailed away to a far-off land in the east toward the rising sun. The same records show that southern

Europe, Asia Minor, and northern Africa were colonized by the white race via Mayax, Central America, and Atlantis. A prophecy states that at a future time this white race will return and claim the land.

Quetzalcoatl, the ancient divine king among the natives of Anahual, taught them the useful arts and the procedures of government. Guatemala was the location of Quetzalcoatl's capital city. Tradition states, "When King Quetzalcoatl, with the very white race, was conquered by the invading darker race, he refused to surrender, saying he could not live in captivity. He could not survive. He then, with as many people as his ships could carry, sailed to a far-off land in the direction of the rising sun. He and his people reached this far-off land and settled there. They prospered and became a great people." Churchward suggests Quetzalcoatl's reign occured between 16,000 and 34,000 years ago.

The Aztecs abandoned their symbol used for the deity. Instead, they adopted the great white King Quetzal as their god. They called his son Tescati. A prophecy told, "Tescati's spirit would return in the body of a white man with many soldiers. He would conquer and retake the country, putting the men to the sword and enslaving the women." At the time of Cortez, the Aztecs were sacrificing more than 30,000 people a year, and they thought Cortez and his soldiers were the prophecy come true. When Cortez and Catholic Bishop Landa arrived in Mexico, they destroyed 27 manuscripts, 5,000 statues, and 197 vases. As a result, the natives today do not know who built the pyramids of Mexico. The name of Quetzal is found in ancient histories of Mexico, Central America, New Mexico, and the Pueblo Indians.

The Empire of Mayax was composed of seven different peoples, all originating from the motherland. They all spoke the Mayan tongue. During the twelve dynasties, the kings and queens of Mayax were all white.

The ruins and pyramids of Mexico are numerous. Today's archaeologists believe the structures were built fifteen hundred years ago. Churchward believes the ruins at Chichen Itza on the Yucatan peninsula were standing 11,500 years ago. Most of the Mayan buildings were adorned with mastodon heads and trunks. Churchward claims the buildings with carvings of feathered serpents are over 15,000 years old and were erected during the Can

(Serpent) Dynasty. The Can Dynasty ended with Queen Moo, who lived during the first century of Egyptian history. According to the *Troano Manuscript,* she was the last of the dynasty who visited the Maga Nile Colony at Sais, Egypt, and met Thoth 16,000 years ago. Plutarch tells us that the priests of Egypt told Solon the lands of the west broke apart nine thousand years ago when Atlantis sank. The resulting mud and seaweed made the Atlantic Ocean impassable. Solon visited Egypt in 600 B.C.

Doctor LePlongeon, an early Yucatan archeologist, found an inscription on a temple wall that read, "This edifice is a memorial commemorating the destruction of Mu, the Land of the West, whence came our sacred mysteries." In Uxmal, an inscription on a wall of the Temple of Sacred Mysteries links ancient man with the early history of Babylonia and Egypt.

What happened to the highly evolved Mayan civilization remains a mystery. It completely disappeared, leaving only stone ruins. Churchward believed earthquakes, volcanic activity, and cataclysmic activity destroyed Mayan civilization about 11,500 years ago. These great waves of water eliminated all life including the white Mayans of the Yucatan. When the land became inhabitable again, the surrounding people migrated and took possession of it. These people included brown races speaking the Mayan language. They were a mixture of three tribes, mainly Mongol. The new inhabitants knew nothing of those who built the historic structures.

Much of the culture of native tribes living on the west coast of South America resemble that of the natives of the Pacific Islands. The 25,000-year-old map of South America discovered in Tibet explains how the streams of Lemurian colonists crossed the center of South America in boats from the motherland to Atlantis through the canals at Lake Titicaca. At that time the region was at sea level, and the Amazon was a sea. The Carians from Mu came directly from the motherland and formed settlements beside the Amazon Sea, along the east coast of South America and Central America. Several major cities were located on the Amazon as verified by the Tibetan map and ancient ruins. On the southwest shore of the Amazon Sea lay the "Jewel City." The "City of Gold," a little inland off the southern shore, was the legendary city of Manoa thought to have been settled by the Caras from Central America. Guatemalan tradition tells of a group of Caras who sailed south to a great river, found a fair land, settled there, and became a great nation. The great city of Manoa was built around fairylike lakes with great golden temples. Churchward believed this occurred 16,000 years ago. The Caribbean Sea was named after the Carians. They also settled in Atlantis, Asia Minor, and the lower part of the Balkan Peninsula, where Greece is now located. Many people of Greece consider themselves the people of Carou.

In her classic *The Secret Doctrine,* H. P. Blavatsky tells that in antiquity three great nations claimed descent from the Kingdom of Lemuria. They were the Egyptians, Phoenicians, and the old Greeks. Some scholars believe that the white race known as the Carians are the Greeks of today.

After leaving South America and Atlantis, the Carians came to the Mediterranean Sea and split into semi-independent tribes. One tribe called themselves Athenians. Egyptian records declare that one of the Athenian capital cities was Athens, which was destroyed by earthquakes and submerged 11,500 years ago, at the same time that Atlantis was submerged. Athens had been built 17,000 years ago. The southeastern part of Mu, the Carian country, included Easter Island. The Greek Herodotus, known as the father of history, claimed to be Carian.

Euclid, in 403 B.C., rearranged the Athenian alphabet to its present form. Today the Greek alphabet today is composed of Cara-Maya vocables, which form an epic commemorative of their forefathers, who lost their lives in the destruction of Mu. One of the Greek alphabet letters is Mu. Plato refers to the lost continent in *Timeus Critiasi* as "The land of Mu (that) had ten peoples."

The North American Indians have many legends about the lost continent of Mu. Legend says the Algonquin Indians lived on Mu when they were given a prophecy about the future flood. The legend says while constructing 138 ships to set out from Mu, "the gates of heaven and Earth were opened . . . The earth rocked to and fro, and the rain fell in torrents . . . the earth was broken. A mighty continent was cut loose from its fastening and the fires of the earth came forth in flame . . . the land sank down beneath the water, to rise no more."

The cliff dwellers were the last colonizers to arrive from the land of Mu. Churchward believes they arrived before the mountains were raised. They spoke the Yucatan-Maya language as depicted by their hieratic alphabet. Archaeological sites show that man lived in Arizona with the mastodon 12,000 years ago. Records of the Pueblo Indians suggest their tribe was a highly civilized and enlightened people. They have some of the oldest records and traditions of any native North American tribe. Tradition tells they came from the motherland. Traditions of the Hopi and Zuni say they also originated from Mu. Their symbols are identical to those of Lemuria. The language of the Pueblos contains many words of the mother tongue. Legends say, "Their forefathers came to America in their ships from across the sea in the direction of the setting sun." The Pueblos, like their motherland, had seven sacred cities, as did Atlantis and India. Hundreds of North American rock writings, according to Churchward, confirm the linkage of Native Americans to Mu. They relate stories of how the first civilization of North America came from a country called Mu, which lay to the west.

Cerve believes Native Americans may have descended from Atlantis as well as Lemuria. He states certain words are common to all the various tribes and only differ slightly in sound and symbol. All these identical words had a religious or mystical meaning. The holidays and ceremonies were also common among the tribes. He asserts the Native Americans may have been descendants from the "Lost Tribes of Israel." Scientists admit that the Indian people came to America thousands of years ago from an unknown country in the west, believing they crossed at the Bering Strait.

Atlantis, settled by the land of Mu, reached its height of civilization about 18,000 years ago. About 6,000 years later a sudden and unexpected cataclysm caused the entire continent of Atlantis to sink in less than twelve years. The Atlantic islands of the Azores, Canaries, and Madeira are remnants of the Atlantean mountaintops. Blavatsky asserts that Atlantis was approaching its greatest days of glory and civilization when the last of the Lemurian continent went down. Churchward and Cerve believe both landmasses went down about the same time.

The ancients believed Mu seeded the whole earth. Negroes lived in southwestern Mu on a cluster of islands called Melanesia, where Negroes still live today. Atlantis' black population lived in the south. Many of the colonizers from Mu sailed along the southern coast of Atlantis. From there they sailed directly to the shores of Africa, which became populated by the Negroes of Mu and Atlantis.

Much evidence suggests a lost continent of Mu greatly influenced our present-day civilizations. It answers the many questions about the unexplained archeological ruins, writings, and legends that modern day science refuses to acknowledge because of its limited paradigm. Researchers of Lemuria may not be entirely accurate in all their facts and dates, but they leave a rich legacy of intriguing hypotheses for modern science to explore

Chapter Two

ATLANTIS
The Lost Continent

The legend of Atlantis remains one of the great mysteries of our time. Whether it is myth or fact has been argued for centuries. The legend began with Plato (427 to 347 B.C.) in his classic dialogues of *Timaeus* and *Critias*. Plato's source of information came from Solon (639 to 559 B.C.), an ancestor of Plato's who was considered the wisest of the seven sages of Greece. The great lawgiver of Athens spent ten years in Egypt during the latter part of his life.

An Egyptian priest in Sais told Solon the story of Atlantis. The priest told Solon that the Egyptian goddess Neith was the same as the Greek goddess Athene. She founded both Sais, located at the division of the Nile River, and Athens eight thousand years earlier and gave both cities their constitutions. History records that a mighty empire waged war against the whole of Europe and Asia. This empire came from an island in the Atlantic Ocean situated in front of the Straits of Heracles (Straits of Gibraltar). The island, which was larger than Libya (Mediterranean Africa) and Asia (Asia Minor) put together, was known as Atlantis. It lay "on the way to an opposite continent, which surrounded the true ocean." Through the efforts of the Athenians, the transgression of Atlantis was halted.

Atlantis was a great and wonderful empire, according to the priest. It subjected parts of Libya, within the columns of Heracles, as far as Egypt and Tyrrhenia. "Your country," the priest said, "stood alone and defeated the invaders, the Kings of Atlantis, and preserved the Greeks from slavery and liberated all the others within the limits of Heracles."

Shortly after the defeat of Atlantis, violent earthquakes and floods occurred. Within a single day and night all the warlike men sank into the earth. The island of Atlantis, in a like manner, disappeared and sank beneath the sea. For that reason, the sea in those parts became impassable because of shallow mud.

The priest told Solon, since that war, nine thousand years had elapsed and many deluges had taken place since the Great Deluge destroyed Atlantis. As a result, small islands remained from the large island of Atlantis.

Solon returned to Greece with a large volume of material about the history of Atlantis and ancient Athens. Because of his age, Solon did not transcribe it to verse, and he died shortly after his return. Plato came into possession of these unfinished manuscripts and undertook the task of writing about Atlantis. Plato transcribed only twenty-two pages of the material before his untimely death. His writings provide the foundation for the Atlantis legend, which is more than two thousand years old.

Proclus (412 to 485 A.D.) writes about Crantor (260 B.C.), a Greek who visited Sais. Crantor saw a column in the Temple of Neith that was completely covered with hieroglyphics, recording the history of Atlantis. Wise men translated the hieroglyphics for Crantor, and Crantor claimed their account fully agreed with Plato's writings of Atlantis. Other historians assert that Plato verified this information on his visit to Egypt.

Since the time of Plato, more than five thousand books have been written about Atlantis, all trying to shed light on this mystery. Legends of many indigenous people tell of a large island in the Atlantic Ocean destroyed by a Great Flood. Archaeological evidence provides clues that a great civilization existed within the confines of the Atlantic. Geologic evidence shows that a great landmass existed above water in the same locale Atlantis is said to have existed. German researcher Otto Muck provides evidence that a great catastrophe occurred about 10,500 years ago in the form of a Great Flood. He cites evidence that it may have been caused by an asteroid impact in the Caribbean near Puerto Rico. The Atlantis mystique heightened in 1882 when Ignatius Donnelly published a book titled *Atlantis, The Antediluvian World.* Donnelly, an attorney, lieutenant governor of Minnesota, and U.S. congressman caught the public's attention.. His best-selling book raised such interest in Britain that according to a British press poll, next to the return of Christ, the discovery of Atlantis would be the most newsworthy item.

All evidence leads to the conclusion that a great civilization existed in an area located west of Europe and east of America, somewhere in the Atlantic Ocean. Geology, archaeology, and indigenous legends left a legacy of evidence that we are still uncovering today.

PLATO'S ATLANTIS

Atlantis, according to Plato's writings, was a large island opposite the mouth of the Mediterranean Sea and believed to be the remnant of a large Atlantic continent. Plato said the island was larger than Libya (Mediterranean Africa) and Asia (Asia Minor) combined. One estimate put the size of Atlantis at 2,650,000 square miles or slightly smaller than Australia, while others estimated it to be the size of present-day Iran.

Poseidon, the god of Atlantis, married a mortal woman named Cleito. They begat five sets of twins, all males. Poseidon divided Atlantis into ten portions, and each son became a king of one portion. Poseidon's oldest son, Atlas, was king of the royal city Poseidonis. Both Atlantis and the Atlantic Ocean were named after Atlas. By Atlantis custom, the oldest offspring inherited the rulership. Atlas headed a large and honorable family in the wealthiest monarchy ever ruled by a king.

The major city of Atlantis was Poseidonis, a magnificent metropolis located on the southern coast of Atlantis. It was surrounded by three concentric circles of water called sea zones. The first sea zone was eighteen hundred feet wide, the second twelve hundred feet, and the third six hundred feet wide. A canal was constructed from the ocean through the zones of land three hundred feet wide, one hundred feet deep, and sixty miles long, so it could handle the largest vessels. At the landward end of this waterway was a harbor. Triemes (galleys with three banks of oars) could easily pass from one zone to another through the canals. The canal and harbors were always full of vessels and merchants. Many triemes and naval stores lined the docks of Poseidonis, and the sound of human voices continued day and night.

The central island, where the palace stood, stretched about one thousand yards across. Stone walls quarried from the island enclosed the central island and each of the two circular zones of land. They were red, black, and white. A light coating of brass covered the outer walls. The walls encircled the island and outward zones for a distance of nine thousand feet. Inhabitants cultivated the enclosed space, and the area facing the sea was covered with villas and storehouses. A dense population thrived on the exterior land zone. Tin plates covered the second land zone's wall, and orichalcum (mountain copper) covered the citadel wall of the central island. Across the circular sea zones stretched bridges with gates and defense towers. The bridge at the principal entrance was approximately one hundred100 feet wide.

The palace lay within the inner citadel, as did the Temples of Cleito and Poseidon, both laced with gold. Measuring six hundred feet long, the Poseidon Temple lay on three square acres. Silver garnished the exterior with the interior roof decorated with ivory, gold, and orichalcum flashing. Statues of gold were found within the temple. A statue of Poseidon standing in a chariot led by six winged horses reached to the roof. Around him stood statues of one hundrerd Nereids (sea nymphs) riding on dolphins. Statues of all ten kings and their wives adorned the exterior of the temple.

Hot springs and fountains of cold water flowed in abundance throughout the city. Great baths accommodated both people and animals, with separate baths for the king, women, and private persons. Horses and other domestic animals had bathing pools of their own.

On each of the two outer land zones of the city lay temples, shrines, groves, and gymnasiums. The temples were dedicated to the gods, and here the original Acropolis was located. Near the middle of the larger zone island was a stadium for horses and chariot races, circumvented by dwellings of court officials and guards. About six hundred feet in diameter, a race course extended all around the island.

Atlantean architecture followed "Cyclopean" style, where buildings were constructed of large, accurately squared stone blocks. The joints were precisely fitted but unequal in size. Enormous monoliths frequently formed gateways.

No mountains were found on the southern coast near Poseidonis. Many lakes, rivers, and marshes beautified the land. A great plain lay in the center of the island, said to be unequaled for beauty and fertility. Surrounding the great plain were mountains that descended toward the sea. The mountains, celebrated for their number, size, and beauty, sheltered Poseidonis from the north.

About six miles from the plain stood a low mountain, where

Evenor and his wife Leucippe lived with their daughter Cleito. After the death of Cleito's parents, she married Poseidon. To show his appreciation for Cleito, Poseidon constructed mounds and ditches for her friends who lived there. Many wealthy people of Atlantis lived in the small rural villages.

Mining was prevalent in Atlantis. Orichalcum was esteemed as the most precious metal, next to gold, and was mined on many parts of the island. Wood was plentiful in Atlantis, and the many carpenters used it for construction in temples, homes, palaces, and docks.

Fruits and flowers thrived in the subtropical climate. Food was abundant, with legumes, coconuts, chestnuts, fruits, and meats being favorites among the Atlanteans. They also grew root foods, grapes, and corn. Their meat came from cattle, sheep, goats, and fish. Large herds of elephants roamed the island.

The fertile plains were cultivated during the many generations of kings. Plato described the plain as rectangular, straight, and oblong. According to Plato's description, Otto Muck estimated the plain to be 370 miles long (northeast to southwest) and 230 miles wide. It followed the course of a circular canal of incredible depth, width, and length. It reached one hundred feet deep, and coursed one thousand miles. Ships navigated the canals to bring wood and produce to the city. Harvest occurred twice a year for fruits and cereals. In winter, the soil was sheltered from rain and floods.

The plains country was divided into 60,000 cantons, each twelve mile's square. All cantons appointed a chief for military service. Inhabitants of the mountains and remainder of the country were also assigned leaders. Six leaders together furnished one war chariot, and all the leaders together provided a total of 10,000 chariots. Each canton supplied two heavily armed men, two archers, two slingers, three stone shooters, three javelin men, and four sailors to help man twelve hundred ships. This was the order of war for the royal city, but requirements differed in the other nine governments. Plato writes that the Atlantean's armed force numbered one million. Otto Muck interpolates from this a population of at least 20 million and most likely nearer to 40 million. He claims the large southern plain could support a population of 40 to 60 million.

Each of the ten kings had absolute control over his citizens. The relationship of the ten sovereigns with one another was regulated by the injunctions set down by Poseidon. Located at the Temple of Poseidon was an orichalcum column inscribed with the laws and penalties of the land. The sovereigns were not allowed to take up arms against one another, and they were all required to come to the rescue if any city attempted to overthrow the royal house. Kings were not to have power of life and death over any in their kingdom, unless the majority of the ten kings approved a special situation. In the Temple of Poseidon, the kings assembled alternately every fifth or sixth year. Here they consulted about public affairs and inquired if anyone had transgressed the laws and passed judgment accordingly.

Bulls played an important role in the rites of the Atlanteans. Before justice was administered by the kings, ten bulls were brought into the sacred zone. Each king made a vow to offer one of these bulls to Poseidon. The bull was led to a copper column and sacrificed without assistance from any iron object. The kings passed the body parts of the bull through a fire and poured blood onto the copper column. Remains of the bull were consumed by fire, while they placed the remaining blood in small vases of gold and splashed it on the fire. The kings drank a small amount of the blood.

Before the decline of Atlantis, the people were virtuous. They cared little for status and had no greed for property and gold, believing materialism only a burden. They obeyed the laws and revered the gods. The Atlanteans were prudent in their foreign relations as well.

After the gods intermingled with the mortals, the divine portion began to fade away, being too diluted with human traits. Human nature dominated, with attributes of unrighteousness, lust for power, greed, lack of honor, deteriorating friendships, rule by violence, and immorality. The wickedness of humanity resulted from extinction of the power of divine ancestors caused by the interbreeding of the gods with the daughters of the Earth.

Zeus, the god of gods, expected all to follow the laws of the land. He observed a most honorable race in a most wretched state, and he wanted to inflict punishment on them. He gathered all the gods together and spoke to them. Afterwards, violent earthquakes, rains, and floods occurred. In a single day and night, all the warlike men sank into the earth as did the island of Atlantis.

LEGENDARY EVIDENCE

Many ancient legends of indigenous peoples support the theory that a great civilization existed on an island in the Atlantic Ocean. The people of Atlantis left their legacy worldwide through colonization in America, Europe, Asia Minor, and Egypt before the Deluge.

Diodorus Siculus (first century A.D.) writes that "the Egyptians were strangers, who in remote times settled on the banks of the Nile, bringing a civilization of their mother country with them such as writing and a polished language. They came from the direction of the setting sun and were the most ancient of men." The discovery of graves of the late pre-dynastic era supported this theory of a master race in the northern part of Upper Egypt. The graves contained anatomical remains of people whose skulls and bodies were of greater size than the natives and earlier inhabitants. The Atlanteans were known to be of large size.

Ancient Egyptian healing priests and shrine bearers learned their medical arts from six different books. They were among forty-two works supposedly brought to Egypt by a different race before the Great Flood. Thoth (Hermes Trismegistus) the god-man of early Egypt was the author. The immortal Thoth claimed he was a former Atlantean. Egyptian priests, according to Herodotus, claim their written history dated to 11,340 years before the era, or nearly 14,000 years before the present. Other open-minded scholars estimate Egyptian colonization by Atlantis began between 14,000 and 30,000 B.C.

John Anthony West writes that researcher Schwaller de Lubicz provided evidence that the erosion of the Sphinx was due to the actions of water, not sand or wind. Therefore the Sphinx must have been constructed prior to the Great Flood of around 10,000 B.C. Schwaller de Lubicz believes the Sphinx was constructed by the Atlanteans centuries earlier.

Other evidence links Egypt with Atlantis. The mystery schools of Egypt are assumed to have inherited their knowledge from Atlantis. Dr. Paul Schieman claims that two papyri found in St. Petersburg showed that Egypt had been a colony of Atlantis. An inscription on the Lion Gate at Mycenae indicated the first temple of Sais was built by Misor, the ancestor of all Egyptians. He was grandson of an Atlantean priest who fled from King Chronos with the king's beautiful daughter and settled on the banks of the ancient Nile. Egyptian records indicate the gods reigned Egypt for thousands of years before the first recorded Egyptian dynasties. Manetho, an Egyptian priest and historian, claims the Egyptians changed their calendar system at the same time that Plato reported the sinking of Atlantis.

Other countries around the world report a legacy from Atlantis. When Spanish explorers arrived on the Canary Islands, they reported a primitive white race with a written language who claimed to be survivors of a former large island that submerged during a great catalclysm.

The Phoenicians are considered by some Atlantologists to be survivors of Atlantis. They referred to a secret island of great wealth, which they called Antilla. Their descendants, the Carthaginians, were the only people among the ancient navigators to sail past Gibraltar into the Atlantic. To keep their trade routes secret from the Greeks, Romans, and Egyptians, they spread rumors about the presence of large sea monsters. Aristotle claimed the Carthaginians visited the island of Antilla, which at one time was part of Atlantis. Anyone divulging the location of their secret land in the Atlantic Ocean received a penalty of death.

The layout of Carthage was almost identical to that of Poseidonis. There was a citadel hill surrounded by zones of land and water, guarded by a great sea wall. There were great cisterns of drinking water and many baths throughout the city. Carthage was a Phoenician trading post established in Tunis in 814 B.C. The names of the Phoenician deities matched the names of Plato's kings of Atlantis. Phoenician legends tell of Thoth being the inventor of the alphabet and the art of writing. Manetho writes that prior to the Deluge, Thoth inscribed all the principles of the old knowledge onto tablets in hieroglyphics and sacred letters. After the Deluge, his successors transcribed the contents of the tablets into the language of the common people. The Phoenician alphabet is the parent of all the European alphabets, which some believe originated from Atlantis, and was conveyed to the Mayans of Central America. The Phoenicians, a Semitic race, called themselves the people of Carou.

Marcellus, an Ethiopian historian, wrote about ten islands in the Atlantic Ocean close to the shores of Europe. The inhabitants of the islands preserved the memory of a much larger Atlantic island. Seven islands were consecrated to the gods Proserpina, Pluto (Hades), and Poseidon.

Arabian legends tell of a land located in the western ocean and believed to be the cradle of civilization. They believed that the people of Ad lived here before the Great Flood and because of their sins were destroyed by the flood.

Diodorus Siculus writes that Atlanteans settled in Africa, and the inhabitants of northwest Africa were known as Atlanteans. For many years they resided in the land of Algiers. In ancient Chaldea, legend speaks of ten antediluvian kings whose fabulous reign extended thousands of years.

Legends abound in Europe of a large Atlantic Ocean island submerged during a great cataclysm. The ancient Celts claim their ancestors came from an earthly paradise in the western ocean, referred to as Avalon, which was ultimately annexed by the sea god. The island contained a great city, Caer Sidi, which was built in a circular form around a great canal. It was overwhelmed by a great flood. Albion, the son of Poseidon, was the original tutelary god of Britain for which Albany, Scotland, was named.

Formorians, in an Irish legend, were the Domnu known as the undersea people from a land that sank below the waves. They were people of gigantic stature, and like the Titans, they waged war upon the gods. They were skilled in magic and dark science. Much of Plato's account of Atlantis is similar to British legend.

Celtic mythology also refers to Atlantis in the saga of *The Voyage of Maildun*. Maildun was an island used by the sea folk for horse racing. The travelers came to an Island of Apples resembling Hesperides. Within the island, a high island divided into four parts with its four walls meeting in the center. There was a wall of gold, a wall of silver, a wall of copper, and a wall of crystal. The legend appears to describe Poseidonis.

Another Celtic legend tells of the sunken city of Ys. It was ruled by Gradlon who was warned of imminent destruction by the approaching sea. He built a large basin to receive overflow from high tide waters. His malevolent daughter Princess Dahut stole the key and opened the sluice gate, allowing the tide to rush in and submerge the city. Gradlon, a Celtic god believed to have been Poseidon, owned a palace resembling the one in Plato's Atlantis. The

Celts believed the abode of the dead lay to the west in the Atlantic Ocean as did the Greeks, Cretans, and Romans.

The Druids are also believed to be of Atlantean origin. Author Lewis Spence wrote that Druidism was the last phase of the Atlantean religion and closely associated with astrology, which probably originated in Atlantis. Like the Atlanteans, the Druids possessed a pillar of orichalcum. They also have legends about the Deluge.

Roman historian Timagenes (first century A.D.) recorded legends of the Gauls telling about an island like Atlantis. One of the three distinct people who inhabited Gaul was from a distant island that had sunk. The Gauls say they came from a remote land in the middle of the ocean.

The Basques who occupied southwest France and northern Spain believed they were descendants of the ancient Atlanteans, whom they refer to as *Atlaintika*. Plato states this part of Europe belonged to the Kingdom of Atlantis. The Basques were the closest neighbors to Atlantis. Ancient Iberians (from which the Druids originated) spoke Basque before the Celtic and Roman conquerors.

The Spainish had legends of Antilla. They referred to it as the Isle of Seven Cities. It was a rectangular island appearing on the maps of the 14th, 15th, and 16th centuries. Columbus possessed such a map before his voyage and was advised by Toscanelli that the island lay midway to the Indies. Many writers believe Antilla was Atlantis. Legends of the Portuguese claim mountain peaks of Atlantis are the present day Azore Islands which lay west of Portugal.

The destruction of the original city of Athens is an accepted historical fact. In Greek mythology, Athene and Poseidon battled for the possession of Attica. Plato, in the third century B.C., wrote that Athens was founded nine thousand years earlier. According to the *Oera Linda Book,* Athens was founded by the Frisian warrior princess Minerva (Greek Athene) in whose honor the Acropolis was built. After the death of Minerva, the loyal people of the Hellenes established her as a goddess, an act that did not meet the approval of their Frisian colonists. Author Murry Hope suggests that Plato's Atlanteans, who waged war on the Athenians and were defeated, were none other than the Frisians.

Diodorus confirmed Plato's flood and states the Hellenic coast opposite the island of Rhodes was greatly damaged by the Flood of Deucalion, which occurred in the seventh generation. Famine, plague, pestilence, and corruption followed.

Aelian writes in *Varia Historia* about Theopompus (400 B.C.) who tells of an interview between Midas the king of Phrygia and Silenus, "The existence of a large continent lying beyond the ocean's stream . . . where splendid cities abound, peopled by gigantic, happy, and long lived inhabitants and enjoying a remarkable legal system."

According to the writings of Lewis Spence, Atlantis also colonized Crete. The Minonan civilization of Crete was patterned after Atlantis. Cretians were Iberians who worshiped the bull. Thera is an island in the Greek Cyclades north of Crete in the Aegean Sea. Below the sea lay remains of an ancient city. In the late 1960s Professor A. G. Galanopoulos and Dr. Spiridon Marinatos announced their theory that these archaeological finds were remnants of the legendary Atlantis.

The Norse and Scandinavians have legends about an ancient Frisian race, written about in the *Oera Linda Book.* The legend tells of a major catastrophe of global proportions that caused their mainland to sink beneath the waves. The land was home to a matriarchal society of fair, blue-eyed people who averaged seven feet tall. They were known as Atlands. Another Viking tradition tells of a strange and magical land to the southwest known as Atli.

Ancient sacred writings of India, the *Puranas* and *Mahabharata* refer to the "white islands." They comprised a continent called Attala located in the ocean half a world away.

The Aztec Indians told the conquistadors of Central America that their race originated on a large island called Aztlan, which some claim lay in the ocean to the east. Toltecs also traced their origins to Aztlan. Aztec is derived from Atzlan. In the Aztec tongue (Nahuatl), "atl" means water, which has the same meaning in the Berber language of North Africa. The Berbers have their own legends of Attala, a kingdom rich in gold, silver, and tin, that now lies beneath the ocean.

Quetzalcoatl, the god of the Aztecs, was said to be a bearded white man who came to the Valley of Mexico from the ocean. Some Atlantologists believe he came from Atlantis.

The Quiche Maya referred to the country in the east as a true paradise where they once lived. Dr. Augustus le Plongeon writes in Queen Moo and the Egyptian Sphinx about how Moo, a Mayan princess in Central America, went to Egypt and helped found the Egyptian civilization. This occurred about the time of the Great Flood. He finds a similarity between the hieroglyphics of the Egyptians and those of Central America.

The Mayan calendar begins on June 5, 8498 B.C., which is thought to correspond to the day that Atlantis was destroyed. A triple conjunction between the Sun, Moon, and Venus took place on that day. Author Otto Muck believes this conjunction influenced the fall of an asteroid into the Atlantic Ocean, causing the Great Flood. It signaled the onset of a new era and the start of a diluvial catastrophe. The Mayan calendar, according to Muck, is five times more accurate than our own Gregorian calendar.

More than one hundred North American Indian tribes have legends of their ancestors coming from a large island in the ocean that was destroyed by a world catastrophe. A myth of the Arawak Indians tells of their god Aimon Kondi scourging the world with fire, which is followed by a flood. Many other myths around the world speak of the drowning of the human race because of its wickedness. The Mandan Indians of North Dakota are believed by some Atlantologists to be of Atlantean heritage. They have a flood legend and use an image of an ark in their ceremonies. The ceremonies reflect the loss of a large land east of the North American continent. Many Mandans were white with gray, hazel, and blue eyes, and some had ash-blond hair. Unlike other Indians, they lived in fortified towns and manufactured earthenware. Some evidence suggests they may be of Irish descent that will be presented later.

Hopi legend tells of their twin gods, Popanghoya and Palongawhoya who guarded the north and south axis (poles) of the Earth. They kept the planet rotating properly. Sotuknang, the nephew of the Creator, ordered them to leave their posts so that the second world could be destroyed because its people had become evil. "Then the world, with no one to control it, teetered off balance, spun around crazily, then rolled over twice. Mountains plunged into the sea with a great splash, seas and lakes splashed over the land, and as the world spun through cold and lifeless space, it froze into solid ice." The Hopis claim the first world was destroyed by fire.

GEOLOGICAL EVIDENCE

Science provides hard evidence to support the legends and theories about the lost continent of Atlantis. The ability to map the Atlantic Ocean floor provides confirmation that a continent did exist above water. Hypotheses by scientists try to explain how such a cataclysm could occur. Some conjecture that an asteroid or comet initiated the catastrophe, while others believe an axis tilt caused it. Archaeological evidence also supports the existence of an advanced civilization. Plato tells of Atlantis suffering violent earthquakes and floods, and in a single day and night Atlantis disappeared and sank below the sea. Could this be possible?

Rapid earth changes on a smaller scale have occurred quite frequently. On November 1, 1775, one of the largest earthquakes of modern times occurred in Lisbon, Portugal. Within six minutes, 60,000 people met their death. A large number of people had gathered on a newly built marble quay. It sank six hundred feet with not one body floating to the surface.

In 1808, a volcano suddenly rose thirty five hundred feet and burned six days on the island of San Jorge in the Azores. Near San Miguel in 1811, a volcano rose from the sea to create an island three hundred feet high. Named Sambrina, it sank below the sea shortly afterwards. Similar volcanic eruptions have occurred in the Azores in 1691 and 1720.

The Earth's surface has a record of successive rising and falling. Near Morocco, the ground opened and engulfed a village of 10,000 inhabitants. In Pennsylvania twenty-three different layers of coal deposits occur within a two thousand foot depth. Each deposit was created when the land rose sufficiently above the sea to maintain vegetation. Layers of rock strata were deposited under water, with some strata measuring hundreds of feet thick.

Ignatius Donnelly quotes Professor Winchel from the Preadmites, ". . . we have seen the whole coast of South America lifted up bodily ten feet or fifteen feet and let down in an hour. We have seen the Andes sink 220 feet in seventy years." Approximately twelve hundred miles of South America beaches have been raised one hundred to thirteen hundred feet.

Dr. Bruce Heezen, an oceanographer with the Lamont Geological Observatory of Columbia University, reports that 11,000 years ago, the sea level all around the world was three hundred feet lower than it is today. The eastern coastline of the United States extended one hundred miles further out into the Atlantic Ocean. The sudden end of the Ice Age caused great quantities of snow and ice to melt and run into the oceans, resulting in a dramatic increase in sea level.

Deep-sea soundings enabled scientists to map the ocean floor. The U.S. ship Dolphin mapped the bottom of the Atlantic Ocean. They found the ocean floor rising about nine thousand feet above the depths surrounding it, with the islands of the Azores, St. Paul's Rock, Ascension, and Tristan d'Acunha all reaching the ocean's surface. This area is referred to as the Dolphin Ridge (Atlantic Ridge) and believed to be the lost island of Atlantis. On July 28, 1877, *The Scientific American* reports this land was once dryland based on the contour of the mountains and valleys which erosion patterns show could only have been formed above water level. Two other ridges on the Atlantic floor, the Challenger Ridge and Connecting Ridge, connect the Dolphin Ridge to South America just north of the mouth of the Amazon. J. Starke Gardner writes in *Popular Science Review* in July 1878, "A great tract of land formerly existed where the sea is, and that Cornwall, Scilly, the Channel Islands, Ireland, and Britain are the remains of its high summits."

In 1989, a layer of sand, discovered in the North Sea off the coast of northern Scotland, was sandwiched between two layers of peat that were above water seven thousand years ago. This landmass was described in the ancient Frisian legend of Scandinavia.

Geologists believe that 200 million years ago, the continents of the world were grouped together in a single landmass called the Pangaea. The lithosphere is the Earth's outer shell, approximately twenty-five miles thick. It is composed of a number of rigid plates, which collide, grow apart, or slide past one another. Beneath the lithosphere is a molten layer called the asthenosphere. Slow convection currents in the asthenosphere exerted great force on Pangaea and caused it to break into separate pieces. When continental plates collide, the Earth's crust buckles and mountains are formed. In 1912, Alfred Wegener proposed his theory of continental drift. He said that changes in the spin of the earth's axis could bring about new directions of continental drift.

Science shows a gradual widening of the Atlantic Ocean. The continental shelves of South America and Africa match, but the shelves of North America and Europe do not. However, their shelves are a perfect match for the Atlantic Ridge.

In 1898, the transatlantic cable snapped approximately five hundred miles off the Azores. While dredging the ocean floor for the cable at a depth of 10,000 feet, a fragment of vitreous lava was brought to the surface. Included was tachylite, a rock of vitreous structure. Paul Termies, Director of the Oceanographic Institute in Paris, asserts the rock must have solidified in free air and could only have been ejected by an above-water volcano. The whole region, he claims, must have sunk more than 6,250 feet at the same time as the eruption or shortly thereafter. The catastrophe must have occurred less than 15,000 years ago. Coming to the same conclusion, Dr. Maria Klenova of the Soviet Academy of Science, after examining similar rocks dredged from the same region.

Other clues to the existence of Atlantis are provided by the Gulf Stream, which warms Europe. Trade winds are a result of a loose coupling between the rotating Earth and encircling air. This coupling sets in motion the Gulf Stream, the sea water drift of the Atlantic Ocean. During the Quaternary period, which began about 20,000 B.C., there was about the same cover of ice on North America and Europe, both buried under huge ice caps. The Gulf Stream originates in the Gulf of Mexico and flows northeast to the North Atlantic. At forty degrees latitude it flows east in the wake of the west winds. This flow occurred in the Quaternary period as it does today. However, it never arrived off Europe on the other side of the Atlantic. Something in the ocean must have blocked it during the entire Quaternary period. It is believed the block came from the great landmass on the Dolphin Ridge that was above water.

Once the landmass sank, the warm Gulf Stream flowed to Europe, and the glacial period ended about 12,875 years ago, according to scientists. This was approximately the transition date from the Quaternary period to the Quinternary age, about 10,000 B.C., near the time the great island of Atlantis was believed to have sunk.

Otto Muck believed the island extended 685 miles north to south. It had ten large peaks, with Mount Atlas (Pico Alto) reaching 16,400 feet. The southwestern part of the island enjoyed a Gulf Stream climate ideal for vegetation, as described by Plato. It brought a mild damp climate to the whole coast, a subtropical climate. The royal city lay near the southeast coast.

What caused this large island to sink? One theory speculates that an asteroid hit the earth. Two large holes nearly 23,000 feet deep and occupying 77,000 square miles, sit on the remains of the fractured Puerto Rico Plateau near Puerto Rico. The Puerto Rico Trench, which has a depth of 30,000 feet, encircles the southern part of the central area. The submerged terrain gives the impression of a large crater. American anthropologist Alan H. Kelso de Montigny and other scientists believe an asteroid hit here about 10,000 years ago. The two similar impact craters are adjacent and were thought to be caused by the asteroid splitting in two. The major axes are elliptical, running from northwest to southeast. Supporting this theory, numerous meteorite craters in South Carolina align with the two larger craters. The Quiche Indians are reported to have seen a huge fire in the sky at the same time as the Great Flood. Other myths tell of a fire in the sky before the flood. Off the coast of the Yucatan Peninsula in the Gulf of Mexico, researchers find evidence of a large underwater crater that some believe may be evidence of an asteroid.

Otto Muck describes the probable scenario. The impact of the asteroid caused a great tidal wave. Volcanic eruptions ran along the entire fracture caused by the asteroid. With the Earth's crust fractured, large masses of magma were released. It took two to three days at the most for the seam to open. The red-hot magma emerged from the depths of the Atlantic producing superheated steam. As the fracture seam continued to burst open, magma, water vapor, and gases continued to increase. The level of the magma beneath the Atlantic floor dropped considerably . Much of it was blown away, resulting in a great depression below the center of the Atlantic basin. The deepest depression was along the fracture which bifurcated around Atlantis. This great depression, resulting from magma depletion, caused Atlantis to sink within twenty-four hours. Today, Atlantis lays two miles below the surface of the Atlantic Ocean.

A great sea of mud resulted from the sinking of Atlantis. When compared with the mud produced in the past century by the huge volcano Krakatoa in the South Pacific, the mud would have lasted an estimated three thousand years. Rumors persisted for a millennium about the mud, and that the ocean was unnavigable beyond the Pillars of Hercules (Gibraltar).

Muck estimates a black cloud drifted eastward containing 3 x

10^{16} tons of volcanic ash and 2 x 10^{16} tons of moisture. In the form of wet, rain-bearing steam it was ejected with the fragmented particles of magma. These minute particles, along with salt crystals, were ideal nuclei for condensation of raindrops. It became a rain cloud of immense dimensions. The cloud drifted eastward across the landmass of the Old World and tropical regions of the New World. It was in these two regions that the rain came, beginning the myths of the Great Flood. This cloud mixture of water and ash would have produced an average rainfall of one hundred feet in northern Eurasia.

In 1928, archaeologist Leonard Wooley carried out his famous excavation at Ur, located in ancient Mesopotamia. Below the tombs of the early Sumerian kings and forty feet below the ground surface, archaeologists found a layer of alluvial clay eight feet two inches thick. It contained no artifacts but evidence of a tremendous inundation from a great flood. Muck believed this could only result from rain and ash occurring 11,000 years prior. He estimated it would take water sixteen hundred feet deep to produce that much mud. The drainage basins of the Tigris and Euphrates rivers were over four hundred miles long. Rainfall of one hundred feet and a mass of sea water could have produced enough water to cause that much mud. Sumerian legends tell of people being turned into mud.

Muck speculated, the dust cloud containing a great amount of water floated at an altitude of 125 to 185 miles. It blocked out sunlight, causing death to plants, animals, and humans. Thickest in the north, it concentrated to the east of the Atlantic Ocean. The original name of Europe meant "world of darkness."

A large asteroid could generate 36,032 degrees of heat, which would have almost instantly melted the Ice Age glaciers in its path. Scientists today theorize that 65 million years ago an asteroid caused the extinction of dinosaurs. In 1989, an asteroid one mile in diameter missed the Earth by 500,000 miles, approximately four hours from a major cataclysm.

An asteroid may have been initiated an axis tilt. Both the Eskimos and Chinese have legends that the Earth tilted violently before the Flood. Ancient Chinese records tell of a time when the sky suddenly began to fall northward, and the sun, moon, and planets changed their course after the Earth had been shaken. Egyptians and Norsemen of ancient times observed the sun rising and setting in a position other than from east to west. The *Oera Linda Book* describes a great catastrophe that involved a tilting of the Earth's axis. It caused climatic changes of great severity within the space of three days.

Greenland is regarded by many to be the northern extreme of Atlantis. It had a subtropical climate in the geological past. A mammoth discovered in a frozen ice field of Siberia died very suddenly, after enjoying a meal of fresh buttercups. During the Quaternary period, Siberia was completely ice-free. The transition from warm to ice occurred suddenly as other mammoths also found in the ice field showed little sign of decomposition.

Some hypothesize that a comet hit the planet. Fifty percent of a comet's mass is composed of ice with the remainder being composed of loosely packed dust and other solids, along with gases such as ammonia and methane. The rapid ice melting would have increased the sea level and created an enormous amount of vaporized water. This would have caused great rainfall and contributed to glacieral melting.

Migration patterns of birds from Europe to South America suggest the existence of a lost landmass. As birds approach the area where Atlantis once was, they begin to fly in great concentric circles to find rest. They do not find it and so continue their journey. The pattern is repeated on their return trip.

Lemmings, Norwegian rodents, gather in hordes during a population explosion and food shortage. They enter the water and swim westward and eventually drown. Legend says they are looking for a land that was once in the west.

If the North Pole was in Hudson's Bay, the South Pole would have been located off Wilkes Coast, which is more than fifteen hundred miles southeast of the South Pole. Much of Antarctica would have been ice-free. Ancient maps have been found that show Antarctica as ice-free, which may have been true during the time of Atlantis.

Writer Lewis Spence believes Atlantis was a much larger landmass than Plato described. He believes it had split into two sections, with the second named Antilla and closer to the North American coastline. Muck believes several great cataclysms at different times caused different portions of the Atlantis landmass to sink. The field of paleomagnetism reveals that the position of the poles has changed at least two hundred times. Sixteen of them have occurred during the last geological period, the Pleistocene epoch.

Atlantologists believe the Sargasso Sea occupies an area Atlantis once occupied and encompasses approximately 2 million square miles of the Atlantic Ocean between the West Indies and the Azores. A calm center in the midst of the Gulf Stream, the sea's name is derived from the sargasso seaweed floating on it.

Archaeological evidence suggests a great civilization existed on what is now the Atlantic floor. Several buildings can be seen below the surface of the ocean off Bimini, an island located east of Florida. In 1968, Dr. H. Manson Valentine discovered an underwater causeway beneath several fathoms of water. The causeway consisted of giant rectangular blocks believed to be a ceremonial road leading to a special site. Fossilized mangrove roots have grown over these stone structures near Bimini. Radiocarbon dating places them at 12,000 B.C. The entire area of the Bahama Bank is believed to have been above sea level during the last glaciation. Underwater buildings have been seen on the northern tip of Andros in the Caribbean.

Pilots flying over the Atlantic Ocean have reported seeing groups of buildings, cities, archways, and pyramids under the ocean surface. Pyramids and huge domes have been seen on the seabed near Cuba and Haiti. West of Gibraltar, in 1974, photographs from the Soviet ship Academician Petrovsky showed walls and steps made of stone blocks that measured about five feet in height and width.

THE RACES OF ATLANTIS

Professor Allan Wilson, a biochemist at the University of California in Berkeley, produced genetic evidence that all present-day humans are related to an African woman who lived 200,000 years ago. Fossil evidence supports the idea that the oldest lineage was African, dating back 140,000 to 290,000 years ago. Tribal legends from Peru, Colombia, Yucatan, Mexico, and Brazil tell of white visitors who were great reformers and leaders and who taught a path of pacification, love, and nonviolence. The legends say these teachers came from an unknown land in the ocean. Churchward claims these white visitors came from Lemuria, while Atlantologists believe they came from Atlantis. Perhaps both are right.

The Cro-Magnon race lived in Europe between 20,000 and

10,000 B.C. A 10,000 year old Cro-Magnon skeleton was found in South America at Tierra del Fuego in 1969/1970. Some Cro-Magnon skeletons average six feet seven inches, and author Murray Hope suggests they may be the giants referred to in the Bible. Otto Muck believes the Cro-Magnon people came from the west and sailed across the Atlantic. They landed at the river mouths in the valleys of Europe. The Neanderthal, whose average height was less than five feet three inches, was believed to have been pushed back to the alpine regions of Europe by the Cro-Magnon. Muck asserts they came either from America, Mesoamerica, or from Atlantis. Europe was largely covered by ice when Atlantis existed.

It was the Cro-Magnon people who made the beautiful cave paintings in Spain and western France. Their skin color was reddish-brown. Lewis Spence writes that the Cro-Magnon man was the first of the immigrant wave to surge into Europe as Atlantis was undergoing its earlier cataclysms 20,000 years ago. The Cro-Magnon people were tall, big boned, muscular, and similar to the red Indian of America. The Egyptians claimed to be rot, or of a red race, and the later dynasties were anxious to preserve the red skin color. Hope believes the Cro-Magnon man was a remnant of an advanced Muan or Lemurian red race.

Other races associated with Atlantis include the Fenians, an Irish race that tradition says comes from the regions of the Pillars of Hercules. The Formorians were people of the deep sea who came to Ireland. They were the Iberian race, the modern form of the Azilian race, which comprises the majority of Ireland. Archaeologist Sergi asserts that the Iberian race originated in western Africa known as the Atlas region. These people also include ancient and modern Egyptians, Berbers, Abyssinians, and Nubians. The Basques claim to be descendants of the Atlanteans, as the ancient Iberians spoke Basque. Spence writes that the Atlantean expansion must be identified with the Iberian expansion.

Many similarities exist between languages on both sides of the Atlantic and worldwide. They suggest a single point of origin. Churchward claims the language originated from Lemuria and spread to Atlantis and other colonies of Lemuria.

THE KINGS AND GODS OF ATLANTIS

Plato wrote that Poseidon, the god of Atlantis, married a mortal woman and begat five sets of male twins. Before the destruction of Atlantis, humanity became wicked because the gods interbred with the daughters of the Earth, which caused humans to lose their divine powers. Zeus, the god of gods, observed that Atlantis was in a most wretched state, and he wanted to inflict punishment on it. Shortly thereafter, Atlantis sank.

A parallel story occurs in the Bible. Genesis 6:2 reads, "That the sons of god saw the daughters of men that they were fair; and they took them wives of all which they chose." Verse four states, "There were giants in the earth in those days; and also after that, when the sons of god came unto the daughters of men, the same became mighty men which were of old, men of renown." Verse five says, "And God saw that the wickedness of man was great in the Earth, and that every imagination of the thoughts of his heart was only evil continually." Verse seven follows, "And the Lord said, I will destroy man whom I have created from the face of the Earth . . . " The Great Flood of Noah followed and destroyed most of humanity. Plato's Atlantis flood and the biblical version of the Flood are very similar, suggesting they may have been the same. Both versions speak of gods, implying they are not the Creator God.

Who were these gods? Ignatius Donnelly gives evidence in his book *Atlantis* that the deified kings of Atlantis were the gods of the Greeks. The history of Atlantis is the key to Greek mythology. According to Donnelly, these gods were like human beings. So where did these gods come from? Author Murray Hope in *Atlantis: Myth or Reality?* suggests that "this divine gene" of Poseidon came from a genus external to this planet. Were these gods extraterrestrials? Zecharia Sitchin's research of Sumerian cuneiform writings also suggests the gods of Sumer, Greece, and Egypt were of genes external to this planet. The Sumerian texts tell where these gods came from and their role with humans. This will be discussed further in chapter four. The mythical cosmology of the Greeks was derived from the Sumerian-Babylonian models. If the Greek gods were the same as the gods of Atlantis, the Atlantean gods would also be of extraterrestrial origin.

For this book, it is important that we look at the deified kings
of Atlantis and see how they relate to mythology despite the many
contradictions that occur in mythology. This occurs partly because
different countries call the same god by a different name and perhaps have a different legend associated with the god. The sons of
Poseidon were all kings. Their names were Atlas, Gadir or Eumolus,
Amphisus, Eudemon, Mneseus, Autochthonus, Elassipus, Mestor,
Azaes, and Diaprepus. Plato states these names had been
Egyptenized from the Atlantean language by the priest of Sais and
subsequently Hellenized by Critias.

Donnelly builds a good case that Greek mythology was the
history of Atlantis. The gods were not looked upon as having created the world but only managed the world already in existence. The
Greek gods dwelt on Olympus much like human beings. They had
palaces, storehouses, stables, and horses. Their social state was similar to the social system on Earth. Olympus was a great island encircled by the ocean. It was the garden of the gods and an island full
of wonders. Olympus was Atlantis, according to Donnelly. Greek
tradition located the island of Olympus in the far west, in the ocean
beyond Africa. Donnelly notes that Olympus and Atlantis are very
similar in pronunciation. Mythology describes Olympus as shaped
like a disk with mountains rising from it. On the highest mountain
lived Zeus, the ruler of the gods. The abode of the deities lay lower
down the mountain on plateaus and ravines. There were twelve
deities comprising the pantheon: Zeus (Jupiter), Hera (Juno),
Poseidon (Neptune), Demeter (Ceres), Apollo, Artemus (Diana),
Hephaestos (Vulcan), Pallas Athena (Minerva), Hermes (Mercury),
and Hestia (Vesta). The Roman names are in parentheses.

Greek mythology tells of Chronos (Saturn), Dionysos,
Hyperion, Atlas, and Hercules being connected with a great
Saturnian continent. They were kings that ruled over countries on
the western shores of the Mediterranean, Africa, and Spain. The
kingdom was divided between Atlas and Saturn, with Atlas ruling
North Africa and the Atlantic islands. Chronos took the northern
shores of the Mediterranean including Italy and Sicily.

Plato writes in *Dialogue, Laws* ". . . God in his love of mankind
placed over us the demons, who are a superior race, and they with
great care and pleasure to themselves and no less to us, taking care
of us and giving us place and revenue and order and justice never

failing, made the tribes of men happy and peaceful . . . for Chronos knew no human nature, invested with supreme power, is able to order human affairs and not overflow with insolence and wrong." Donnelly writes, "In other words, legend refers to an ancient time when the forefathers of the Greeks were governed by Chronos, of the Cronian Sea (the Atlantic), King of Atlantis, through civilized Atlantean governors . . . who by their wisdom created a golden age under the control of the demons (the knowing wise ones)." In Greek mythology a demon is an intermediate between god and man.

In this era of the gods, Chronos, Uranos, and Zeus passed through a Golden Age, a time of plenty, and then they entered a Silver Age of peace and happiness. An Iron Age of struggle followed, and finally Zeus sent a Great Flood to punish the people for their sins. The whole of Greece lay underwater according to Greek mythology. Donnelly asserts that the history of Atlantis could be reconstructed out of the mythology of Greece. It is a history of royalty, love, adultery, wars, murders, rebellions, palaces, agriculture, and other human endeavors.

Uranos was the first god. He was at the beginning of all things, and his symbol was the sky, who was the son of Gaea (Earth). Uranos parented three races — the Titans, Hekatoncheires, and the Cyclops. The empire of the Titans was the empire of Atlantis. Leading mythologists believed the post-diluvian world was partitioned among Shem, Ham, and Japeth — the sons of Noah. Pre-diluvianl partitioning was among Zeus (Jupiter), Poseidon (Neptune), and Pluto. Zeus, the most potent of the brothers, received Asia. Poseidon ruled the sea and its islands, and Pluto was believed to have ruled Spain.

The empire of the Titans, which most Atlantologists believed was Atlantis, was extensive, according to the ancients. They possessed Phrygia; Thrace, a part of Greece; Crete; Spain, part of Africa; and Sanchoniathon, which adjoins Syria. Mythology tells us that the Titans were defeated by Saturn (Chronos) and then retreated into the interior of Spain. The names of the Titans were Oceanus, Chronos, and Atlas, all the sons of Uranos.

Oceanus and Tethys were the children of Earth and Heaven, and their offspring were Chronos and Rhea. Chronos, the harvest god, married his sister who gave birth to Zeus, Pluto, Poseidon, Hestia, Demeter, and Hera. Uranos was deposed from the throne, and his son Chronos succeeded him. The Romans knew Chronos as Saturn who ruled over a great Saturnian continent in the western ocean. Chronos came to Italy and changed it from a barbaric society to a peaceful one. Plato confirmed that the Atlantean rule extended to Italy, home of a civilized, agricultural, and commercial people. The civilization of Rome was an outreach of Atlantis.

Zeus was the third and last ruler on the throne of the highest god, and was called the thunderer. During the time of Zeus, Atlantis was at the height of power, and Zeus was recognized as the father of the entire world. Zeus was righteous, merciful, truthful, faithful, and kind. His offspring included Artemis (Diana), Aphrodite (Venus), Hermes (Mercury), and Hercules.

Poseidon was the first king of Atlantis. He was a brother to Zeus and son of Chronos and fell heir to the Ocean and its islands. Poseidon, often portrayed carrying a trident while riding in a chariot, was god of maritime, commerce, and agriculture. During his reign Poseidon founded many colonies along the shores of the Mediterranean. He settled Attica and founded Athens named after his niece Athena, daughter of Zeus. Temples were erected to Poseidon in nearly all the seaport towns of Greece. The *Iliasi* portrays Poseidon as ruler of the sea who inhabited a brilliant palace in its depths.

The nymphs of Greek mythology were between god and humans and were communicated with and respected by both. Donnelly believed they were the female inhabitants of Atlantis who lived in the plains and were called Atlantides, the offspring of Atlantis. He writes, "The entire Greek mythology is the recollection, by a degenerate race, of a vast, mighty, and civilized empire, which in a remote past covered large parts of Europe, Asia, Africa, and America."

Tradition suggests that the Atlantean people worshiped the sun. The goddess Neith gave birth to Ra, the sun god, while Isis was the mother of Rat, the female sun. Isis was a goddess of Egypt, believed to have come from Atlantis.

Most students of Atlantology believe that the Titans and Atlanteans were the same. Prometheus, according to Greek mythology, played a role in the origin of humanity. During the revolt of the Titans, Prometheus remained neutral, which resulted in his admittance to the circle of immortals. He maintained a grudge against those who destroyed his race and favored humankind rather than the gods. Legends have Prometheus fashioning people in the likeness of the gods. The Egyptians believed Prometheus was a son of Poseidon.

Historian Diodorus Siculus of Sicily gives nearly as much history about Atlantis as did Plato. His writings in *Historical Library* present a general history of the world as known in his time. He concurs that the genealogy of the Atlanatean gods did not differ much from legends of the Greeks. The Atlanteans, Diodorus writes, inhabited a rich country bordering the ocean and were noted for their hospitality to strangers. They claimed the gods were born among them, and Uranus was their first king. According to Diodorus, Uranus was Poseidon, and both were fathers of Atlas. Uranus civilized the people and caused them to live in the cities and till the soil. Uranus, the Roman god of the sky, fathered Saturn. Under his dominion lay greater part of the world, especially toward the west and north. Being a great prophet, Uranus was addicted to the study of astrology. He instituted the solar year and lunar months. The people admired him and paid him divine honors by naming the starry heavens after him following his death. Uranus had forty-five children by various wives, and eighteen of them were by Titea or Terra. They became known as the Titans.

Uranus's most celebrated daughters were Basilea and Rhea (Pandora). Basilea was known as the Great Mother and was elected queen of the people after the demise of Uranus. Writer Lewis Spence believes Basilea was the mother goddess revered by the entire Mediterranean and known as Astaroth, Astarte, Diana, Venus, Aphrodite, and Isis. She was the great maternal figure with many names. She married her brother Hyperion and gave birth to Helio and Selene, who later became the gods of the Sun and Moon. Upon the death of Hyperion, the children of Uranus divided the kingdom among themselves. Atlas took control of the country bordering the ocean and called its inhabitants Atlanteans. A great mountain named Atlas arose from the land.

Atlas married his sister Hesperius, who begat him seven daughters called the Atlantides. Busiris, the Egyptian king, fell in love with the Atlantide maidens and sent pirates to kidnap them. Hercules intercepted the pirates and rescued the young women returning them to Atlas. In appreciation, Atlas, a wise astrologer, taught Hercules the art of astrology. The Egyptians told Herodotus that Hercules was one of their most ancient deities and one of the twelve produced from the eight gods. This happened 17,000 years before the reign of Amasis. The seven Atlantides became the first ancestors of several nations including Greece. They were known as the seven stars of the Pleiades who were adored as goddesses. In other myths, Atlas was alluded to as son of Iapetus and Clyme, and brother of Prometheus and Epimethus. Atlas and the Titans made war against Zeus.

Saturn (Chronus) was the brother of Atlas, who married his sister Rhea and fathered Jupiter (Zeus). Jupiter displaced his father Saturn and became King of Atlantis. Saturn made war against Jupiter but was overcome in battle, and Jupiter conquered the world.

The writings of Pomonius Mela tell that Albion, the Titan, was son of Poseidon. He was the original tutelary god of Britain, and his brother Iberius was the tutelary god of Ireland. Albion and Iberius were the Celtic gods considered to be giants.

The gods of Atlantis began to be overlaid with a hierarchy of deities. These were gods of virtues and vices, gods of trades, gods of agriculture, and so on. Once the gods became connected with a planet, they were regarded as powerful deities. They strove to direct the action of man into harmony by means of their own great plan. Later, the dynasties of Sumer, Greece, Rome, Egypt, Babylonia, Mexico, and Central America all began with legends of the lives and deeds of the heavenly descended monarchs. Were the giants of the Bible, originally called the Nefilim, the Titans of Atlantis? Were they the Anunnaki, who the Sumerians called gods from another planet? Perhaps the Atlantean gods and Sumerian gods were one and the same.

OTHER MYSTERIES OF ATLANTIS

America's best known seer, Edgar Cayce, provided historical information about Atlantis through his many trance like clairvoyant readings. He died in 1945 leaving over 14,000 documented records of his clairvoyant statements on more than 8,000 people over forty-three years. Cayce predicted that remnants of Atlantis would be discovered in a not-too-distant future in the Atlantic Ocean, east of Florida. He said that Atlantis occupied an area between the Gulf of Mexico and the Mediterranean Sea. In 1968, ruins were found off the coast of Bimini, not far from where Cayce had predicted; many believe these ruins to be traces of Atlantis.

Cayce gave many readings about the continent of Atlantis. Atlantis encompassed great stone cities with modern advantages such as mass communications and transportation via land, air, and undersea. Atlanteans were very scientific and had the ability to neutralize gravity. They knew of electricity and atomic power and used laser technology. They developed a means of spiritual communication between the finite and infinite through huge reflective crystals known as the Tuaoi Stones. Scientists could generate power from these great crystals, which radiated energy across the land without wires. The crystals became known as Firestones or the Great Crystals. One huge crystal located in the Temple of the Sun in Poseidonis, became the power station of the country. It was suspended in the center of the building under a dome, which could be rolled back for exposure to the sun. Its energy powered ships at sea, aircraft, and pleasure vehicles. Energy was transmitted throughout the land through invisible beams, similar to radio waves. The crystal's energy also rejuvenated the human body, but it also became a tool for torture and punishment. It started many fires deep within the Earth, which precipitated volcanic eruptions.

Cayce said the deterioration of the Atlantean civilization was largely responsible for its destruction. Civil discontentment, enslavement of workers, and interbreeding of humans with animals occurred. Human sacrifice, widespread adultery, fornication and misuse of the forces of nature also contributed to the deterioration. He said the mixing of races, the "sons of god and daughters of men" caused degeneracy of a perfect race in Lemuria, which disappeared beneath the Pacific Ocean and a new era commenced in Atlantis. The misuse of the crystals helped cause two of the cataclysms that eventually destroyed Atlantis. The spiritual evolution of the Atlanteans, Cayce said, did not keep pace with their mental and physical evolvement, hence they were destroyed.

Chapter Three

SUMER
The First Civilization

How the world's first recorded civilization advanced so rapidly in the land of Sumer remains a great mystery of ancient history. Before the middle of the 19th century, historians were unaware of this ancient culture. Sumer comprised the lower half of Mesopotamia, a land today occupied by modern Iraq, north of Baghdad to the Persian Gulf, an area of approximately 10,000 square miles. In classical times Sumer became known as Babylonia. Two major rivers, the Tigris and Euphrates, provided its lifeblood. The climate was hot and dry, the soil arid and windswept. No trees grew to provide timber resources, and large reeds covered many marshes. Beginning in the fourth millennium B.C., the ingenuity of the Sumerians transformed this forsaken land into a garden of Eden.

Sumer was the land of firsts. It provided recorded history with the first written documents; it provided the first schools, the first political congress, the first taxes, the first law code, and humanity's first cosmogony and cosmology. As one compares this ancient civilization with today's modern society, many things have not changed over the millennium. Historians believe Sumer laid the foundation for our current civilization.

Scholars are bewildered about how a great civilization could arise from nowhere in such a short period of time. They have no idea where the people of Sumer originated. Excavations in the Indus Valley of India, similar to those in Sumer, suggest these two civilizations originated from a common source, but Sumer was much earlier and may have colonized the Indus Valley. Legends that explain the genesis of civilization in Mesopotamia infer there was an influx of people from the sea. One must wonder if they inherited this great civilization from Atlantis.

Lower Mesopotamia is a vast plain of alluvial mud brought down by the Tigris and Euphrates Rivers. Seven thousand years ago

51

all of what is now southern Iraq was under water, and the Persian Gulf reached north of Baghdad. The fertile silt brought down by the two rivers changed the sea into marshes, and islands began to appear allowing habitation and agriculture. As the land gradually dried, the marsh barriers disappeared and communities formed. They began to interact with one another, which helped unify the country. Few stones were found in Mesopotamia, so buildings were constructed almost entirely of mud brick which was sun-dried or kiln-baked.

Because mud was so prevalent in Sumer, it was used for tablets to record the cuneiform Sumerian writings. Approximately 99 percent of the tablets dealt with economic issues such as contracts, deeds, notes, and receipts. Literary texts comprised only 1 percent of the quarter million tablets excavated, with many still to be unearthed. The cuneiform script began as pictograph writing. Each sign, a picture of one or more objects, represented a word closely related to the object. Over time the Sumerians modified the meaning of the pictographs.

Mesopotamia was not easily accessible to Europeans, which accounted for the late discovery of Sumer. The heat could reach 120 degrees Fahrenheit, and the constant threat of hostile Bedouin tribes discouraged foreigners. In the early 1850s William Kennett Loftus discovered ruins of the ancient Sumerian city of Erech. Shortly afterward, George Rawlison discovered the biblical city, Ur of the Chaldees, the birthplace of Abraham. In 1855, J. E. Taylor discovered the ruins of Eridu. During the 1870s and 1880s, governments, universities, and museums, financed archaeologists and organized expeditions from many countries. The first significant excavation on a Sumerian site began in 1877 at Telloh, where lay the ancient ruins of the Sumerian city of Lagash. Between 1877 and 1900 Earnest de Sarzes conducted eleven major campaigns that unearthed 40,000 tablets and splendid statues.

Archaeologists from the University of Pennsylvania conducted the second major Sumerian excavation at Nippur beginning in 1889. The four campaigns resulted in 30,000 tablets from an era spanning from the second half of the third millennium B.C. to the last centuries of the first millennium B.C. The German scholar Grötefend first decoded the secrets of the cuneiform writings in the 1850s. Correct deciphering of the Sumerian language by other scholars continued for fifty years. The task was difficult because several different languages comprised the tablets. Throughout southern Iraq a frenzy of archaeological activity occurred between the years of 1920 and 1939. Dr. Samual Kramer became the leading scholar of Sumer and published numerous scientific papers and books. He was a Professor at the University of Pennsylvania and curator of their museum.

Sumer had not been heard of for two thousand years. There was no trace of its people, language, or civilization in the biblical, classical, or post-classical literature. No one knew until the mid-19th century that the people of Sumer existed. Scholars had begun to suspect that the cuneiform system of Babylonian writing was invented by a non-Semitic people who preceded the Semites in Babylonia.

HISTORY

The gods controlled the city-states of Sumer. As in Atlantis, during the pre-Flood era, the kings were gods themselves. Some scholars believe more than one major flood occurred, the latest being approximately 10,000 B.C. After the last Flood, the gods appointed the kings to represent them to rule the city-states.

Excavators at Ur found a list of Sumerian kings that gave their length of reign. Eight antediluvial (pre-Flood) kings reigned for a total of 241,200 years. Twenty-three kings ruled after the Flood, during the First Dynasty of Kish. The First Dynasty of Erech (mentioned in the Bible) had twelve kings who ruled for 2,310 years, while the First Dynasty of Ur (about 3100 to 2930 B.C.) had four kings who ruled one hundred seventy years. Dumuzi, an antediluvian god, is listed as a postdiluvian ruler of Erech, as is Gilgamesh, who was part god and part man.

The fact that the scribes recorded antediluvian kings and mentioned cities that existed before the Flood signifies that the Sumerians occupied the country before the Deluge. Scholars originally discounted the King's List as being fabricated myth because of the length of each king's reign. However, their minds began to change after excavations substantiated the kings mentioned on the list, suggesting the reality of the antediluvian gods. (The next chapter will discuss how these kings could have such long reigns, as they were the ancient gods. The history of only a few kings has been discovered.)

King Etana of Kish, who ruled for fifteen hundred years, was the first ruler of Sumer whose deeds were recorded. The King's List describes him as the king who stablized all the land. Scholars believe him to be the first known empire builder. Legend says he ascended to heaven.

Meskiaggashar, the son of Utu (the Sumerian sun god), was the first ruler of Erech and reigned for 325 years. He was known for his ambition and greed. Erech was a major city in southern Mesopotamia. Meskiaggashar's son, Enmerkar, succeeded him and was famous for his campaign against Aratta, which lay on the Caspian Sea. Enmerkar forced Aratta to surrender its independence and become a vassal of Erech. He used his sister, Inanna, the goddess of love, to threaten destruction of Aratta.

King Lugalbanda succeeded Enmerkar to the throne of Erech. He was followed by Dumuzi, a king married to the goddess Inanna. He reigned for 100 years. Gilgamesh succeeded Dumuzi. His deeds became world renown as he was the supreme hero of Sumerian myth and legend, becoming a symbol of man's drive for fame, glory, and immortality.

According to the King's List, the first three Sumerian dynasties after the Flood were of Kish, Erech, and Ur. The first dynasties of Kish and Erech overlapped. Kish, according to Sumerian legend, had received kingship from the gods immediately after the Flood. Erech, which lay far to the south, grew in prominence until it seriously threatened Kish's supremacy in Sumer.

The first postdiluvian settlements in Sumer occurred about 4500 B.C. and remained until Sumer's people no longer existed around 1750 B.C. By the year 3000 B.C., strong independent city-states such as Kish, Eridu, Ur, Erech, Umma, Larsa, Adab, and Nippur existed. At the zenith of Ur's expansion, one-half million people lived within four square miles of Ur. Comparable populations lived in Nippur, Kish, Eridu, and Lagash.

The cuneiform tablets recorded the history of Lugal-zaggisi who ruled for twenty-five years during the Third Dynasty of Erech about 2630 B.C. He was considered the King of Four Quarters (of the Universe) and exercised kingship over the entire world. All the foreign lands paid tribute to him because he brought peace to the people. He built temples for all the great gods and restored Sumer as a great civilization.

Sargon the Great was one of the most remarkable political figures of the ancient Near East. He was a Semite who founded the powerful Dynasty of Akkad. Sargon conquered the Lugal-zaggisi Dynasty resulting in the Semitization of Sumer, which eventually led to the end of the Sumerian people. Considered a genius in military leadership, Sargon's conquests destroyed the cities of Erech and Lagash. Armies invaded Egypt, Ethiopia, and India. Talented in administration and building, he left a historical legacy in deeds and achievements. Sargon's two sons later succeeded him and commemorated his military victories by erecting the most famous temple of Sumer, located at Nippur, in honor of the great god Enlil.

Not far from Kish, Sargon built the city of Agade, which in a brief span of time became the most prosperous and splendid city of the ancient world. Most of Agade's population were Semites related to Sargon by blood and language. From the name "Agade," or the biblical counterpart "Akkad," the word "Akkadian" has come to designate the Semites of Mesopotamia.

Sargon's grandson Naram-sin assumed rule from his father and brought Agade to new heights of power and glory until its tragic and bitter end. He defeated a powerful coalition of rebellious kings from Sumer, but his demise came from the demoralizing and destructive invasion by Gutians, a barbaric horde from the mountains to the east. A historical poem entitled *The Curse of Agade: The Ekur Avenged* describes the ordeal. Naram-Sin had sacked Nippur and desecrated and defiled Enlil's sanctuary. The god Enlil solicited the Gutians to come down from the mountains to destroy Agade and avenge Enlil's beloved temple. To soothe the spirit of their ruler, Enlil, eight of the important deities of the Sumerian pantheon placed a curse upon Agade so that it should remain forever desolate and uninhabitable. Inanna was the tutelary god of Agade who forsook her temple and the city of Agade.

The defeat of Naram-Sin at the hands of the Gutians resulted in political confusion and anarchy in Sumer. Under the Gutians rule, Lagash became the favored city for nearly a half century. A savior by the name of Utuhegal of Erech arose in Sumer, broke the reign of the Gutians, and brought back kingship to Sumer. After seven years of rule, Utuhegal's reign was usurped by Ur-Nammu, who founded the last important dynasty of Sumer known as the Third Dynasty of Ur. Ur-Nammu, a great builder, an outstanding administrator, and capable military leader, promulgated the first law code in man's recorded history. His leadership initiated a cultural renaissance that produced magnificent new buildings in Lagash, Umma, Nippur, and Ur. Shulgi, Ur-Nammu's son, inherited the kingship and ruled for forty-eight years, bringing relative peace and prosperity to Sumer. The Third Dynasty of Ur had twenty-three rulers and lasted from 2278 to 2170 B.C.

From 2170 to 1950 B.C. the Dynasty of Isir endured, founded by Ishbi-Erra who claimed rulership over Sumer and Akkad. The dynasty controlled Ur, the old imperial capital, and Nippur, Sumer's spiritual and intellectual center. Lipit-Ishtar assumed kingship for eleven years and claimed control over the deities of Sumer, proclaiming himself King of Sumer and Akkad. A new Sumerian law code was promulgated that was a model of the renowned code of Hammurabi.

To the north in the previously unimportant city of Babylon, an outstanding Semitic ruler named Hammurabi came to prominence. His legacy left the famous Hammurabi law code. His military force defeated the Elamites who had previously ended the last Dynaty of Ur. The kingdom reached from the Persian Gulf to the Habus River in the north and lasted from 1728 to 1686 B.C. With Hammurabi, the history of Sumer ends and the history of Babylonia begins. Babylonia was a Semitic state built on a Sumerian foundation.

Assyria was an ancient kingdom of northern Mesopotamia linked culturally with Babylonia. Lying between the Tigris and Euphrates Rivers, Assyria's first capital was Assur and later Ninevah. Assyria came into existence toward the end of the Sumerian reign about the time of Babylonia's rise. Between 700 and 530 B.C., the power of Assyria reached its zenith, controlling the whole Near East, including Egypt. Both Assyria and Babylonia struggled bitterly for supremacy throughout the second millennium B.C. Babylonia became a vassal state of Assyria, but in 612 B.C. it became independent after destroying Ninevah, thus beginning an era of prosperity. Assyrians, also Semitic, spoke Akkadian as did Babylonians. The people of both countries were characterized by their aquiline noses and high domed skulls. The decipherment of the Sumerian language came through the decipherment of Semitic Akkadian, also written in cuneiform.

THE PEOPLE OF SUMER

Three classes of people comprised the population of Sumer. Government officials, priests, and soldiers made up the patrician order, while merchants, school masters, farmers, artisans, and laborers comprised the burgher class. Slaves were the inferior class.

Sumerians believed their primary life purpose was to serve the gods. Religion, an important part of Sumerian life, instilled high values. Goodness and truth, law and order, wisdom and learning, courage and loyalty, mercy and compassion were all valued and practiced by Sumerians. Love and respect tied members of the family closely together as they committed themselves to family obligations. Cooperation between individuals and communities was a hallmark attribute of Sumerians. They valued personal rights and resented any encroachment upon them.

Their love for their home city and intense patriotism was a strong moving force in Sumerian thought. Sumerians, a competitive and aggressive people, strove for success, victory, and prestige, all reflected in their wealth and possessions. Sumerians valued rich harvests, well-stocked granaries, and stalls filled with cattle. Families of nobility owned huge estates that measured hundreds of acres, usually obtained by purchase from less fortunate citizens. Ordinary citizens owned about half the land not owned by the nobility or temples.

Parents arranged marriages. The betrothal became legally recognized when the groom presented a bridal gift to the bride's father. The groom forfeited the gift if he broke the engagement. A wedding ceremony consisted of writing and sealing the marriage tablet. A short courtship occurred before marriage, and premarital sex was quite common among young people. Often a special clause in the marriage contract protected the wife against the husband's creditors. This prevented him from disposing of joint property without her consent. Wives were allowed to engage independently in business and to keep or dispose of their own slaves. Under certain conditions, such as a payment for a debt, a husband could sell his wife and hand her over as a slave for three years. A husband could divorce his wife based on little grounds, unless she was protected by a special clause in the marriage contract. It was more difficult for her to divorce him. A barren wife could be divorced only after returning her dowry and giving compensation. In Sumer, monogamy was the law of the land. During the Third Dynasty of Ur, women who committed adultery were punished by drowning. However, there was tolerance for men to have concubines. Overall, the Sumerian laws protected the legitimate wife.

Children were under the absolute control of their parents, who had the right to disinherit them or even banish them from the city. Parents could sell their child into slavery or rent them out temporarily as slaves to pay off debt. Adoption was encouraged and safeguarded by law. Many children were adopted as a result of temple prostitution. This helped solve the dilemma of illegitimate children whose fathers were unknown. The temples of Sumer housed many prostitutes, and religion gave the profession a place of honor. Sumerian law also gave the children the right to inherit their deceased father's estate.

Slavery was a recognized institution in Sumer. The wealthy, nobility, royalty and temples owned and exploited slaves. Many slaves were prisoners of war, captured from a neighboring city defeated in battle. Sometimes free Sumerians could be reduced to slaves as punishment for committing a criminal offense. Slaves were the property of a master who usually treated them well, as it was to the owner's advantage to keep the slave healthy and strong. However, owners could brand their slaves and subject them to flogging for disobedience. Slaves had little protection against ill treatment. Children of slaves who married a free person became free. Sumerian law did give slaves some rights. Slaves could protest their sale and appeal it to the courts. They could give evidence in court, borrow money, engage in business, and they could buy their freedom.

Sumerians were often called "black heads" because of their dark hair. Many were short and stocky with a tendency to be fat in their middle age. Men usually had potbellies and prominent noses and eyes. Beards were common except among the priests.

Women in the higher class wore loose-fitted gowns that bared one shoulder. Other women usually wore flounced skirts, overlaid by long felt cloaks in early Sumer, but long skirts later became the style. Women often wore elaborate headdresses consisting of hair ribbon, beads, and pendants. Lip rouge and eye shadow were common, and wealthy women often enhanced themselves with oils, perfumes, and fancy jewelry.

The average Sumerian house, a small, one-story, mud-brick structure, consisted of several rooms built around an open court. Houses were often built on an artificial platform, above water level. The wealthy lived in two-story structures composed of about a dozen rooms. Furniture consisted of low tables, high-back chairs, and beds with wooden frames. Often there was a lack of furniture even among the rich. Reed mats, skin rugs, and wool hangings adorned floors and walls. Below many houses lay mausoleums where families buried their dead.

From Sumer, writing spread throughout the world. About the middle of the third millennium B.C. writing was formally taught, and shortly thereafter the Sumerian school system matured and flourished. Numerous school textbooks, unearthed in the ancient Sumerian city of Shuruppak, dated from 2500 B.C. The original goal of the Sumerian school system was to train scribes, as most graduates became scribes. Thousands of scribes worked throughout Sumer, ranging from junior scribes to high scribes to royal and temple scribes to highly specialized scribes. Scribes recorded the legacy of Sumer on clay tablets. The Sumerian vocabulary was complex, and their tongue was was monosyllabic and agglutinative, similar to Turkish, Finnish, and Hungarian.

The schools were known as *edubba tablet houses*. They became the centers of culture, creative writing, and learning in Sumer. Many ancient scholars' livelihoods depended on their teaching salaries, but education was not mandatory or universal. Most of the students came from wealthy families, since the poor could not afford the tuition, and the fathers of the scribes were usually the wealthiest citizens. The head of the school was called the "school father" and the student was the "student son." Discipline was a major problem in the schools, and the rod was not spared. Students met from sunrise until sunset, and attended school from early youth to young manhood.

Scribes and learned teachers often relocated from Sumer to the schools of neighboring lands, while scribes from other countries came to Sumer to learn and study the writing craft. Most of the peoples of western Asia, the Akkadians, Assyrians, Babylonians, Hittites, Hurrians, Cananites, and Elamites borrowed the cuneiform script. As a result, Sumer's culture and literature disseminated widely.

SUMER'S ECONOMY

Southern Mesopotamia was a fertile alluvial plain composed of silt layers deposited by the Tigris and Euphrates Rivers. When it came to agriculture, the Sumerians were extremely innovative. To protect themselves from both flooding rivers and time of drought, they constructed intricate systems of canals, dikes, and reservoirs.

When water in the irrigated fields subsided, they released oxen to trample the wet ground, eliminate weeds, and level the surface. Farmers followed with pickaxes to smooth the hoofmark. Fields were plowed twice with two different types of deep soil plows pulled by oxen. Three harrowings and rakings followed. Farmers seeding was done with a plow attachment that released seed from a container to a narrow funnel and down into the furrow. After the seeds sprouted, farmers prayed to Ninkilim, the goddess of field mice and vermin. During harvest, three men worked as a team: one a reaper, one a binder, and one who arranged sheaves. For threshing they drew a wagon back and forth over the mounds of barley, separating the grain from the chaff. Barley was the most important crop, but Sumerians also grew wheat, millet, spelt, and other vegetables. They used grains for bread and beer, and grapes were used in wine. Date gardens in Sumer were plentiful, as were sheep, which produced abundant wool.

Land was owned by either individuals, the temple, or the king. Commercial land was often under collective ownership, while outsiders cultivated some land for speculation purposes. A poor man often borrowed for seed and equipment, and he was protected from creditors until after harvest. If the harvest failed through no fault of his own, creditors excused him from interest on the loan.

Northern trade routes led up the Tigris and Euphrates. Merchants from the south had branch offices in distant cities. Sumerians coined no money but bartered for goods and services. Local trade was usually reckoned in barley, while gold and silver exchanged for out-of-town transactions, with the shekel of silver being the standard. A witnessed, written agreement confirmed all transactions. Even in ancient times interest was charged to borrowers. The maximum legal rate of interest for barley was 33 percent, and for silver it was 20 percent. Government institutions always tried to maximize rents an entrepreneur could charge for homes, ships, wagons, land, and commercial sites. Wages could also be regulated. Overall, the Sumerian economy was relatively free, and private property was the rule. Private enterprise and individual drive determined success or failure, wealth or poverty.

Textiles were one of the most important industries of Sumer. Clothing was one of the their most important trade commodities, cherished by surrounding countries. Weaving appeared first in Mesopotamia around 3800 B.C., and Ur processed thousands of tons of wool annually. Trade commodities were transported by sledge, wagon, chariot, and boat. The most common boat was the *guffa*, still used today in Iraq.

Petroleum technology was an important industry of Mesopotamia. Fuels, bitumens and asphalts that seeped to the surface, made Sumer technologically supreme. Sumerians began using petroleum products around 3500 B.C. They used them in road building, waterproofing, caulking, painting, cementing, and molding. Fuels were basic to an advanced chemistry and medicine.

Sumerians, proficient in metallurgy, processed gold, silver, tin, lead, copper, and bronze. By the beginning of the third century B.C., copper works were highly developed. Precious metals and minerals were imported from surrounding countries. Much of the ancient commerce was devoted to metal trade. Metals formed the basis for the development of Sumer's banking and first money, the shekel. Industrious artisans and craftsmen sold their metal handiworks in the free market.

THE GOVERNMENT

In the earlier days of Sumer, political power lay in the hands of free citizens and a city governor known as an *ensi*. Later, struggles developed between various city-states as Sumerians became extremely patriotic toward their city. These struggles became bitter and violent, usually over land, water, and trade. Populations of the cities swelled, and water became an issue, especially when the climate changed to lengthier dry seasons. This inter-city-state struggle eventually led to the undoing of Sumer, as each city-state refused to give up its independence. During times of threat, barbaric people to the west and east of Sumer pressured the city-states to unite under leadership of the king, who established a regular army.

The first political congress in man's recorded history met in 3000 B.C. Composed of two houses, it included a senate comprised of an assembly of elders, and a house consisting of arms-bearing male citizens. One tablet tells of congress meeting to take a stand on war or peace. The senate voted to pursue peace at all costs, opposite of what the king wanted. He then brought the matter to the lower house, which voted to declare war.

At one time, Sumer had no paid army, as each citizen was a potential soldier and all were liable to be called up. In time of war, the king often road in the forefront of battle. Chariots were the main offensive weapons of a heavily armored infantry. Victories on the battlefield were followed by the wholesale slaughter of prisoners. The fortunate survivors became slaves. In later times, the army recruited from the higher class of citizens; in return for their service, they received land parcels and had to cultivate them under penalty of forfeiture. Captured Sumer soldiers were often ransomed by their captors for the prisoners' own private fortunes. Citizens, under absolute control of the king, could not escape military service when called upon.

Sumerians became the first people to compile written laws to avoid misunderstandings. The custom began with legal documents for deeds of sales and contracts between various parties. By 2400 B.C., the promulgation of laws and legal regulations was common. The laws were usually liberal and upheld the rights of the individuals. By the end of the Third Dynasty of Ur, the king of Sumer was responsible for law and justice. The *ensi* administered the laws in his locale.

As in today's society, Sumerians did not escape taxation. To raise and supply armies, the citizens' wealth and property were taxed heavily. Property belonging to the temple was often appropriated. During times of war, citizens offered little opposition to heavy taxation. Government inspectors seized boats from boatmen, cattle from farmers, and fish from fishermen. If a man divorced his wife, he paid a tax of five shekels to the *ensi*. Tax collectors were everywhere. When a dead man was brought to the cemetery, numerous officials made it their business to collect taxes from the bereaved relatives. Barley, bread, and date wine were often paid to the officials. The first recorded tax revolt occurred in the city-state of Lagesh during the 24th century B.C. when the bureaucrats levied such high taxes and appropriated so much temple property that citizens overthrew the Ur-Nanshe Dynasty. It was replaced by the rule of Urukagina, who restored order in the city and provided freedom for the citizens.

The king appointed judges, and higher government officials had judicial authority as well. The court usually consisted of three or four judges, sometimes one or two. Judges came from all types of occupations, as there was no such profession as a judge. A *mashkin* was like a county clerk and prepared the case for court. The judges often quoted legal precedents to support their decision after listening to the witnesses give testimony under oath. A judge could not reverse his decision under penalty of fine or dismissal. Lawsuits were common in Sumer.

Numerous Sumerian laws regulated real estate, slaves, servants, taxation, marriage, inheritance, boat rentals, oxen rental, and much more. The most famous law code unearthed was the Hammurabi law code, written around 1750 B.C. The code was an Akkadian compilation of laws based on Sumerian prototypes, similar to the laws of the Bible. The inscribed stele is now on display at the Louvre in Paris. Ethics and morals of the Sumerians paralleled those of the Hebrews. The Ur-Nammu code, the oldest law code discovered, was promulgated by King Ur-Nammu in 2050 B.C. and promoted the welfare of the citizens.

The Liptar-Ishtar law code, promulgated around 1900 B.C., contains such laws as regulating illegitimate children: "If a man's wife has not borne him children (but) a harlot (from) the public square has borne him children, he shall provide grain, oil, and clothing for that harlot; the children which the harlot has borne him shall be his heirs, as long as his wife lives, the harlot shall not live in the house with his wife." Regarding a second wife, "If a man has turned his face from his first wife . . . but she has not gone out of the (house), his wife which he married as his favorite is a second wife; he shall continue to support his first wife." Regarding slaves, " If a slave girl of a man has fled into the heart of the city and it has been confirmed that she dwelt in the house of another man for one month, he shall give slave for slave." Regarding oxen rental, "If a man rented an ox and damaged its eye, he shall pay one half of its price." Regarding hitting a man, "If a man hits another man accidently he shall pay ten shekels of silver."

Punishment was often harsh for criminal offenses. During one period of Sumer history the death penalty was imposed for homicide, theft, adultery, and bearing false witness. Punishment for some crimes resulted in mutilation of the body. There was a heavy penalty for committing perjury, as the state did its best to prohibit abuse of the courts. Sumerians recorded each sentence setting a precedent for future rulings. The guilty could always appeal.

An offense committed against the higher class was punished far more severely than if committed against a lower class. If a member of the higher class committed an offense, the individual received punishment far more severe than his social inferior. An "eye for eye" bound the upper class while the middle class might escape with a monetary fine. A builder or contractor could lose his life for poor workmanship if the house collapsed and killed someone. A surgeon who bungled an eye operation could have his hand cut off. Laws of Sumer protected women. They held property, engaged in business, and qualified as witnesses. By the year 2000 B.C. the law based on an "eye for an eye" gave way to a more humane form of punishment, monetary fines rather than physical punishment.

SCIENCE AND ART

Sumerians were the people of firsts, but scholars have a difficult time explaining how this civilization became so advanced. They first developed the wagon wheel, the potter's wheel, the plow, the sailboat, the arch, the dome, and the vault. Sumerians also developed castings in copper and bronze, soldering, stone sculpture, and engraving. They originated a system of writing on clay. Sumerians invented construction modalities such as brick molds and fashioning huge marsh reeds into huts. They also invented a calendar.

The Sumerian year was divided into two seasons. Summer began in March, and winter commenced in September. Months were lunar based, being twenty-nine or thirty days in length. Sumerians introduced an intercalary month at regular intervals to compensate for the varying lengths of lunar and solar years. Their day began at sunset and was twelve double hours long. They divided night into three watches of four hours each. A water clock or *clepsydra* measured time.

They used a sexagesimal number system with the factor six and ten: 1, 10, 60, 600, 3600, 36,000, etc. It permitted flexible number writing, which enabled Sumerians to tabulate reciprocals, squares, square roots, cubes, and cube roots. Scholars believe this system was the forerunner of the Hindu-Arabic decimal system now in use. The Sumerians first divided the circle into 360 degrees.

Famous for their knowledge of astronomy, the Babylonians inherited this knowledge from Sumerians and their generations of observing the clear night skies of Mesopotamia. Astrology and astronomy peaked in Babylonia and Chaldea during the last half of the first millennium. Sumerians believed the stars affected the lives of humans. The sun, moon, and planets were identified with the gods. Changes in the faces of heaven reflected the disposition of the gods, who were directly responsible for the events on Earth.

Sumerians also believed in magic and omens. Each kind of accident, every chance event had a meaning and had bearing on the future. Generations of priests made records of these events, and compiled books of omens for future guidance.

Sumerian physicians used botanical, zoological, and mineral sources for their healing modalities. Medicine was taught at medical schools with the aid of clay organ models. The medical texts gave instruction on removing cataracts. Sick people could choose between a water physician and an oil physician. Sodium chloride, river bitumens, and crude oil were some of the favorite minerals for the oil physician. Wool, milk, turtle shells, and snakes were commonly used for healing by water physicians, while botanical medicine came from thyme, mustard, pears, figs, and pine. Physicians, familiar with elaborate chemical processes, could separate chemical components from natural substances. The first recorded physician was named Lulu, dating back to 2700 B.C. Physicians used magic spells and incantations to help the healing process. They believed all sickness was caused by malignant spirits prevalent in another dimension that preyed on man. The doctor used various techniques to exorcize demons and thereby rid the body of physical symptoms.

Sumerians did not have theoretical science nor did they possess general scientific laws. Science was straightforward, as textbooks of fish, trees, plants, vegetables, and stones have been unearthed describing only their physical characteristics.

Musical instruments such as beautiful harps and lyres have been uncovered. Drums, tambourines, pipes of reed and metal also made up their musical repertoire. Song and poetry flourished in the schools with most hymns directed to gods and kings.

Sumerians, noted for their impressionistic sculpture, used foundries capable of four-piece molds. Jewelers often worked with gold and silver. Another form of art was quite practical, the cylinder seal which became a trademark of Mesopotamia. A small engraved cylinder produced a clear and meaningful design when rolled over a clay tablet. Sumerian officials and merchants used them as identification. The pictographs found on the cylinder seal provided researchers with a great insight into Sumerian civilization.

RELIGION AND GODS

Scholars have discovered many religious stories of Sumer written on cuneiform tablets that are similar to the stories found in the Bible. The story of Creation, the Flood, Adam and Eve, and the Tower of Babel are examples common to both Sumer history and biblical writings. Sumerian texts help provide meaning to biblical verses once a mystery to religious scholars. Historians also agree that Greek and Roman mythology originated in Sumer, but as we shall see in the next chapter, these gods were very real.

The life purpose of a Sumerian was to be of service to the gods. Their religion was polytheistic; they worshipped innumerable gods. The gods were recognized and honored throughout the land. Each city had a patron god who lived in the temple ziggurat, the shrine built in his honor. Patron gods owned the temple and served as the lord of the land, the governor of the state, and a leader in war.

The Sumerian gods were close to man and anthropomorphic, meaning they had human characteristics. They lived a normal human life, lived off the sacrifices made by humans, and married human women who bore them children. Gods often went to battle with men. The defeat of an enemy was not complete unless the enemy's god was brought as an honored captive into the palace of the city god. Gods shared prosperity with humans in good times and suffered with them in times of disaster. They rewarded the virtue of humanity and punished wrongdoing. Similar to man, gods made plans and acted, married and raised families, supported large households, and were addicted to passions and weaknesses. Though gods were believed to be immortal, they could become sick to the point of death, and in battle they could be wounded or killed.

Each of these superhuman beings had a purpose. They controlled one component of the universe and subjected man to the rules and regulations that governed that component. All gods were not of equal importance and rank. Each had a cosmic responsibility such as being in charge of heaven or Earth; of sea or air; of astral bodies such as the sun, moon, and planets; of atmospheric forces such as wind, storms, and rain; of Earth attributes of rivers, mountains, and plains; of cultural functions such as cities, states, farms, fields, dikes, and ditches; and of mundane artifacts such as the ax or plow.

From the beginning of written records, the Sumerian theologians assumed as axiomatic the existence of a group of human beings who were humanlike in form, superhuman and immortal, and guided and controlled the cosmos. The Sumerian pantheon consisted of twelve gods led by a king. Seven of them decreed fate. Four gods of the pantheon were creative and the remainder were noncreative. The basic four components of the cosmos were heaven, Earth, sea, and atmosphere. Each cosmic phenomenon could exist only within one of these realms. The four gods in charge of these components, the creative gods, planned the creation of every other cosmic entity. A minor deity acted as a mediator between humans and the city god, as the city god was too great to be approached by mere mortals. Each human had his or her own tutelary god. To this god humans bared their hearts in prayer and supplication, and through this personal deity humans found personal salvation. A close relationship existed between man and his god. Ethics and morality were preferred by the major gods, since they themselves were assumed to be moral in conduct. However, there were gods who planned evil, falsehood, violence, and oppression.

The four creative gods included Anu, the heaven god, and Great Father of the gods; Enlil, the air god who was a son of Anu; Enki, the water god, another son of Anu; and Ninhursag, the great mother goddess, half-sister and lover to Enlil and Enki. Anu, the supreme ruler of the pantheon, conferred most of his power on Earth to Enlil. All the creative deities had to do was lay the plan, utter the word, and pronounce the name.

Enlil, the air god, led the gods who carried out the creative gods' decrees. Kings and rulers of Sumer boasted that Enlil gave them kingship of the land, and he made the land prosperous. Enlil was regarded as a beneficial deity responsible for the planning and creating of the most productive features of the cosmos. He made the day come forward, took pity on humans, and established abundance. Enlil made plans that brought forth the seeds, plants, and trees from the earth. Many scholars have cast Enlil as a destructive deity, but Sumerian researcher Samuel Kramer believes this is a misconception. He portrays Enlil as a fatherly deity who watched over the safety and well-being of humans. Enlil and his half sister, Ninhursag, planned for the creation of man, animals, plants, and civilization. On the other hand, Enlil carried out the decree of the gods to destroy man and earth.

Enki, the brother of Enlil, and the god of wisdom stood for the creative forces of the world. He was in charge of the abyss, the Abzu, where gold was mined in Africa. He organized the Earth in accordance with decisions of Enlil and established law and order. The details and execution of the divine plan were left to Enki, and he directed the construction upon Earth. Enki filled the plains with plant and animal.

Ninhursag (Ninmah), half sister and lover to Enki and Enlil, was exalted as the mother goddess. She was the daughter of Anu. Ninhursag, regarded as the mother of all living things, played an important role in the creation of man. Early Sumerian rulers described themselves as being nourished by the trustworthy milk of Ninhursag. Scholars believe her name was originally Ki, Mother Earth. Anu and Ninhursag were perceived as being parents of all the gods.

Other important gods include Nanna, the son of Enlil, known as the moon god Sin. His son was Utu, the sun god, and his daughter was Inanna, the love goddess also known as Ishtar. The wife of Anu was Antu, Enlil's wife was Ninlil, and Enki's wife was Damkina. Marduk was the first born of Enki and became the patron god of Babylonia. The Sumerians tell of fifty great gods but did not give names to them. They seem identical with the Anunnaki, the children of Anu. By the end of the third millennium, there were hundreds of named deities.

Each city-state had a patron god. Erech was Anu's main seat of worship. At Nippur, the main temple was dedicated to Enlil, and Eridu was Enki's home. Ur was home to the patron goddess Nanna, while Babylonia's patron deity was Marduk, the first son of Enki. Shamash, the god of justice, lived at Larsa. The supreme deity of each city often tried to usurp the province of others.

Sumerians accepted their mortal limitations and believed they had little control when it came to death and divine wrath. Life was governed with uncertainty and insecurity by unpredictable gods.

Life after death, they believed, was no better than the present physical life. The departed ones went to the nether world, where again
they had to placate the gods and important priests. After death, the
newly arrived deceased had a special place assigned to them in the
nether world where they were instructed on the protocol and laws.
Rules and regulations were abundant there. While in the nether
world, the dead were in a sympathetic world to Earth from where
they came. They could suffer anguish and humiliation, and could
cry out against the independent gods.

Sumerians believed the nether world was a huge cosmic space
beneath the Earth and corresponded to heaven, a huge cosmic space
above the Earth. The deceased souls descended from their graves to
the nether world, where there were important cities with gates and
special openings. Before entering, the soul needed to cross a river
by ferry. Rulers of the nether world were Ereskigal (Inanna's sister)
and Nergal, who had a special entourage of deities including seven
Anunnaki. As did the gods in the sky and mortals on Earth, these
deities needed food, clothing, weapons, jewelry and much more.
Ereshkigal held court in a palace with seven gates. A hierarchy existed among the dead, with the highest seats occupied by dead kings
and high priestly officials. Though dark and dreary during the
nether world's day, the sun shone brightly at night. Judgment was
performed by the sun god Utu. If a favorable decision was made, the
human's soul would live in happiness and contentment. Sumerians
did not believe there would be a blissful life in the nether world,
and most were convinced that it was a dismal, wretched reflection
of life on Earth.

Those earthlings who descended to the nether world could
not wear clothes, had to annoint themselves with good oil, needed
to carry a weapon or staff, had to wear sandals, and needed to make
a noise. They were to behave normally toward members of their
families who resided there. The dead, they believed, on special occa-
sion could be raised temporarily to the physical world of Earth. An
unbroken rule of the nether world was that no one who had entered
their gates could return to the world above unless he produced a
substitute to take his or her place.

Rites and rituals played a predominant role in the Sumerian
religion. Sumerians believed their only purpose was to serve the
gods. Service must be performed in a perfect manner that pleased
the master deity.

The god owned the land, but the priest administered the city on his behalf. The *patesi,* the chief priest of the temple who was the god's direct representative on Earth, assumed the position and power of civil governor. The priests were the scientists, engineers, physicians, and guardians of skills and crafts. Only the priest knew when to reap; when to prepare for floods; where to dig the canals; when to build; when to make war or negotiate peace; and how to build a ziggurat, a palace, or irrigation canal. The high priest of a large temple usually held great political importance, and he usually came from the royal house. The church and state of Sumer were intermingled.

There were numerous priests and priestesses. The *kala* priests were responsible for temple chants while the *baru* priests interpreted omens, an important part of religious life. No enterprise began without reading and interpreting the omens. Such omens included examining the liver of a sacrificed animal, or observing the flight of birds, or noting the patterns of a substance when poured from a jar. Some priests performed ritual ablutions. Around 3000 B.C., 736 priests served the goddess Bair, but in later times three thousand staffed Marduk in Babylonia. The Sumerian priests and holy men were noted for their colorful and complex rites, rituals, and ceremonies that served to please and placate the gods.

The temples, the center of their religion, contained a sanctuary for the god's emblem or statue with a mud brick table for offerings that lay in front. It sat in a space surrounded by many subsidiary rooms and an altar. During the Third Dynasty of Ur, large cities contained temples with vast building complexes. Temples were always the largest and tallest buildings of the city. The Nanna Temple of Ur measured 600 feet by 1,200 feet, and it contained a ziggurat and many shrines, storehouses, courtyards, and dwellings. The ziggurat itself measured 150 feet by 200 feet and was 70 feet tall. The temples owned a great deal of land, often rented to sharecroppers. The greatest calamity to befall a city and its people was the destruction of a temple.

The deceased were buried in graves dug as a rectangular pit. The corpse was wrapped in a matting and placed in a coffin of clay, wood, or basket work, and laid on its side in the position of sleep. Death pits led to the royal tombs. Humans who had given up their lives in honor of the royalty were buried on the ramp leading to the tomb. Most, being people of rank, were buried with elaborate jewelry and garments. Splendid chariots and wagons were also found in the pits. Scholars found evidence of butchering and conjecture that these people were sacrificed.

One of the hallmark achievements of the archaeological finds, according to Kramer, was the background it gave on the origin of the Bible. Many Sumerian writings parallel those of the Bible. Though the Sumerians ceased to exist long before the time of the Hebrews, they influenced the Canaanites who preceded the Hebrews. The Sumerian paradise, the land of Dilmun thought to be found in southwest Persia, may be the biblical paradise. A Sumerian poem describes the goddess Ninti, the lady of the rib, who healed Enki's rib. Ninti is thought to mean "the lady who makes live". Scholars believe the story of the biblical Eve originated here. Both the Sumerians and the Bible told of people fashioned from clay and imbued with the breath of life and whose purpose was to serve the gods.

The Sumerian Flood story is similar to the biblical version. The Sumerian King Ziusudra of Shurupak, the Noah of Sumer, was saved by the gods. He preserved the seeds of vegetation, animals, and humanity.

Sumerians thought of themselves as the chosen people. Abraham was born in Ur and thought to have brought Sumerian lore to Palestine. Sumerian traditions tell of their antediluvian rulers who lived extraordinary life spans, similar to the biblical antediluvian patriarchs.

The Sumerians tell a story similar to the biblical account about the Tower of Babel and the dispersion of humanity. The Tower of Babel, a ziggurat, represented a bond between heaven and Earth, between god and man.

The only time Sumer is mentioned in the Bible is in chapters ten and eleven of Genesis, which is written "Shin'ar," believed to be Sumer, according to the scholars.

Many ancient countries speak of the gods who played an important role in their lives, and the Bible also refers to the gods. The Sumerians believed the gods were real, and as we shall see they were real and of extraterrestrial origin, coming from Nibiru, the twelfth planet of our solar system.

Chapter Four

THE ANCIENT GODS
Visitors From Another Planet?

Ancient history records the important role gods played in early civilization. Sumer, Babylonia, Egypt, Greece, Rome and many more civilizations have had a mythology of gods. The Bible refers to gods in Genesis, and Plato writes of gods being rulers of Atlantis. These gods remain a mystery to scholars, with most believing they were a fabrication by humans to help them understand unexplainable events. In recent times, the research of Zecharia Sitchin gave reality to the gods. Sitchin, a multilinguist historical researcher, is one of the few people with command of the Sumerian cuneiform language, as well as Hebrew and several other ancient languages. This chapter is based on Sitchin's research, which he recorded in seven books.

Sumerian texts, according to Sitchin, tell about the DIN.GIRs, who are "the righteous ones of the rocket ships." They came to earth from their own planet, and chose Mesopotamia as their home away from home. They called it KI.EN.GIR, "the land of the lord of the rockets." The Sumerian texts date their arrival to 432,000 years before the Deluge when the DIN.GIR came down to Earth from their own planet. The planet's name was Nibiru, which Sumerians considered the twelfth member of the solar system. As we will see, Sitchin's Sumerian research gives us answers about the creation of our planet, the creation of man, the ancient gods, and the mysteries of the Bible.

THE CREATION OF EARTH

Sumerian texts say our solar system consists of the sun and eleven planets, counting the moon. Nibiru, the twelfth planet, the planet of the DIN.GIRs, whom Sitchin calls the Nefilim. Nefilim is a term used in Genesis, traditionally thought to mean giants.

However, the literal translation in Hebrew means "those who were cast down." Genesis 6:4 reads, "There were giants (Nefilim); and also after that, when sons of God came unto the daughters of men, and they bare children to them . . ." The sons of God were the Nefilim. The biblical writings parallel the Sumerian texts that tell of the Nefilim cohabiting with the daughters of men and bearing children.

The creation of Earth preceded the creation of man. The writings of Sumer tell of an unstable solar system, consisting of a sun and nine planets, invaded by a large comet like planet from outer space. This invading planet was Nibiru, which the Babylonians called Marduk, and it had seven satellites. It was on a collision course with a large planet named Tiamet, a planet with water called the "water monster" between Jupiter and Mars. The two planets did not collide, but one of Nibiru's satellites smashed into Tiamet that left Tiamet fissured and lifeless. Nibiru's passage brought it into the gravitational pull of the sun, and it hit Tiamet on its next orbit around the sun, causing Tiamet to split in two. Another of Nibiru's satellites hit one of the separated halves of Tiamet, which carried this celestial body to a new orbit where no planet had orbited before. This became Earth. The other half suffered a different fate, when on the next orbit of Nibiru, the two bodies collided and left the Tiamet half in many pieces. This collision resulted in the asteroid belt the ancients called the "Great Band" or "Bracelet." The collision caused Tiamet's chief satellite, Kingfu, to fall into the gravitational pull of Earth to become the moon. The remaining pieces of Tiamet became comets. The Sumerian scenario explains the concentration of continents on one side of Earth and a deep cavity on the other side, the Pacific Ocean. Tiamet is where Earth got its water.

Because of the collision, Nibiru was now bound to the gravitational pull of the sun. The direction of its elliptical orbit ran opposite that of the other planets. A forty-five-hundred-year-old Sumerian depiction of the twelve celestial bodies shows the twelfth planet orbiting between Mars and Jupiter. Its orbit takes thirty-six hundred years.

Astronomers have long been looking for evidence that another planet existed between Mars and Jupiter. Mathematical calculations, called Bode's law, predict a planet should exist between Mars and Jupiter. Historically, all the planets beyond Saturn were first discovered mathematically and not visually. Three thousand asteroids have been discovered, believed to be debris from a planet shattered to pieces and for which scientists have no explanation. Astronomers have failed to see Nibiru visually because of the lack of sun reflection.

THE COLONIZATION OF EARTH

The planet Nibiru was in a thirty-six hundred-year elliptical orbit around the sun. It generated its own heat from an abundance of radioactive elements in its depth. Volcanic activity provided Nibiru with an atmosphere that ancient texts describe as a halo clothing Nibiru. It could generate its own heat and retain it because of the atmosphere. The Sumerian writings do not tell if Nibiru was colonized after its collision with Tiamet or if there were survivors. At any rate, the atmosphere began to wane, and the shield that trapped the heat began to dissipate. The only solution to prevent dissipation was to suspend gold particles in the atmosphere. Nibiru needed gold! They developed a space program with the sole purpose of providing gold to the twelfth planet.

Anu, the ruler of Nibiru, chose his son Ea, who became known as Enki, to be the leader of the first mission to Earth. He was a brilliant scientist and engineer. The first colonizers arrived 432,000 years before the Flood, with the original plan to extract gold from the waters of the Persian Gulf. They named the first settlement Eridu, in the land of Sumer. All the ancient texts agree that the god Enki waded ashore to the edge of the marshland and said, "Here we settle." Fifty Anunnaki astronauts accompanied Enki.

The colonists worked hard once they arrived. They dredged stream beds, they filled marshes, and they built dikes. Enki spoke of much flooding when he first arrived on Earth, during an ice age. Later, the ice began to melt, accompanied by much rain. Enki enjoyed the water and later was assigned as the god in charge of the watery deep. He purified the Tigris River and preferred to travel by boat. Enki and the first group of Nefilim remained on Earth for eight Shar's, or 28,800 years. One Nibiru year equaled thirty-six hundred years, the time it took for one orbit of Nibiru to orbit the sun. While Enki endured hardships on Earth, Anu and Enlil watched the developments from Nibiru. Enlil, Anu's son and Enki's brother, was really in overall charge of the Earth mission.

Enlil descended to Earth to take personal charge of the mission. He settled in Larsa, also located in Mesopotamia, and stayed there for six Shar (21,600 years). The mission control center was established nearby at Nippur. An epic poem tells of Nippur being protected by awesome weapons. An artificially raised platform, found at the mission control center, was the communication center, the bond between "Heaven and Earth." Once established, it became a supply depot with abundant supplies brought down by shuttle craft. Sippar, the spaceport of the Nefilim, was located northeast of Nippur.

Sumerian seals depict boxlike divine objects transported by boat and pack animals. Sitchin describes the depictions as similar to the ark of the covenant built by Moses with directions from God. Implications now suggest the Ark of the Covenant was a communication box, electrically operated, that no one was to touch or they would die immediately by electrocution. Therefore, it was carried by wooden staffs passed through four golden rings. The Ark was supernatural equipment that enabled communication with a deity.

A winged globe symbolized the planet Nibiru. Wherever archaeologists discovered remains of Near Eastern civilizations, they found the winged symbol. It was dominant on temples, palaces, king's thrones, chariots, and cylinder seals. The rulers of Sumer, Akkad, Babylonia, and Assyria all revered the symbol.

When Nibiru approached Earth on its thirty-six hundred year orbit, it signaled upheaval, great change, and the beginning of a new era. The Great Flood occurred when Nibiru made its nearest orbit to Earth. It was a predictable event. The planet could be seen from Earth in the daytime, and the Anunnaki referred to it as the Day of the Lord. The most important religious event of Sumer was the twelve-day Near Year's Festival celebrating the orbit of Nibiru. It coincided with the spring equinox.

The gods originally planned to acquire gold from the sea, but they soon realized it was not feasible. They discovered gold deposits in the mountains of southeastern Africa near grassy plains and lush vegetation. The main deposit was found at Mount Arali where mining soon commenced, and the land became known as Abzu. The Sumerian pictograph of Abzu was of an excavation, deep into the ground, mounted by a shaft. Working hard, the Nefilim did the mining themselves. Special cargo ships carried the gold back to

Mesopotamia where the ores were cast into ingots. Enki's son, Gibil, was in charge of smelting the gold to ready it for transportation back to the space station, where the Anunnaki transferred it to spaceships en route to Nibiru. The twin peaks of Mount Ararat were used as a landmark for the spacecraft, and all the Sumerian cities were laid out to form an arrow pointing to the spaceport at Sippar. Enki became a frequent commuter between Sumer and Abzu, overseeing the gold project. Scientific studies show that mining occurred in Swaziland (South Africa) about 70,000 to 80,000 B.C. The cuneiform texts suggest the Nefilim also mined radioactive material such as uranium or cobalt. Pictographs show powerful rays emitting from a mine, and the gods attending Enki used a screening shield.

The Sumerian writings describe the Anunnaki as the rank-and-file gods who settled the earth, numbering six hundred. These few gods performed the physical labor. Another three hundred Anunnaki astronauts, called the Igigi, remained in the spacecraft providing support.

The Anunnaki toiled hard and long. Digging was the most common chore, the most arduous, and they all abhorred it. The lesser gods dug the river beds to make them navigable. They dug canals for irrigation, and they dug in Abzu to bring up the minerals. They worked for forty Shar or 144,000 years. They reached a point where they could not tolerate it anymore, and they cried out, "No more!"

THE CREATION OF HUMANS

When the Nefilim settled Earth, humans did not yet exist, according to the Sumerian writings. Humans originated because of a mutiny by the Anunnaki who refused to work, organized at a time when Enlil was visiting. It upset Enlil so much that he wanted to resign, especially when Anu sided with the Anunnki. Enki offered a solution to the crisis. He suggested that a primitive worker be created to take over the manual labors of the Anunnaki. It was a very popular suggestion with the ruling gods, who voted unanimously to create such a worker. They were to be called man.

Enki and his half-sister Ninhursag, the Mother Goddesss, were given the task of creating the primitive worker, man. The great experiment took place in the laboratory through genetic engineering.

Scholars have searched for the missing link in human evolution, which Sitchin believes the Sumerians manipulated genetically in the laboratory 300,000 years ago.

After much experimentation, Ninhursag purified the essence of the sperm of young male Anunnakis. She then mixed it into the egg of a female ape. Once the egg became fertilized, they implanted it into the womb of a female Anunnaki for the remainder of the pregnancy. When the hybrid creature was born, she lifted the infant up and shouted, "I have created it. My hands have made it." It had taken the Anunnakis considerable trial and error to achieve the perfect model. Fourteen Anunnaki birth goddesses were implanted with the genetically manipulated eggs of an ape-woman.

When the hybrid babies grew up, they put them to work in the mines. Originally they sent the slave workers to Abzu to work the mines. As a result, they mined more ore in Africa resulting in a greater workload in the processing facility in Sumer. The Anunnaki workers in Sumer began to clamor for slave workers, but Enki initially refused. Enlil, wanting the additional workers, attacked the African mines, resulting in an agreement where workers labored in both lands. In Sumer, the genetically engineered slaves were used for processing the ores, digging canals, and raising food.

Sitchin believes the Sumerian writings give validity to both the theory of evolution and to the biblical story of creation. It was a deliberate creation of the gods and the link in evolution. They created humans to do the work of the gods and be their servants. The decision to create humans was made by an assembly of gods. In the Book of Genesis, the Elohim said, "Let us make man in our image, after our likeness." Elohim is the plural of deity. The biblical story of creation originates from Sumer.

The new being was called the "Adam" because he was created of the Adama, the Earth soil. Humans were similar to the gods, both physically and emotionally, because the gods created them that way.

Science has determined that Homo sapiens appeared inexplicably some 300,000 years ago. The Nefilim landed 450,000 years ago, toiled for 144,000 years, and created humans 300,000 years ago. The Nefilim, under the direction of Enki, took an existing creature, the Homo erectus, and manipulated it in the image of the gods by means of genetic engineering. However, they needed a quick process for mass production of the new workers, and continued to

experiment. Non-Sumerian texts tell of hideous beings being created. Some had two wings, some had two faces, some had goat horns,
and some had horses' feet. The Nefilim tried to hybridize the new
creature with other animals.

Enki and Ninhursag, in their experimentation, created six
deformed humans. Once they achieved the perfect human, named
Adapa, the mother goddess gave humans the skins of gods. In the
final product, the Nefilim were genetically compatible with the
daughters of man. They were able to marry them and have children
with them. This was only possible if humans had developed from
the same seed of life as the Nefilim. Humans were a mixture of a
godly element and the clay of the earth.

Anu referred to Adapa as the human offspring of Enki. Ninki,
Enki's wife, was pregnant with the first Adapa. It was the perfect
mold and gods clamored for more. Duplicates were either male or
female, and Eve was made from Adam's essence. The divine element
came from the male genes, and the earthly element came from the
female genes.

Anthropologists have scientific evidence that man evolved and
emerged in southeast Africa. The Sumer texts also suggest the creation of man took place in Abzu, in the Lower World, where the
mines were located.

Enlil wanted to keep the humans sexually suppressed. Enki,
on the other hand, wanted to bestow upon humanity the "fruits of
knowing," procreation. Enki genetically engineered humans so
they were able to have children. This unauthorized deed angered
the gods, and they arrested Enki. The enraged Enlil ordered the
expulsion of the Adam, the homo sapien earthlings, from Edin the
"abode of the righteous ones." Humans were no longer confined to
the settlements of the Anunnaki, and they began to roam the world.

EARLY HUMANS

Ancient texts tell of the god's blood being mixed into the clay
so as to bind god and humans genetically to the end of days. Both
the image (flesh) and likeness (soul) of the gods would be imprinted upon humans in a kinship of blood that could never be severed.
The Akkadian term for clay is "tit," referring to the ovum of a
female ape (Homo erectus) fertilized by the genes of a god's sperm.

As long as Adam and Eve lacked knowledge about sex, they were allowed to live in the Garden of Eden. The Sumerians called the god's abode Edin, the home of the righteous ones. Enki decided to give humans the ability to procreate, which angered Enlil. Sitchin suggests that the metaphor of the serpent in the Bible represents Enki who gave Adam and Eve the knowledge of procreation. The deity represented Enlil, who cast Adam and Eve out of Edin, the abode of the gods. Procreation was a crucial step in man's creation.

At some point, the banished humans were allowed to return to Mesopotamia and live alongside the gods to serve and worship them. In the Bible during the days of Enosh, "the gods allowed mankind back into Mesopotamia to serve the gods." Enki had taken Adapa (Adam) by spacecraft to see Anu in Nibiru. After his return, humans proliferated. Humans, no longer just slaves in the mines and fields, performed all tasks. They built houses and temples for all the gods, and learned how to cook, dance, and play music for the gods.

In the fourth generation after Enosh, according to Genesis, the firstborn son was named Enoch. He walked with the deity, and did not die on Earth but was taken by the deity. The Book of Enoch expounds on this and details his first visit with the angels of God to be instructed in various sciences and ethics. After returning to Earth to pass on this knowledge and the requisites of priesthood, he was taken up permanently to join the Nefilim in their celestial abode.

Young Anunnaki lacked female companionship and began to have sex with the daughters of man. The Sumerian writings parallel those of Genesis: In those days, when the Nefilim were upon the Earth, they cohabited with daughters of the Adam, and they bore children with them. They were mighty ones of eternity, the people of the shem (shem meaning sky vehicle). The good life was the main concern of the Anunnaki, and humanity became too infatuated with sex and lust. Genesis describes the taking of wives by the Nefilim. After awhile, the genetic perfection of humans began to deteriorate. The increased sexual relations between the male Anunnakis and the daughters of man upset Enlil. He cried, "Enough!"

The Bible reflects this concern by Enlil when the Lord said, "I will destroy the Earthlings whom I have created off the face of the Earth." Enlil saw his chance to eliminate man when a scientific station at the tip of Africa reported an ensuing natural calamity. Sitchin believes they saw that the growing ice cap over Antarctica had become unstable and was resting on a layer of slippery mush. Because Nibiru was making a close pass, the gravitational pull would cause the ice caps to slip into the ocean, resulting in mass flooding.

The author offers the hypothesis that Nibiru was returning close to Earth within the asteroid belt, and the gravitational pull may have veered an asteroid towards Earth. Perhaps the Anunnaki detected an asteroid was about to hit the planet as described in an earlier chapter.

At any rate, the Deluge became a predictable but an unavoidable event. The gods conspired not to tell humanity of the upcoming disaster, as this was their chance to eliminate humans from Earth. Before this opportunity of elimination, Enlil had called for plans of natural disasters to decimate humans through pestilence, sickness, drought, and starvation. But now there was an even better plan offered by Enki who told the assembly of ruling gods about the upcoming flood. The gods swore Enki to secrecy, forbidding him to tell man of his upcoming demise.

Enki, determined to save his creation, humanity, was also obligated to follow the wishes of the gods. In the temple where he hid behind a screen, he instructed his Noah, King Ziusudra of the city Shuruppak. Enki whispered urgent instructions to Ziusudra to construct a submersible boat, a submarine, that could withstand an avalanche of water. Precise dimensions were given. He called for a boat roofed over and sealed with tough pitch. There were to be no decks or openings. Enki provided Ziusudra with a navigator who was to direct the vessel to Mount Ararat, the Mount of Salvation. The sons of Zuisudra and their families also aboarded the vessel.

When the storms that preceded the Deluge commenced, the Nefilim boarded the shuttle craft and orbited the Earth until the waters subsided. As the fleeing gods watched the destruction of Earth from above, they trembled from the noise caused by the Deluge. They then realized how much they had fallen in love with the planet. Ninhursag was said to have wept with other Anunnaki as they were all humbled.

When the water subsided, Enlil saw the ark on Mount Ararat and was filled with anger. Only after Enki convinced Enlil to make peace with the remnants of humanity did Enlil accept the fact that humans would survive.

The families of Ziusudra were sent out to settle the mountain ranges flanking the inundated plains of the Tigris and Euphrates.

They were to wait until the plains were dry enough to cultivate before they inhabited them. Cereals and grains were brought down from the mountains and planted under the direction of the god Ninurta. Seed, stored in Nibiru before the Deluge, was reintroduced to Earth. Ninurta also damned the mountains and drained the plains. Genesis describes sowing and harvesting as divine gifts to Noah. Scholars place the origins of agriculture about thirteen thousand years ago, about the time of the Deluge in the mountain terrains. They can't explain the earliest grains nor the domestication of animals. Enki introduced domestic herds. The plan for recovery was introduced, and life began to normalize.

Enki returned to Africa to access the damage. He turned his attention to the Valley of the Nile and used his knowledge to recover this great area. The Egyptians acknowledge that their great gods came from the "olden place."

The Nefilim decided it was time to establish an intermediary between themselves and humans. Before this decision was made, there was no kingship in the land. The rules came from the gods. After Anu made a visit to the Council of the Great Gods, who thought the Anunnaki were too lofty for humans, they decided upon kingship.

The gods decided that Enki must share the divine formula of civilization with the other gods so they could reestablish their urban centers. Civilization was to be granted to all of Sumer. They made the decision to establish new cities alongside the older ones that had been destroyed in the Deluge. The first city established was Kish, which fell under the control of Ninurta, the son of Enlil. It became Sumer's first administrative capital. The urban center of Ur was established next under the control of Nannar/Sin, the firstborn son of Enlil. Ur became Sumer's economic capital. The men who were appointed kings of the cities by Enlil were called Lugal. Genesis, chapter 10 of the Old Testament, confirms the Sumerian writings:

"Kish begot Nimrod
He was first to be a mighty man in the land
And the beginning of his kingship
Babel and Erech and Akkad
All in the land of Shin'ar (Sumer)."

At one time all humanity spoke one language. Initiated by Enlil, the gods decided to divide the tongue and disperse humans told in the Sumerian texts and the biblical story about the Tower of Babel (Hebrew for Babylonia). The original Akkadian definition of Bablli meant "gateway of the gods," the place where the gods were to enter and leave Sumer. The Bible tells of a group of perpetuators who planned to construct a tower, whose top would reach into the heavens. These ancient words describe a ziggurat. This happened sometime between 3450 and 3600 B.C. After the people settled in Sumer, they learned the art of brick making, built cities, and raised high towers. They had planned to make for themselves a shem (rocket) and a tower to launch it. According to Sitchin, the Sumerian meaning of "mu" and its Semitic derivative "shem," refers to the heavenly journeys of the gods by sky vehicles. Sumerian pictographs verify multistage rockets and flying vehicles that roamed the Earth's skies. Unearthed artifacts show pictures of rockets with wings or fins, reached by a ladder, and sculptures show a god to be inside a rocket-shaped chamber. Both the Bible and Sumerian writings infer the flying machines were meant for the gods and not humanity. Humans could only ascend to the heavenly abode upon the wish of a god.

The gods became quite concerned about this action and feared the human race would unify in culture and purpose. For this reason, they thought they could control man better with the philosophy of divide and rule. As a result, man was dispersed and given a divided tongue.

Several major civilizations were seeded from this decision of the gods. About 3200 B.C. kingship and civilization made its first appearance in the Nile Valley. Another advanced civilization occurred in the Indus Valley of India and encompassed large cities, developed agriculture, and flourishing trade. It commenced about one thousand years after the Sumerian civilization began. Scholars believe that the seeds of these two civilizations originated from Mesopotamia. This is confirmed in the Bible. Following the Deluge, humans were divided into three branches, led by the three sons of Noah. The people of Shem inhabited Mesopotamia and the Near Eastern lands. Ham inhabited Africa and parts of Arabia, while the third son, Japeth, settled the Indo-European lands of Asia Minor, Iran, India, and Europe. Each of these lands was assigned to one of the leading deities. The single Sumerian language was differentiated into three different languages following the Tower of Babel incident: Sumerian, Egyptian, and Indo-European.

Following the Deluge, the Nefilim held lengthy council regarding the future of gods and humans on Earth. They decided to create four regions including Mesopotamia, the Nile Valley, Indus Valley, and a fourth region dedicated to the gods alone. Trespassing by humans could lead to their quick death. This land was called Tilmun (the place of missiles) in the Sinai. A new spaceport was established here after Sippar was destroyed in the Flood. Tilmun came under the command of Utu/Shamash, grandson of Enlil and father of Inanna, the god in charge of fiery rockets. In many Sumerian tales, humans try to reach this forbidden land, believing they would acquire immortality among the gods of heaven and Earth.

To end the feud between the Enlil and Enki families, the gods drew lots to determine over which region they were to have dominion. Asia and Europe were assigned to Enlil and family, while Africa was given to Enki. Ninuta, Enlil's son, was assigned the lands of Elam, Persia, and Assyria. Enlil's son Nanna was given the land of Sumer. Nanna was a benevolent god who supervised the reconstruction of Sumer and rebuilt the prediluvian cities on their original sites. New cities were also constructed. The youngest son of Enlil, Ishkur (Adad), was given the northwest lands of Asia Minor and the Mediterranean islands that spread to Greece. Like Zeus, he was depicted riding a bull and holding forked lighting.

Enki's son Nergal was given southern Africa, and Gibil, another son, was given control of the African gold mines. Marduk, Enki's favorite son, learned from his father all the sciences including astronomy. His Egyptian name was Ra, according to Sitchin, and he presided over the Nile Valley. Later, around 2000 B.C., Marduk usurped the lordship of Earth from Enlil and was declared supreme god of Babylonia.

Only in the 20th century was the third region unearthed in the Indus Valley, and two major cities were found, dominated by an acropolis. The Sumerian goddess Inanna, whom the Akkadians knew as Ishtar, ruled this area. This region lasted only one millennium, and by 1600 B.C. the civilization no longer existed.

A NUCLEAR CATASTROPHE

Sitchin presents Sumerian evidence that the biblical story regarding the destruction of Sodom and Gomorrah was in all likelihood a story about a nuclear holocaust. The story begins when Abraham camped near Hebron. Here the Lord disclosed to him the true purpose of his journey: to verify the accusations made against Sodom and Gomorrah. The Lord disclosed to Abraham the upcoming destruction of the two cities and told Abraham if there were fifty righteous ones in the city, he would call off the holocaust. Abraham bargained with the Lord to get the number down to ten, and the Lord agreed.

Two emissaries of the Lord visited Lot in Sodom. An unruly crowd gathered outside Lot's home and tried to break in. The emissaries persuaded Lot and his wife to leave the city without delay and to escape to the mountains without looking back.

The weapon of the gods was discharged, and all the people, cities, and plant life were destroyed by its tremendous heat. Lot's wife looked backed and was turned into a "pillar of vapor." The Bible says it was a "pillar of salt," but Sitchin asserts the correct Hebrew interpretation is a "pillar of vapor."

Abraham got up the next morning after the blast and viewed Sodom and Gomorrah, fifty miles away. He saw smoke rising from the Earth and that the once populated valley with five cities was now part of the Dead Sea. Today, it is still nicknamed "Lot's Sea."

Archaeological evidence shows the region was abruptly abandoned in the 21st century B.C. and was not reoccupied for several centuries. The water that surrounds the Dead Sea is still contaminated with radioactivity, enough to cause sterility. The holocaust occurred in 2024 B.C., the sixth year of the reign of Ibbi-Sin, the last king of Ur.

The Sumerian texts give background on why this catastrophe happened. During the sixth year of Ibbi-Sin's reign, Marduk returned to Babylon for the second time, as the omens had predicted. For twenty-four years Marduk had been in exile among the Hittites. He wished to bring peace and prosperity back to the land. To ensure Marduk's return, Amorite supporters of Marduk swooped down the Euphrates Valley toward Nippur. The god Ninurta influenced the rulers to organize Elamite troops to fight the invading force, and the two troops met each other at Nippur. Ekur, the shrine to Enlil, was destroyed in battle. Ninurta falsely accused Marduk of desecrating Enlil's holy of holies at Nippur, but in actuality it was Ninurta's ally Nergal that caused the destruction. Enlil became so enraged that he sided with Ninurta against Marduk and his son

Nabu. They secretly planned to destroy the centers of support for Marduk at the Canaan cities on the Jordan plain, the location of Sodom and Gomorrah.

Meanwhile, at the Council of Gods, Nergal recommended the use of force against Marduk. Enki lost his patience at the meeting and ordered Nergal to leave his presence. Nergal knew the location of seven awesome weapons that he planned to use. The weapons were created by Anu and hidden underground in the mountains. Gibil warned Marduk about Nergal's scheme, and Marduk rushed to his father, Enki, who did not know where the weapons were stored. However, Enki knew they would make the land desolate and cause the people to perish.

Ninurta returned to the Lower World (Earth) and found that Nergal had already primed the seven awesome weapons. The council warned Nergal that the weapons could only be used against specific targets approved by the gods. Humanity was to be spared. Nergal agreed to notify the Anunnaki and the Igigi manning the space station, but he refused to warn Marduk. Nergal used words identical to those the Bible attributed to Abraham when he tried to have Sodom spared.

Nergal's strategy was to deny Marduk his greatest prize, the spaceport located on the Sinai. When Nergal presented the plan to the gods, Ninurta was speechless, but Anu and Enlil approved the plan. The first target was the spaceport, and Ninura detonated the first nuclear bomb. Nergal then blew up Sodom and Gomorrah.

The Anunnki guarding the spaceport were warned, and escaped to the orbiting space station. The spaceport was obliterated, the runways demolished, and all vegetation decimated. Today a black scar remains on the face of the Sinai where the explosion blackened the soil.

The explosion had a profound affect on Sumer and essentially caused its demise. The blast gave rise to a great radioactive wind that blew from west to east. Sumer became the ultimate victim. Unearthed lamentation texts describe the ordeal in Ur, Nippur, Uruk, and Eridu, which experienced a sudden concurrent catastrophe. Cities were without people, the pastures were without cattle and sheep, the rivers were bitter, the fields turned to weed, and the plants withered. Resident gods abandoned the cities.

The source of this unseen death, a brownish cloud, appeared

in the skies of Sumer, and at night, the cloud had a luminous edge. A fast howling wind, described as an evil wind caused by a huge explosion from the awesome weapons, accompanied the cloud. The death episode lasted twenty-four hours.

Upset, Ninhursag wept with bitter tears and Nanshe cried. The texts describe Inanna's departure from Uruk to Africa in a submarine ship while complaining that she had to leave her jewelry. The resident deities had instructed the people of Uruk to run away and hide in the mountains. Enki left Eridu, and he too wept with bitterness. He led the displaced survivors to the desert, instructioning them to hide underground. Ningal and Nannar spent a nightmarish night in the ziggurat at Ur. Upon departing the city, they saw death and desolation with dead bodies melted away. All of southern Mesopotamia was incapacitated, its soil and water poisoned, its cities desolated, and the reed marshes rotted. A great civilization had come to pass.

THE INTERACTIONS OF GODS

The Sumerian tablets reveal relationships among the gods that make modern-day soap operas look rather tame. Gods were allowed any number of wives and concubines, but a certain protocol had to be followed. Lovemaking between brother and sister was allowed, but marriage was prohibited. However, marriage between a god and his half-sister was condoned. The birthright of an offspring stemmed from a code of sexual behavior based not on morality but on sexual behavior. A first male offspring from a relationship between a god and his half-sister took priority over the firstborn son of a god. The son of a god and his half-sister had fifty percent more of a pure seed. If a god married more than one person, he had to select one as his official spouse, preferring a half-sister for the role. The god's official spouse was honored with a feminine aspect of his title. Anu's wife was named Antu, while Sud, the nurse who married Enlil, was named Ninlil. They married because Enlil raped her on the first date and impregnated her. Enki's wife Damkina was known as Ninki.

Enki was the firstborn son of Anu whose mother was Id, one of six concubines of Anu. Anu's half-sister Antu bore him Enlil. Anu had eighty children, sixty-six by his concubines and fourteen by

Antu. By the Nibirun code of succession, Enlil became the legal heir to Anu rather than Enki. A strong rivalry and jealousy developed between the two half-brothers. When Anu decided to bring Enlil to Earth, heated arguments arose from Enki.

Ninhursag was a daughter of Anu, but not of Antu. She was a half-sister of Enlil and Enki. Ninhursag was one of the original Great Anunnaki known as the Mother Goddess and a member of the Pantheon of Twelve. Enki desired to have a son with Ninhursag but she bore him a daughter. Frustrated, Enki mated with his daughter who also gave birth to a daughter. Not willing to give up, Enki made love to his granddaughter who presented him with another daughter. This incensed Ninhursag who put a curse on Enki, which the gods later made her remove. Enlil had better luck with Ninhursag when she gave him a son named Ninurta, who became the rightful heir. Enki's firstborn son with his wife Ninki, was Marduk. Nannar, also known as Sin, was the firstborn son of Enlil by his wife Ninlil. He later became sovereign over Sumer's best-known city-state of Ur and was responsible for Ur's great prosperity.

Enlil possessed the Tablets of Destiny which gave him power over Earth. A god named Zu stole the tablets, thus usurping the power of Enlil. Enlil's son Ninurta retrieved the tablets, resulting in the banishment of Zu. Zu possessed a flying machine from which he engaged Ninurta in battle. Scholars believe Zu may have been a contender for the Enlilship of Earth.

Inanna was one of the most colorful gods of Sumer. She was a daughter of Utu, the sun god, and granddaughter to Enlil. The Greeks knew her as Aphrodite and the Romans called her Venus. She was goddess of war and love to Sumerians. Scholars believe her domain, a land east of Sumer known as Aratta, is the Indus Valley. She desired to be goddess of Uruk, where she occupied Anu's temple and shared his bed.

Inanna wanted the divine formula for civilizations that Enki possessed. She tricked Enki by getting him drunk. Before passing out, Enki parted with one hundred of the formulae. After Enki woke, he realized what he had done, but it was too late. Inanna was on her way back to Uruk in her flying machine.

Inanna was infamous for sleeping with various rulers to advance her position. Her ultimate goal was to become a member of the Pantheon of Twelve Gods which she finally accomplished.

Inanna was cunning, beautiful, ruthless, and often depicted as naked by the Sumerians. The writings describe Inanna as flying place to place in her "boat of heaven." She often flew by herself, but normally her pilot/navigator was Nungal. The ruler of Uruk, Enmerkar, sent Inanna to Aratta to convince them to surrender to Uruk without bloodshed.

Inanna instituted the custom of the "sacred marriage," which was a sexual ritual in which the priest or king became her spouse for only one night. Enmerkar was the first of many invited by Inanna to share her bed under the guise of "sacred marriage." One of the most famous rulers of Erech, Gilgamesh, two-third's god and one-third man, also had a love affair with Inanna. He became famous for his quest for immortality.

Around 2400 B.C., Sumer became a country in need of strong leadership because of all the turmoil between the city-states. Inanna discovered Sargon I, a Semite, and the perfect person to fill the role. He built a capital near Babylon called Agade. Sargon satisfied both Inanna's bedtime and political ambitions as she used him to create her an empire. A temple was erected for Inanna in Agade to serve as her noble abode.

Historical records of Sargon's many conquests describe Inanna's presence on the battlefield. The empire spread well beyond Sumer but Sargon did not receive Tilman, the land of the gods. He also avoided Babylon, controlled by Ninurta but claimed by Marduk. Sargon ruled for fifty-four years and after his death, Inanna put one son after another on the throne.

For several years Inanna created havoc in her conflict with Marduk of Babylon. She married a god named Dumuzi, a son of Enki, of whom Marduk disapproved. Inanna descended to the nether world to visit her sister, which eventually led to the death of her husband. She blamed Marduk for Dumuzi's death and she wanted revenge. Inanna persuaded the gods to bury Marduk alive inside the Great Pyramid without food and water. After a frightful time inside the pyramid, Marduk was eventually rescued.

Marduk returned to Babylonia from exile and fortified it, making it impervious to attack. He also enhanced the underground water system to help him withstand a prolonged siege. The Anunnki gods did not want to use force to remove Marduk from the divine seat in Babylonia. Instead they sent Nergal, Marduk's brother, to convince Marduk to leave Babylonia, which he did. However, Nergal entered a forbidden underground chamber after Marduk's departure and removed a radioactive source of energy, a "brilliant weapon," also mentioned in the Old Testament. As a result, the day turned into dark, flooding occurred, the land was laid waste, and the gods became angry. This ended the conflict between Inanna and Marduk, and she also made peace with Nergal.

Inanna put her son Naram-Sin on the throne who commenced to conquer city after city. He entered the Sinai where the spaceport was located. An assembly of gods was called to deal with Inanna's exploits. Fearing she would be seized, Inanna fled Agade for seven years. She deliberately defied the authority of Anu and Enlil by asking her son Naram-Sin to dismantle E-Anna (House of Anu) in Erech and to attack Enlil's temple in Nippur. The angry Enlil ordered hordes of Gutiums to lay waste to Agade which they had controlled for ninety-one years. Inanna's mother and father took her back to Sumer ending the era of Inanna.

After nuclear catastrophe befell Sumer, it took several centuries for the land to recover and be resettled. The power shifted northward to Babylon, and a new empire rose with the ambitious Marduk as the supreme deity. He restored his position as the national god of Sumer and Akkad at the beginning of the second millennium B.C. The other gods, required to pledge allegiance to him, resided in Babylonia where their activities could be supervised. Marduk usurped the Enlilship of the planet and initiated a large-scale forgery of documents to make it appear that he, rather than Anu or Enlil, was the Lord of Heaven, the Creator, and the Benefactor. Marduk assigned himself as the deity of Nibiru, and the planet became known as Marduk to the Babylonians. The Babylonian *Epic of Creation* credited Marduk, rather than Nibiru, with crashing into Tiamet to create the planet Earth.

In Babylonia, Marduk ordered King Nebuchadnezzar II to march his army toward Jerusalem. In Jerusalem, the word of the Lord Yahweh came through the prophet Jeremiah. Yahweh called Nebuchadnezzar his servant and announced to Jeremiah that Jerusalem would be punished because of its people's action. In 586 B.C., the army of Babylon came into Jerusalem and destroyed the temple and city. Its desolation lasted seventy years.

EGYPT AND THE SUMERIAN GODS

The gods of Sumer had great influence over Egypt's civilization. Tilmun, the land of the gods and location of the new spaceport, was located on the Sinai peninsula following the Deluge. According to Manetho, the ancient Egyptian historian, the Egyptian god Ptah reigned over the lands of the Nile 17,900 years before Menes of the First Dynasty, which would make it 21,000 B.C. Nine thousand years later, Ptah handed over his rule to his son Ra. About 11,000 B.C., the rule of Ra was interrupted for about one thousand years. This corresponded to the time of the Flood. Egyptians believed Ptah returned to Egypt to help in its reclamation after the Deluge. Sitchin believes that Ptah was none other than Enki, who had divided Africa between his six sons when the lands became habitable again.

Some scholars believe Marduk, Enki's firstborn son and legal heir, was the Egyptian god Osiris. Sitchin believes Marduk was actually Ra, Egypt's sun god. Marduk rose to prominence when the Great Pyramid played an important role in his career.

Sitchin believes the Anunnaki built the pyramids some 10,000 years ago in conjunction with the spaceport, located on the Sinai. Egyptologists believe the pyramids were built during the Sixth Dynasty by Khufu (Cheops), by his successor Chefra (Chephren), and the third pyramid by Menkara (Mycinus). Sitchin provides proof that the Great Pyramid and the Sphinx already existed when kingship began in Egypt and that they were known in Mesopotamia. According to the Sumerian ancients, the Giza Pyramid and the Sphinx served as landmarks for spacecraft in the Sinai. The Great Pyramid contained instrumentation that helped guide the shuttle craft. An inscription on a stele near the Sphinx credit's Ra as the engineer who built the protected place in the sacred Tilmun from which he could ascend beautifully (spaceport) and traverse the skies.

Mesopotamian texts describe the Pyramid Wars after Enlil and Enki agreed to end their hostilities and allow peace on Earth. The followers of Enki were no longer to inhabit the lands of Enlil. In exchange, the sovereignty of Enki and his descendants over the Giza complex would be recognized for all time. Enlil agreed, with one condition. Marduk, who had brought on the Pyramid Wars and used the Great Pyramid for combat purposes, should be barred from ruling Giza. Enki agreed to the proposal.

Enki appointed a young son to be Lord of Giza and Lower Egypt. His title was NIN.GISH.ZI.DA, and he became guardian of the secrets of the pyramids. This god was also Thoth, who had married Enki's daughter, begot after Enki made love to his sister Ninhursag. Manetho writes that Thoth replaced Horus on the throne of Egypt about 8670 B.C. when the Second Pyramid War ended. Thoth's reign was a peaceful time for Egypt, when the Anunnaki established settlements relative to the new space facilities. Manetho assigned a reign of thirty-six hundred fifty years to the demigods who belonged to the Dynasty of Thoth. Thoth departed Egypt during the First Intermediate of Egypt (2160 to 2040 B.C.) when Ninurta asked Thoth to erect a temple for him at Lagesh. It was to be built from the humble dry clay of Mesopotamia, not of stone. At this time, Egypt abandoned the worship of Osiris and Horus, and moved the capital Memphis to Heliopolis.

Enlil and Enki came to another agreement. Enki and his sons would be allowed to freely enter Sumer if Enki returned the site of Eridu to Enlil's control. Enlil agreed, and in return for his hospitality, Enki brought prosperity to the land of Mesopoatamia.

From that day on, the land of the spaceport was known as Sin's land, the Sinai Peninsula. After the Flood, command of the new mission control center was given to Sin's son Shamash and located in Jerusalem (Ur-Shulim). Shulim meant the "supreme place of the four regions." It replaced Nippur as the mission control center and acquired the title of "the naval of the Earth." A new beacon city was built, called the city of Annu, and renamed Heliopolis by the Greeks. It was located outside of today's Cairo.

Sumerian legend says their civilization began with an influx of people from the sea. The Atlanteans, Sumerians, and Egyptians all had gods as their prediluvian rulers. The gods of Atlantis were similar to the gods of Greece, and scholars acknowledge that Greek mythology originated in Sumer. One must assume that during antediluvian times when Atlantis existed, the gods of Atlantis were the gods of Sumer. Egyptian legend describes their early rulers as gods who originated in both Atlantis and Mesopotamia.

The writings of Sumer date the creation of man approximately 300,000 years ago, while the ancient Nacaal writings assert the civilization of Mu began more than 200,000 years ago. Archaeological finds in Africa date Homo sapiens to approximately 250,000 years ago, the earliest evidence of modern man. The Nefilim arrived on the planet 432,000 years before the Deluge, when Mu was a continent in the Pacific Ocean considered the "Mother of all Civilizations." Evidence suggests Mu colonized Atlantis which in turn colonized Egypt. One can only suppose the gods of Sumer were the original inhabitants of Mu.

Chapter Five

EGYPT
The Land of Secrets

Egypt, like Sumer, was a complex civilization that came into existence fully developed. All aspects of Egyptian knowledge were in place from the beginning with no signs of an evolvement period for the sciences, art, architecture or hieroglyphics. The civilization was based upon complete and precise understanding of universal laws. Science, art, and religion were all interrelated and fused into a single organic unity. The Egyptian civilization appeared to be a legacy from another advanced civilization.

Open-minded Egyptologists believe this legacy came from Atlantis, while orthodox Egyptologists scoff at such an outlandish theory. As we will discover, the most logical explanation for this intriguing mystery is that Egypt is the land where Atlanteans preserved the remnants of their lost civilization.

EARLY HISTORY

As mentioned in the Atlantis chapter, the Greek Solon (fifth century B.C.) was told the story of Atlantis by an Egyptian priest in Sais. From this information Plato based his writings about Atlantis. Diodorus Siculus (first century B.C.) writes, "The Egyptians were strangers, who in a remote time settled on the banks of the Nile, bringing a civilization with them of their mother country such as writing and a polished language. They came from the direction of the setting sun and were the most ancient of men." Ancient Egyptian healing priests learned their medical arts from six books brought to Egypt by a different race, before the Great Flood. They were among forty-six works written by Hermes Trismegistus (Thoth), the early god-man of Egypt. The immortal Thoth claimed to be a former Atlantean. Two papyri found in a St. Petersburg museum tell of Egypt being a colony of Atlantis. An inscription found on the Lion Gate at Mycenae indicates that the first temple of Sais was built by Misor, said to be the ancestor of all Egyptians. Purportedly the grandson of an Atlantean priest, he fled from King Chronos of Atlantis with the king's beautiful daughter to settle on the banks of the Nile.

Some of the best evidence about ancient Egypt comes from Manetho (third Century B.C.), an Egyptian high priest in Heliopolis who wrote a book in Greek entitled *Egyptian History*. The name Manetho means the "Truth of Thoth." According to scholars, Manetho lived in Egyptian Ptolemic times and wrote an excellent and accurate history of Egypt. At that time, he had access to records of all kinds, including papyri in the temple archives, hieroglyphic tablets, wall sculptures, and innumerable inscriptions. No one but an Egyptian priest could read these records. Manetho also incorporated historical traditions and popular legends into his writings. He tried to set the record straight regarding the Egyptian history written earlier by Herodotus and other Greek historians. Orthodox Egyptologists and historians have trouble believing all Manetho's writings because of the long reigns he attributed to the rulers. The scholars believe the years Manetho writes about were lunar years and not solar years. They do agree with many of his writings regarding later Egyptian history because the writings support their beliefs.

Manetho writes that before the Flood, the Egyptians claim a line of gods, demigods, and spirits of the dead ruled them for more than 20,000 years. He tells of five Egyptian tribes who formed thirty dynasties which included gods, demigods, spirits of the dead, and mortal men. Manetho claims that the earliest rulers of Egypt were the gods.

Haphaestrus, the first king, ruled for nine 9,000 years and discoverered fire. Helios was his successor, followed by Sois. Then came Cronus, Osiris, Typhon (brother of Osiris), Agathodaemon, and finally Horus, the son of Osiris and Isis. The gods ruled for an unbroken succession of 13,900 years. The demigods included Ares, Anubis, Heracles, Apollo, Ammon, Tithos, Sosus, and Zeus. Also included in this category were the kings referred to as Spirits of the Dead. The demigods and Spirits of the Dead ruled for 11,000 years.

Syncellus writes in the *Old Chronicles* that Manetho may be in error. He claims thirty Egyptian dynasties with 113 generations reigned a total of 36,525 years. Greek historian Diodorus Siculus ascribes 23,000 years to Egyptian civilization.

The ancient Egyptians described a bridge linking the world of humans to the world of gods. The Followers of Horus, who carried down intact the traditions and secrets of the gods, maintained this bridge. According to researcher Schwaller de Lubicz, they carried a knowledge of divine origin and unified the country with it.

Verifying the authenticity of prehistoric Egypt is difficult. The ancient historians believed Egypt existed before the Flood, and the gods and demigods ruled for a lengthy period of time. If these gods were from the planet Nibiru, as the Sumerian texts claim, this would account for their lengthy reign. One Nibiru year equals thirty-six hundred Earth years. Modern scholars have tried to condense Manetho's years into lunar years to fit their hypothesis about Egypt.

One of the few king lists that has survived to the present day, the *Turin Papyrus*, dates back to the second millennium B.C. Scholars badly damaged the papyrus, but one fragment lists the names and reigns of the gods. It ascribes 3,126 years to Thoth and 300 years to Horus, the last fully divine king of Egypt. A second register of kings, devoted to the Followers of Horus, the *Shemsu Hor,* claims the Followers ruled for 13,420 years. The reign of rulers before the Shemsu Hor lasted 23,200 years.

The *Building Texts of Edfu,* discovered at the Temple of Edfu, describe a temple that existed at the beginning of the world, constructed by the gods themselves. The wisdom god, Thoth, copied down the words of the seven sages (gods) into a book that codified the location of certain sacred mounds along the Nile. The text contained records of the Great Pyramid mound itself — the place, it said, where time began. The seven sages, as divine beings, knew where the temples and sacred places were to be created. Assisted by Thoth, they initiated the construction of the Primeval Mound, the original temple of the First Time. They also constructed an edifice called *hwt-ntr,* the "mansion of the god." The texts describe the Flood waters gradually receding as the Primeval Mound emerged. Some scholars have identified the Primeval Mound with the Great Pyramid.

The seven sages and other gods, according to the texts, came from an island that was the homeland of the primeval ones. Their civilization came to a sudden end, and most inhabitants drowned. The few survivors arrived in Egypt and became the Building Gods. Like the Followers of Horus, the Building Gods could constantly renew themselves. Scholars find a strong similarity between these two groups. Their purpose was to pass on knowledge, tradition, and wisdom from the earlier epoch. The seven sages also had plans and designs that were used for all future temples, a role also ascribed to the Followers of Horus. The texts claim that the "new world" created by the sages after the Flood was conceived of and designed by its creators as the rebirth of the previous world of the gods.

Tradition in India tells of seven sages, called Rishis, who survived the Flood. Their purpose was to preserve and pass down to future generations the wisdom found in the antediluvial world. James Churchward received his information about Lemuria from tablets in an Indian Rishi temple. Babylonian tradition also tells of seven sages surviving the Flood who built the sacred city of Uruk.

The recorded history of Ancient Egypt began when Upper Egypt and Lower Egypt became one country under one ruler, King Menes, which began with the First Dynasty of pharaohs and ended when Alexander incorporated Egypt into his empire, thirty dynasties later. A total of 330 monarchs reigned. There is little history about many of the pharaohs, but Egypt was a land of tradition, and Egyptians maintained little changed since the time of the gods.

The Nile River gave life to Egypt, and was considered the benevolent master. By overflowing its banks each year, the Nile ensured Egypt with food for the coming years. Considered almost a miracle, the flood would occur each year just when the land was being parched by the summer sun. Besides irrigating crops, the Nile provided water to springs and wells. It flowed four thousand miles before emptying into the Mediterranean Sea, making it one of the largest rivers in the world.

The papyrus plant was another blessing from the Nile. Egyptians chewed the lower part of the plant, much like sugar cane. However, they used it mainly to manufacture paper for writing and drawing. The paper, nearly indestructible, lasted almost indefinitely. Dense clumps of papyrus plants were once found in the delta of north Egypt, with stems sometimes five or six times the height of man. But now the plant has completely disappeared from that region.

Hieroglyphic writing was invented toward the end of the prehistoric period. It was used frequently during the reign of King Menes of the First Dynasty. At the age of twelve, Jean Francois Champollion had a premonition that he would be the first to decipher the hieroglyphics. He mastered all the languages, both ancient and modern, that he thought would lead to this goal. The solution came in 1822 when the Rosetta Stone was discovered, a Ptolemaic relic upon which the same inscription was recorded in three languages: hieroglyphics, dremotic (vernacular for hieroglyphics), and Greek. Working back through Greek, Champollion deciphered the hieroglyphics, and Egyptology was born. Shawallwer de Lubicz discovered that hieroglyphic symbolism conveyed a subtle metaphysical reality found in the sacred science of the pharaohs. It carried a Hermetic message, kept alive by the Gnostics, Sufis, Kabbalists, Rosicrucians, and Masons.

THE SPHINX

The Sphinx is an enormous statue of a lion's body with the head of a man. Carved out of limestone bedrock on the Giza Plateau near the three Great Pyramids, it measures two hundred forty feet long, sixty-six feet high, and thirty-eight feet wide at its shoulders, and has a gaze directed east along the thirtieth parallel.

It includes a complex that consists of a Sphinx Temple, to the east of the Sphinx and a Valley Temple south of the Sphinx Temple. The Sphinx Temple is almost square measuring one hundred thirty feet on each side. Both roofless temples are approximately forty feet high, built of massive limestone, and at one time were fitted with inner and outer castings of granite. The two temples are constructed from gigantic megaliths estimated to weigh two hundred tons.

Scholars have a difficult time comprehending how Egyptians lifted the blocks into place, as today's technology would have difficulty accomplishing this task. Most of today's cranes can pick up a maximum load of twenty tons, and few cranes in the world can lift two hundred tons. Egyptologists conjecture builders used earth ramps and many workers to move the gigantic monoliths. A slope of one foot elevation in ten feet would be the maximun feasible gradient for such a heavy load, and the ramp would have had to be of material harder than limestone. Scholars estimate it would take eighteen hundred men to move the blocks, almost impossible to do in such a small space.

A rock face was cut away from the limestone to form the hollow where the Sphinx was carved. Both the Sphinx and rock face, carved before the severe weathering , show deep smooth erosion.

John Anthony West calculated the time the Sphinx has been

buried as five thousand years. Until Napoleon arrived in Egypt, the Sphinx lay buried to its neck in sand. In 1816 it was excavated. Because the Sphinx is carved out of a single ridge of rock, only the upper portion rises above the otherwise level ground. Once the hollow of the Sphinx is cleared of sand, it takes twenty to thirty years to fill again. Excavations of the sand occurred in 1853, 1888, and 1916. Without constant attention, the Sphinx becomes covered with sand and therefore immune to erosion of wind and sand.

A controversy has recently arisen regarding the age of the Sphinx. Because of its erosion marks, geologists have dated the Sphinx thousands of years older than the age ascribed by orthodox Egyptologists. The erosion marks were first noted by Schwaller de Lubicz who researched the Egyptian ruins for two decades following his first visit to the Temple of Luxor in 1932. His landmark research, according to John Anthony West, proves that all accepted dogma concerning Egypt is wrong. His findings show that the whole of Egyptian civilization was based on a complete and precise understanding of universal laws, the very knowledge that modern science lacks.

Schwaller de Lubicz observed that severe erosion of the Great Sphinx's body was due to water and not wind and sand. This statement led West, years later, to organize geological research to help determine the age of the Sphinx. West writes in *Serpent in the Sky*, "If proven, the water erosion of the Sphinx is to history what the convertibility of matter into energy is to physics." West thought if water had eroded the Great Sphinx, it must have been constructed before the Great Flood, which was responsible for the erosion. An uphill temple connected to the Sphinx showed identical erosional effects. After West showed photographs of the erosion to geologists, they agreed that the damage was typical of water eroded surfaces. However, erosion by wind and sand could produce marks similar to erosion by water.

Egyptologists believe the Sphinx was constructed by King Cheop's successor, Pharaoh Khafre, also credited with building the second Great Pyramid. The Greeks knew Khafre as Chephren, who reigned from 2520 to 2494 B.C. Egyptologists believed that the facial features of the Sphinx were of Khafre himself, based on a sculpture of Khafre, even though the face of the Sphinx is badly damaged. Professor Mark Lehner, a renowned Sphinx researcher from the Chicago University Oriental Institute, used a computer to reconstruct the face of Khafre on the Sphinx. Critics say that with a computer they could have reconstructed almost any pharaoh's face on the Sphinx, and nothing was proven. Lt. Frank Domingo, a senior forensic artist of the New York Police Department, denies that the Sphinx's face represents Khafre's face.

Lehner asserts, "There is no way to date the Sphinx itself because the Sphinx is carved out of natural rock." However he is certain that it dates back to the Fourth Dynasty, even though Egyptologists are confronted with a complete absence of Old Kingdom texts. He assigns it to the Fourth Dynasty because of a single syllable carved on a granite stele found between the front paws, despite the fact that the stele was not contemporary with the Sphinx itself. The first syllable was Khaf, the first syllable of Khafre.

There is no Early or Middle Kingdom reference to the Sphinx. It came into historical prominence with a stone stele erected between its paws by King Tuthmosis IV about 1400 B.C. The tablet describes a vision Tuthmosis had in which the Sphinx appeared to him, promising him the crown of Egypt if he removed the sand that covered it. Two centuries later Ramses II erected another stele, found in front of the Tuthmosis tablet. This inscription said the Sphinx was consistently kept clear of sand.

Herodotus did not mention the Sphinx in his visit to Egypt during the fifth century B.C. During the Ptolemic times of Rome, a clumsy repair of the paws was undertaken in 300 B.C. Christianity became the official religion of Rome in 333 A.D., so West surmises the Sphinx was buried in sand from 300 to 1800 A.D.

Only wind of sufficient velocity to carry sand can cause perceptible damage, which happens one month of the year when the Khamsin winds blow. They blow from the south, but the temple complex essentially protects the Sphinx from these winds. West concluded, even if the Sphinx had been clear of sand for forty-five hundred years, the effect of wind-blown sand erosion would be minimal. The damage would have been confined to six feet above ground level. Only one erosion mark on the Sphinx is typical of wind erosion and is located on the back of its neck. A hollow appears six feet above the plateau level, suggesting the Sphinx was buried in sand. Nowhere else in Egypt does a statue or temple exhibit weathering as does the Sphinx and its temple. The erosion of the

Sphinx and core blocks of the Valley Temple were caused by the same weathering agent.

The Edgar Cayce Foundation funded Dr. Mark Lehner, then field director of the American Research Center in Egypt, and Dr. K. Lal Gauri, the director of the Stone Conservation Laboratory at the University of Louisville. Their research concluded that three major repair campaigns were conducted on the Sphinx. The weathering, they said, was due to water reacting with the material salts in the limestone. They hypothesized that the water was groundwater leached into the body of the Sphinx from below. Lehner insisted that until the past few decades, no substantial weathering had taken place on the Sphinx since the first repair campaign. Lehner concluded this left only a five hundred year span when the Sphinx could have eroded. West did not believe that underground water could cause this type of erosion, so he consulted a geologist.

He summoned geologist Dr. Robert Schoch of Boston University to render a professional opinion. A stratigrapher and paleontologist, Schoch specialized in the weathering of soft rock, such as the limestone found on the Giza Plateau. West believed only a dozen geologists could properly analyze the erosion of the Sphinx.

A brief visit to Egypt in 1990 convinced Schoch that water had weathered the Sphinx, but not water leaching from the ground. A later visit further confirmed that only water could produce such weathering. The deep vertical fissures along the ditch wall surrounding the Sphinx could have been produced only by running water, coursing down the plateau and cascading over the ditch wall of the Sphinx. The limestone Sphinx sustained three feet of weathering to its body, while only a few miles away mud bricks of the same era received no damage. The water erosion, claims Schoch, was caused by rainwater and not flooding. Schoch was ready to go on record that the Sphinx was older than Dynastic Egypt.

Tentatively he said the Sphinx was carved, at a minimum, 5,000 to 7,000 B.C. A minimum date was established because weathering does not proceed in a linear fashion. West disagrees with Schoch on the date and believes it to be much earlier. He conjectures that the rain that accompanied the Great Flood caused much of the Sphinx erosion, and this occurred about 10,000 B.C. The Sphinx, he concluded, must predate the breakup of the last Ice Age.

The story does not end here. Accompanying Schoch on the research team was geophysicist and seismologist, Dr. Thomas L. Dobecki. Seismology picked up readings of a cavity deep in the bedrock, between the paws and a tunnel along the sides of the Sphinx. The cavity measured twenty-seven feet by thirty-six feet buried fifteen feet below the surface. They believed it might be manmade.

They also found that the limestone bedrock floor immediately behind the Sphinx, showed only half the depth of weathering as did the sides. Schoch and Dobecki concluded that the back of the Sphinx was cut out at a later date. Weathering patterns suggested this portion of the Sphinx was cut out no later than Kaphre's time, some forty-five hundred years ago.

Egyptian traditions assert that the Giza monuments stand as a last and grand memorial to a highly evolved civilization that the Great Flood destroyed. Legends also tell of a "Hall of Records" with recorded knowledge and wisdom of the lost civilization concealed somewhere at Giza, either beneath the Sphinx or in the Great Pyramid.

Arab chronicles from about the 9th century also continue this tradition. They assert the Great Pyramid was built before the Flood as a depository of ancient scientific knowledge. When Caliph Al Mamoun forced a tunnel into the north face, it became the first recorded entry into the Great Pyramid in 820 A.D. He believed he was entering a relic of antediluvial time that contained secrets of ancient science.

A number of hieroglyphic inscriptions on papyri claim hidden chambers called the Chamber of Archives and Hall of Records lay beneath the Sphinx or nearby. Coptic legends maintain that a single subterranean chamber under the Sphinx leads to all three pyramids. A statue of amazing abilities guards each entrance.

The clairvoyant readings of Edgar Cayce tell of a number of Atlanteans who escaped the destruction of Atlantis and reached the Nile Valley in Egypt during the eleventh millennium B.C. Cayce said Egypt was a repository for records concerning Atlantis and ancient Egypt. Around 10,500 B.C., a vast underground repository had been established, containing a library of wisdom from Atlantis.

Cayce describes its location: "This in position lies, as the sun rises from the water, the line of the shadow falls between the paws of the Sphinx." Cayce reports on a chamber or passage from the right forepaw to the entrance of the record chamber. The chamber, he predicted, would be discovered and entered when the time was fulfilled. This would occur just before the end of the 20th century. The discovery of the Hall of Records would be linked to a series of events that would preclude "the second coming of Christ." The cavity detected by the seismograph lay exactly where Cayce said it would be. Cayce said the contents of the Hall of Records would not be shared with the public until many years after it was first entered. He described the ones who were to first enter the chamber as "those who make the perfect way of life."

Egypt's director of antiquities, Dr. Zahi Hawass, acknowledges the hidden tunnels around the Sphinx and pyramids. Hawass appeared on a short video titled Secret Chamber in December 1995, shown standing inside the Sphinx and entering a tunnel that had never been opened. He said, "No one really knows what is inside this tunnel, but we are going to open it for the first time." Hawass is aware of the Cayce readings, and it was rumored that the Edgar Cayce Foundation financially helped him obtain his doctorate at the University of Pennsylvania. Hawass denies this, but acknowledges he has visited with Edgar Cayce's sons. The Edgar Cayce Foundation did help support Dr. Mark Lehner's education.

THE PYRAMIDS

The enigma of the Egyptian pyramids of Giza remains one of the world's great mysteries. Scholars still debate their purpose and builder. They are an architectural wonder built on the principles of sacred geometry that today's scientists have difficulty comprehending. The Great Pyramid's architects had information about the Earth that took scientists a millennium to discover. The architects knew the mean distance from the Earth to sun, the weight and density of the Earth, the polar diameter of the Earth, the direction of true north, and Pythagorean mathematics.

Ancient historians did not agree when the Great Pyramid was built. Manetho (280 B.C.) writes that Suphis, the second king of the Fourth Dynasty, was the builder. Herodotus (fifth century B.C.) asserts Cheops built it, while Diodorus Siculus (56 B.C.) claims the Eighth King, Chemmis of Memphis, built the Great Pyramid.

Today's orthodox Egyptologists believe the first Great Pyramid was built by King Cheops, the second pyramid by his brother King Khafre (Chephren), and the third and smallest pyramid by King Mycerinus, the son of Cheops. Pliny the Elder wrote it took eighty-eight years and four months to build the three pyramids. These three Egyptian pharaohs reigned around 2,500 B.C. However, ancient Egyptian legends say the three Pyramids of Giza were constructed by survivors of Atlantis to preserve their sacred knowledge.

The Great Pyramid sits in the exact center of all the world land areas. It is located on the north-south axis (31 degrees 9 minutes east of Greenwich) which is the longest land meridian, and the east-west latitude (29 degrees 51 minutes 51 seconds north), the longest land parallel. Being only three arc minutes off true north, it lies one-third of the way between the equator and North Pole.

The Great Pyramid's base covers thirteen acres. The blocks of limestone that make up the pyramid along with huge granite blocks, weigh six and one-half tons. There are enough blocks to build thirty Empire State Buildings. Each side of the base measures 755 feet with only an eight-inch variance between the longest and shortest side. Its height measures 481.39 feet. The height in relation to its base perimeter (3023.16 feet) is the same relation as a circle's radius is to its circumference; that is, the relationship is two Pi (481.39 x 2 x 3.14 = 3023.16 feet).

A ratio of 1:43,200 exists between the dimensions of the pyramid and the dimensions of the Earth. The pyramid height of 481.39 feet (0.091 miles) multiplied by 43,200 is 3938.69 miles, an estimate of just under eleven miles of the polar radius of the Earth (3949 miles).

The perimeter of the base (3023.16 feet) multiplied by 43,200 is 24,734.94 miles, within 170 miles of the true equatorial circumference of the Earth (24,902 miles).

The corners set at almost perfect right angles on corner sockets, were engineered for the stress and strain of the pyramid. The pyramid was aligned to the cardinal points, with the average deviation being off by only three arc minutes.

Legend says the pyramid's reflection of the sun is visible from the moon. Some scholars believe that a great sundial once perched on the truncated top of the Great Pyramid, which served as a timepiece for Egypt. At high noon during a summer solstice, the sun casts no shadow.

At one time, casing stones of dense white marble-like limestone covered the exterior of the Great Pyramid. The stones were quarried near the Nile. They weighed up to sixteen tons, numbered 144,000, and covered twenty-two surface acres. These casing stones were eight feet thick, and the joint edges had an area of thirty-five square feet. When fitted next to an adjacent stone, there was only one-fiftieth of an inch of separation. In 1301 A.D., a powerful earthquake shook lose the casing stones.

The average land elevation on Earth is estimated to be 455 feet. The top of the unfinished Great Pyramid (the builders left it unfinished) is 454.5 feet.

The mean temperature of all the earth's surface is sixty-eight degrees Fahrenheit. Scientists consider this the ideal temperature for man's existence. The permanent temperature in the King's Chamber is sixty-eight degrees Fahrenheit, which is one-fifth the temperature between the freezing and boiling points of water. Two air channels, when cleared of sand, maintain that temperature.

The core masonry of each side of the pyramid is hollowed-in by 35.76 inches, meaning it is slightly concave. Computations show the radius that would produce this slight curve is equal to the radius of the Earth.

The unit of measurement employed to construct the Great Pyramid was the Egyptian Royal Cubit, and the linear unit was the Sacred Cubit. The cubit is one-ten-millionth of the distance from the center of the Earth to the pole (3949.89 miles). One Sacred Cubit (twenty-five pyramid inches) is 25.0265 British inches.

The slope of the Great Pyramid, determined from the remaining facing blocks along the north face, measured 51 degrees 51 minutes. The slope angle of the pyramid equals Pi (3.14165). As mentioned before, the ratio of the vertical height to its base perimeter is the same ratio of a circle radius to its circumference. Pi is related to the more interesting Phi, the so-called Golden Section, discussed later.

How they constructed the pyramids of Giza remains a mystery. Herodotus (430 B.C.) clears up some of the questions. He describes how King Cheops quickly brought Egypt into a state of misery by shutting down the temples and preventing sacrifices to the gods. Cheops ordered all Egyptians to help construct the pyramids. Many were enjoined to drag huge stones from quarries in the

Arabian mountains to the Nile. Others received the stones and brought them by ship via the Nile. He writes that 100,000 men labored at one time, in three month shifts.

It took ten years to build the infrastructure of roads along which the stones were dragged. During this period, they constructed underground chambers on the hill where the pyramid now stands. A tomb within an underground chamber was made for the Pharaoh, situated on an island formed from a constructed subterranean channel of the Nile.

Construction of the pyramids took twenty years. Stairs facilitated them in elevating the gigantic stones. Herodotus speaks of "engines" made of short timbers that were used. From the ground, they raised the stones to the first level of stairs. They were set on an "engine" at this level and drawn up to the second level. There were as many "engines" as levels of stairs. He said the pyramid was completed from the top down, the top of the pyramid finished first.

Cheops' reign lasted fifty years. Building a pyramid was an expensive endeavor, and at times he lacked money. For example, sixteen hundred talents (41,884 kg.) of silver were spent on just radishes, onions, and garlic for the laborers. Over the years, Cheops had become so obsessed and wicked that he put his daughter to work in a brothel to help raise money. Her reputation flourished, and each man that came unto her gave a present of one stone. From these stones, traditions tell, pyramids were made.

Diodorus Siculus tells how building mounds near the pyramids made pyramid construction possible. After the mounds were no longer needed, laborers returned the mound material to where it came from. A total of 360,000 men were employed in construction over a twenty-year period. Diodorus Siculus writes that the stones came over a great distance from Arabia. Sledges transported the stones to the river. Approximately fifty men pulled each stone.

Each of the three pyramids had a causeway leading to it, which linked a temple to the pyramid. Each causeway ranged in length from one-quarter mile to one-half mile and was fashioned out of huge blocks of limestone. The causeway of the third pyramid runs directly east; the second pyramid causeway points fourteen degrees south of east; and the causeway of the Great Pyramid points fourteen degrees north of east. Egyptologists assume the causeways were used for the funerary journey of the pharaoh's corpse from the Valley Temple to the Mortuary Temple, where the final embalming ritual took place. Some believe the causeways were initially used as a base for hauling the huge stones.

The interior of the pyramid is as intriguing as the exterior. The Great Pyramid has a complex array of passageways and galleries that house three major internal chambers. The passageways of all three pyramids slope twenty-six degrees. One passageway leads to a subterranean chamber below ground level. The King's Chamber of the Great Pyramid measures thirty-four feet four inches by seventeen feet two inches, and is nineteen feet one inch high. The one hundred fifty-three-foot Grand Gallery connects the King's Chamber to the lower level of the monument. At the base of the Grand Gallery, a horizontal passage, three feet nine inches high and one hundred twenty-seven feet long, runs into the Queen's Chamber.

A well shaft lays at the junction of the horizontal passage of the Grand Gallery. A near vertical tunnel, less than three feet in diameter, joins the Descending Corridor almost one hundred feet below ground level. The one hundred twenty-nine foot Ascending Corridor slopes downward from the Grand Gallery and measures a little more than three feet in height and width. It meets the junction of the Descending Corridor which leads to the Subterranean Chamber, situated in bedrock one hundred feet below the surface plateau. The Subterranean Chamber is a square pit reaching a depth of ten feet. Over the King's Chamber are five relieving spaces. In four of the spaces are hieroglyphics, written in red paint.

Excavators found an empty sarcophagus in the Queen's Chamber, a type used in Egypt at the time the pyramid was built. The capacity of the coffin equals that of the Ark of the Covenant.

Four shafts were found in the Great Pyramid, two exiting from the King's Chamber and two from the Queen's Chamber. Around 2,500 B.C., the north shaft of the Queen's Chamber pointed to the star Kochab, which the ancients associated with cosmic regeneration and immortality of the soul. The southern shaft pointed to Sirius in the constellation of the Great Dog. Sirius is associated with the goddess Isis.

In the King's Chamber, the north shaft points toward the ancient pole star, Thuban (Alpha Draconis), associated by the pharaohs with cosmic pregnancy and gestation. The south shaft points to Al Nitak (Zeta Orionis), the brightest of the three stars in Orion's Belt. Ancient Egyptians identified Orion with Osiris, the god of resurrection and rebirth.

According to authors Graham Hancock and Robert Bauval, this star configuration confirms that the pyramid was strongly connected with the period of 2500 B.C., the approximate date orthodox Egyptologists assign to the building of the pyramids.

Robert Bauval found an interesting association between the three pyramids and Orion. An overhead view of the three Giza pyramids shows the Great Pyramid and Second Pyramid stretch out at a diagonal, running 45 degrees to the south and west of the Great Pyramid. The Third Pyramid is offset to the east of the line. This pattern mimics the sky where the three stars of Orion's Belt stretch out at the same angle. The first two stars, Al Nitak and Al Nilam, are in direct alignment as are the First and Second Pyramid. The third star, Mintaka, lies offset to the east as does the Third Pyramid from the first two pyramids. Bauval asserts that the Pyramids of Giza are a successful metaphor on the ground of Orion's Belt.

The Edgar Cayce Foundation funded Egyptologist Mark Lehner to study the pyramids. Fifteen samples of ancient mortar containing fragments of organic material were taken from the Great Pyramid. Southern Methodist University and a lab in Zurich perfermed radiocarbon 14 dating. Their dates ranged from 3809 to 2869 B.C. and are off two hundred to twelve hundred years from orthodox Egyptologist's chronology. Lehner concluded the pyramids were built four hundred to four hundred fifty years too early to be Old Kingdom pyramids.

In 1872, Wayman Dixon retrieved a small metal hook, a stone sphere, and a piece of wood from within the Great Pyramid. The piece of wood was lost and could not be carbon dated. In 1837, Col. Howard Vyse and two civil engineers discovered an iron plate while clearing the mouth of the southern shaft. They concluded it must have been left during the construction. In 1989, a fragment of the plate was subjected to rigorous chemical tests, and the report suggested that the plate was incorporated into the pyramid at the time it was built. The British Museum refused to believe the report.

In 1993, Rudolf Gatenbrink discovered another piece of wood on the floor of the north shaft of the Queen's Chamber by sending a small robot mounted with a camera up the shaft. At about two hundred feet he discovered a door with a peculiar metal fitting and a small gap beneath it. A red laser spot projected by the robot seemed to disappear. A fiber-optic lens would need to be added to see what lay behind the door. After reporting his findings, Gatenbrink was not allowed to pursue the research, although it would have been inexpensive to extract a piece of wood and perform carbon dating. He also offered to donate his robot to the Egyptian government and train a technician if they would do the research, but was turned down by authorities. Finally in 1996, Dr. Zahi Hawass, director of antiquities, declared that Gatenbrink's find was of great interest. He said the door would be opened in September of 1996, and the multinational research team would be lead by Egyptian geologist Dr. Farouk El Bal.

SACRED SCIENCE

Egypt possessed knowledge whose principle was responsible for the created universe. This sacred knowledge was not written down in books but exhibited in the mathematical principles found in Egypt's pyramids, temples, and art. Today we call these Pythagorean principles sacred geometry, knowledge that modern science ignores. These are the laws of harmony and proportion, first attributed to Pythagoras (580 to 500 B.C.), but known by Egyptians millennium before.

This sacred knowledge was referred to as number mysticism, a theory that numbers have innate meaning. During the Cathedral Age (11th to 14th centuries), the cathedral builders possessed these secrets which were widespread in Europe but disappeared as abruptly as they had appeared. The alchemists, Kabbalists, Rosicrucians, and Freemasons preserved the secret knowledge. The Knights Templar came into possession of these mysteries which they found at King Solomon's Temple in Jerusalem. This sacred information was applied to the European cathedrals and architecture. Because of persecution by state and church, the Knights Templar were forced underground and eventually evolved into the Freemasons.

R. A. Schwalle de Lubicz (1891 to1962) realized Egypt had discovered these mystical principles. His fifteen years of research at the

Temple of Luxor culminated in a multivolumed work entitled *Le temple de l'Homme* (The Temple of Man). John Anthony West believes this is the single most important work of scholarship this century. West clarified Schwalle de Lubicz's findings in his book *Serpent in the Sky* and believes the Egyptians were taught this knowledge from a greater civilization, predating Dynastic Egypt. He writes that it is now possible to prove Atlantis's submersion is the historical reality of the biblical Flood.

Schwaller de Lubicz was born in Alsace in 1891, adopted by a Lithuanian prince, and trained in mathematics and chemistry. He came to Egypt in 1937 and saw the Parthenon of Egypt in Luxor. The Pythagorean mathematics of number, harmony, and proportion held the key to the ultimate mystery of the universe according to Schwaller de Lubicz. He believed that ancient civilization possessed this knowledge, and transmitted it in the form of myth, art, and architecture. If Egypt did possess this knowledge, it would be written into their temples with harmony, proportion, myth, and symbol. To prove his theory, Schwaller de Lubicz first studied the dimensions and proportions of the Temple of Luxor located on the Nile, several hundred miles south of Cairo. He set out to look for Phi.

Phi controls the proportion of innumerable organisms, according to Schwaller de Lubicz. The spiral of our galaxy is a Phi spiral, while orbits in the planets of the solar system are in a complex Phi relationship to one other. The ratio of adjacent bones to one another in both man and animal is equal to Phi. Phi is also found in plant growth and flower petal arrangement. Proportions of Gothic temples are governed by Phi. Science has shown that if people are given a large array of rectangular shapes, they will tend to choose, as most satisfying, the one whose ratio of length to width is equal to the Phi ratio.

Phi, also known as the Golden Section, is obtained by dividing a line (AC) at a point (B) in such a way that the whole line (AC) is longer than the first part (AB) in the same proportion as the first part (AB) is longer than the remainder (BC). $AC/AB = AB/BC = 1.618$.

Dividing a square in two can determine Phi. A diagonal of each half square is swung down to the base line, creating Phi or the Golden Section.

The mathematical formula of Phi is one-half + square root $5/2 = 1.61803$. The square of Phi is equal to itself plus one, while the reciprocal equals Phi minus one.

Phi is also achieved from the Fibonacci series, which principle the ancient Egyptians knew. The Fibonacci series is a sequence of numbers beginning with zero and adding one, which equals one. The two ones are then added giving a sum of two. The sum of two and the previous one equals three. This is repeated to give the sequence: 0, 1, 1, 2, 3, 5, 8, 13, 21, 34, 55, 89, 144, etc. As one goes up the series, the ratio of adjacent numbers settles toward a more constant figure, 1.61803, which is Phi. The geometric form of the Fibonacci series is the spiral, as demonstrated by the spiral of our galaxy.

Phi is not considered a number, but a function. It is called an irrational number and defined by its interactions between numbers. The number one represents the absolute and unity. It creates multiplicity and becomes two. Two creates polarity and becomes conscious of itself. Three represents the relationship established between opposing forces. Four accounts for matter, represented by the four elements: fire, air, earth, and water. Five was the sacred number of Pythagoreans, and members were sworn to secrecy about its mysteries upon penalty of death. The Phi function generates five geometrically, and five is the number of creation. It is the number of love, and was the union of the first male number three and the first female number two. Five was the first universal number. Six is the number of time and space, symbolized by the hexagram. Seven signifies the union of spirit with matter. Thoth was master of eight, which symbolizes the mysteries of the manifested world, of which Thoth gave to man. Eight is the number of justice. Nine represents completion.

Scwaller de Lubicz believed the Phi ratio was a symbol of reproduction and of the eternal ongoing creative function. His research at the Temple of Luxor did prove that the Temple construction was based on Phi. Every aspect of the covered temple was measured as was each pavement stone. The dimensions of each figure in the Temple complex was recorded, including the height of the naval, forehead, crown, and so on. Qualified professionls checked all measurements and data collected. Schwaller de Lubicz's research did prove that ancient Egyptians possessed advanced mathematics and scientific knowledge, and that the Phi relationship underlaid the Temple of Luxor.

The Pyramids of Giza were also shown to be based on different Phi relationships. Ancient sources claimed that Egypt was the original source of geometry, and Pythagoras acknowledged he acquired much of his knowledge from Egypt. Egyptian civilization, according to Schwaller de Lubicz, was based on a precise knowledge of the mysteries of the Creator.

Every aspect of knowledge in the arts and sciences of Egypt was held secret beyond a certain level. The rules, axioms, theorems, and formulas never became public. Dangerous ramifications lay behind the secret knowledge of Pythagorean numbers if it fell into the wrong hands. This knowledge of harmonic law was given only to a class of initiates who would be responsible in controlling its effects. They preserved this knowledge in architecture, art, music, painting, and rituals. The underlying principles of Egyptian knowledge were kept secret, but manifested in works. Knowledge recorded in books belonged to those whom had earned the right to them, the keepers of the secrets.

All Egyptian art and architecture were first laid out upon grids to precisely determine proportion and scale with nothing left to the whim of the artists. It was the anonymous sage who was the artist. They designed the temples, statues, and wall friezes. Egyptian art was based on knowledge and not inspiration. The primary theme of art and architecture was reincarnation, resurrection, and the journey of the soul to the underworld. Man's purpose was to return to the source.

The Old, Middle, and Late Kingdoms' art work operated on a grid of nineteen squares. Nineteen demonstrated Pythagorean properties and related to the cosmic measurements regarding the cycle of time and to the twelve signs of the zodiac. Mayan art was also laid out on a grid of nineteen squares.

The temples of Egypt were torn down and rebuilt according to plan. Sages, not Christian zealots as Egyptologists ascribe, ordered the effacement of reliefs and inscription. This priestly secret society made the decision, not the reigning pharaoh. Temples were dismantled carefully and deliberately after the predetermined symbolic significance had passed. Egyptians perpetually engaged in taking down old temples and constructing new ones, often on the site of the old one.

Schwaller de Lubicz referred to The Temple of Luxor as the Temple of Man. This vast stone symbol incorporated within it the total wisdom of Egypt, including science, math, geometry, astronomy, astrology, art, and symbolism. Through its proportions and harmonies it tells the story of the creation of man and his development stage by stage. The temple measures eight hundred feet in length and was built in stages to a sacred architectural design. Every aspect of the temple aligns with one of three axes. By design it evokes an understanding of creation and the creative power in the beholder. According to Schwaller de Lubicz, the temple proportions are those of the Adamic man, man before the Fall, the perfected man, and man who regained his cosmic consciousness.

The Great Pyramid also demonstrated a direct geometric relationship of the appropriate relationship between Pi and Phi. Because the architects chose the Pi angle slope of the pyramid (51 degrees 51 minutes), the Phi ratio became an inevitable consequence. The ratio between the slope height and half the base is 1.61899, or Phi. The cosine of the Pi angle is 0.618.

Peter Lemesurier wrote in *The Great Pyramid Decoded* that every one of the Pyramids' basic and internal measurements can be expressed as a function of Pi and 365.242 (the number of days in a year). Every primitive inch along the floors of the passageway represents a year. Some researchers believe the pyramid was a monument of prophecy and a graphic chart of the ages, representing both past and future events. By establishing the Zero Year (beginning of Adam) with geometry and with each pyramid inch representing a year, the passageways reflected man's history and future.

Ancient Egyptians were quite advanced in the principles of astronomy. They understood the heavens and possessed three calendars. Egypt worked according to the lunar calendar, which had alternating twenty-nine and thirty day months. The lunar calendar ran in twenty-five year cycles of 309 lunations. They also consulted a moving civil calendar of 365 days that had five additional days, when the neters (gods) were said to be born. The third calendar was based on the helical return of the star Sirius, which returned every 365 1/4 days.

The Egyptian New Year allowed one to determine the date when Upper and Lower Egypt were unified. The three possibilities were 4240, 2280, or 1320 B.C. West believes the date to be 4240 B.C., but orthodox Egyptologists believe the date was 2280 B.C.

Egyptians regarded Sirius as a greater sun than our solar system sun. Some scholars also suspect Sirius is a great sun around which our sun orbits. Sirius is a double star with one large, low-density half and a smaller, extremely bright half that makes it one of the brightest stars in the heavens. The annual Nile flooding usually coincides with Sirius's appearance on the horizon, which occurs around July 20.

Ancient Egyptians were aware of the precession of the equinox. Because the Earth does not spin true on its axis, the spring equinox rises against a gradually shifting background of constellations. The anomaly was approximately five minutes longer than the sidereal year. Therefore, it takes 2160 years for the equinox to precess through one sign of the zodiac, and 25,920 years for the spring equinoxes to traverse through the complete constellation. The cycle is called the Great Platonic Year. The precession of the equinox gave names to the various ages. Pisces began around 140 A.D.; Aries, 2000 B.C.; Taurus, 4000 B.C.; and Gemini, 6000 B.C. Scwaller de Lubicz discovered that the earliest dynasties knew about the precession of the equinoxes, as it shaped Egyptian artistic and architectural policy.

The unification of Upper and Lower Egypt in 4240 B.C. coincided with the establishment of the Sothic (Sirius) year, and marked the precessional exit from Gemini into Taurus. While in Gemini (the sign of the twins) there had been an emphasis on duality. Egypt unified under King Menes, the founder of the First Dynasty, and a new era of architecture began. The symbolism of Mentu, the bull (sign of Taurus), became the characteristic feature of Egyptian art, and architecture became monolithic. Many kings incorporated Mentu, the bull, in their names. The Age of Mentu ended after Mentuhoteps I to V.

Another great change took place around 2100 B.C. when the equinox moved into Aries. Mentu the bull disappeared from art, name, and architecture, and the ram of Amon made its appearance. The ram was the sign of Aries. The pharaohs incorporated Amon in their name: Amenhotep, Amenophis, and Tutankhamen. Egyptian astronomy was a sophisticated science on which the meaning of astrology was based. Scwaller de Lubicz concluded that Egypt's astronomy and astrological significance influenced the course of art and architecture.

Graham Hancock and Robert Bauval explain in *The Message of the Sphinx* that the orientation of Orion's Belt to the Milky Way in

10,500 B.C. mirrored the relationship of the three pyramids to the Nile River. At that time, the Orion star Al Nitak crossed the meridian at an altitude of nine degrees twenty minutes, which is the lowest position in the star's precession.

The Age of Leo (the lion is Leo's sign) began around 10,500 B.C., the only epoch where the east-facing Sphinx would manifest exactly the right symbolic alignment. On spring equinox 10,500 B.C., when the sun rose over the horizon, ninety degrees to the south, the three stars of Orion's Belt formed a pattern in the sky identical to the grand plan of the Giza Pyramids. This marked the beginning of the age of Leo and the upward precessional cycle of Orion's Belt. Why would the Egyptians have aligned the pyramids to these three stars of Orion? Hancock and Bauval explain: In a Hermetic text, Thoth remarks to his disciple Asclepius. "Do you know Asclepius that Egypt is an image to Heaven? Or, so to speak more exactly, in Egypt all the operations of the power which rule it work in heaven have been transferred to Earth below?"

In the ancient *Book of What is in the Duat,* an initiate receives explicit instruction to build on the ground a replica of the hidden circle of the Duat. "Whoever shall make an exact copy of these forms . . . and shall know it, shall be a spirit and well equipped in heaven and Earth, unfailingly, regularly, and eternally. Whosoever shall make a copy . . . it shall act as a magical protector for him both in heaven and earth."

Hancock and Bauval suggest immortality may have been the real motive for the construction of the three Pyramids at Giza. The constellations of Orion and Leo dominated the Duat sky-region, and both were imaged on the ground at Giza.

The Duat envelops the stars of Orion and Sirius, and the ancient Egyptians considered the Duat to be active only at the time of summer solstice, when Orion and Sirius rose helically. Helical means the apparent rising or setting of a star due to its nearness to the sun. The day Sirius rose with the sun at dawn, after a period of invisibility, was considered the beginning of ancient Egypt's New Year.

Ancient Egyptians speak with certainty of an epoch called Zep Tepi, when the gods inhabited the world. The god Osiris was associated with Orion, and Isis with Sirius. Egyptologists call the Duat the underworld, ruled by Osiris. Because Osiris ruled this world after death, Egyptians placated this great god to achieve immortality. Evidence suggests the pharaohs and chosen ones constructed the three pyramids to help them attain this immortal state, and provided the setting for initiation into immortality.

Chapter Six

THE PHARAOHS AND GODS
A Journey to Immortality

To understand the mysteries of Egypt, one needs to comprehend the roles of the pharaohs and gods of Egypt. This awareness helps provide answers to the deepest secrets held by the pyramids, Sphinx, and temples.

Evidence has been presented that Egypt inherited its traditions from another advanced civilization. Sumerian texts suggest that Sumer had an early influence on Egypt after the Flood, as both civilizations rose almost instantaneously without a period of development. Sitchin believes this rapid development occurred because the gods, who originated from the twelfth planet, Nibiru, brought their heritage. The gods, according to the Sumerian texts, were here long before the Flood.

Plato writes that the gods ruled Atlantis until its demise, and that many gods of Atlantis were identical to the gods of Greece. If the gods existed before the Flood, one might assume the gods of Egypt, Sumer, and Greece originated from Atlantis. Evidence has been presented that a great flood, thought to be the biblical Flood, destroyed Atlantis around 10,500 B.C. Survivors from Atlantis went to Egypt, according to ancient documents and tradition, and in Egypt they preserved their sacred knowledge.

PHARAOHS

The rulership of Egypt can be categorized into three distinct eras. Prior to the Great Flood, the gods ruled Egypt similar to the traditions of Atlantis and Sumer. This era, lasting nearly 14,000 years, began with Hephaetus and ended with Horus. During the second era, the demigods and Spirits of the Dead reigned for approximately 11,000 years. Mortal kings were the last to reign.

Manetho writes that Egypt's civilization endured 36,525 years, from the time of the gods to the pharaoh's last dynasty. Greek historian Diodorus Siculus ascribes 23,000 years to the Egyptian civilization, with mortal kings accounting for less than 5,000 years.

The Followers of Horus, the Shemsu Hor, defined the second era of kingship, which took the divine Horus lineage through the ages until Menes, the first human pharaoh. Egyptians believed one purpose of the Followers of Horus was to carry the extraordinary knowledge that they had inherited from the gods through the ages. These powerful and enlightened individuals were selected by an elite academy, who had undergone a rigorous initiation. The Followers of Horus established themselves at the sacred site of Heliopolis several millennium before the beginning of recorded Egyptian history. Pythagoras, Solon, and Herodotus had all studied ancient records at Heliopolis that told of significant events that happened long ago. They knew the pharaohs and their priests were guardians of these ancient records of the Followers of Horus.

The Followers of Horus were equated with beings who were sometimes divine and sometimes human. Considered a bridge, they linked humans to the world of the gods. Sometimes called the Souls of Heliopolis, they assisted the kings to ascend to the heavens into the Kingdom of Osiris. This Heliopolitan Brotherhood prepared and initiated the generation of Horus kings to help them resurrect to the former world of gods.

Menes was the first pharaoh of the First Dynasty following the unification of Upper and Lower Egypt. Thirty dynasties followed, ending with the conquest of Egypt by Alexander the Great. In all, there were three hundred monarchs. The King's List of Manetho names the pharaohs and gives their length of reign, but little is known of their history.

The Bible described the master of Egypt as the pharaoh, a term used today to refer to Egypt's kings. In official stelae, inscriptions often refer to the king as nefer, the perfect god. Egyptians consider the pharaoh above all other humans, immediately after the supernatural gods.

The royal infants were not conceived as were other children. According to tradition, the real father of Queen Hatsheput was Amen-Ra, the king of gods, who took the form of the reigning King Tuthmosis I. He resolved to give Egypt a new sovereign only after summoning the Great Ennead of twelve gods and notifying them of his intentions. The god Thoth led him to the queen, who was lying in splendor in the royal palace, and "The god's love flowed through her limbs, and he revealed to her the name of the divine majesty to whom she would give birth." The theory of divine birth had existed in the Old Kingdom. Queen Hatsheput later became responsible for some of the most beautiful buildings in Egypt.

The god Ra was reported to have impregnated a mortal daughter of an Egyptian priest. Ra instructed several goddesses to assist in the birth, which produced triplets. The three infants later reigned in succession at the beginning of the Fifth Dynasty. King Cheops tried to seize the children, without avail. He failed because the gods controlled the birth of the heir to the throne.

The coronation ceremony consecrated the authority of the king to his subjects, and tradition claims the gods performed a parallel ceremony. On the day of coronation, the names to be assumed by the new king were proclaimed. Until then, the heir to the throne had only his birth name. The day of coronation was considered the beginning of a new era, which makes it difficult for scholars to be exact in dating.

After the king was enthroned, he lived in the palace, which was probably inherited from his father. The pharaoh's ambition was always to construct a palace of his own.

The kings of the Old Kingdom all resided in Memphis. During this kingdom most kings married their sisters. The general rule seemed to have been that the pharaoh, the son of Ra, could only marry a princess who claimed to be of divine origin. Kings were permitted to have two or more wives at the same time, and they were allowed to enjoy themselves on the side.

The average length of the dynasties between King Menes and King Cambyses was just under a century. Egyptians, who wanted change, did not always wait for an absence of a male heir before ousting a royal family from the throne. Historically, attempted assassinations and plots to overthrow the king were common.

Even though private individuals owned a large part of the country, the pharaohs considered all property in Upper and Lower Egypt their own. This included livestock, buildings, land, tools, and even people. They could do as they wished with them. The king was the biggest landowner, and royal estates were clearly marked.

Egypt was divided into provinces called nomes, ruled by a governor who collected taxes for the pharaoh. With every new reign, the number of official posts increased. Appointments were usually made from within the king's family or aristocracy, and often the king would help the high ranking officials build their own tombs.

The pharaoh spent much of his time on tasks that gave pleasure to the gods. It was his duty to display his gratitude. In thought and deed, the pharaoh behaved as an obedient and respectful son to the gods. In theory, he was the only intermediary between the gods and man, as the pharaoh was considered to be part divine. In practice, professional priests carried out the ritual worship.

Priesthood was not an easy profession, as the priests needed to know everything about the god they served. They recited hymns, prayers, and magic formulae. Their priestly function closely aligned with requirements of their particular god. Never did they preach a moral code, as they were not celibate, and they were encouraged to eat, drink, and be merry. They were usually sons of other priests.

Priests entered the temple daily to wake up and dress the god with various garments, headdresses, and insignia. At night, the god was undressed and put back into the shrine. The gods were fed three or four times a day. Priests accepted the fact that priests of other gods should exist side by side with them.

The temple was the abode of the god, often based on the design of the pharaoh. A gateway led to an inner court covered with inscriptions and bas-reliefs extolling the power of the gods. The important gods had altars located either in the temple or town. A relatively large staff maintained the temple.

Priests were assigned to increase the possessions of the gods. By the time of King Ramses III, the priesthood had acquired tremendous wealth. The servants of Amun, the God of Thebes, numbered 86,000 men and 400,000 beasts. They lived on the estate of the god that comprised 10 percent of Egypt and had fifty-three small towns. The estate boasted of hundreds of gardens and eighty-three ships.

The essential duty of the king was to build and keep up the temples. To provide a means of support, he needed to constantly replenish the offering tables. By building a temple a king could cooperate with the gods, as the gods instructed the pharaoh about where to locate and how to design the temple. Kings of the Old Kingdom supported polytheism and built temples in honor of local gods. Pharaohs often declared themselves sons of the gods of every city.

Herodotus believed the Egyptians were the most religious of all people. They had more gods, goddesses, sacred beings, and sacred objects than any of the people who built such magnificent temples for their deities. Each of the thirty-two *nomes* had its official deity, with Thebes and Memphis each possessing many gods.

The kings of the Old Kingdom and Middle Kingdom built pyramids to ensure their immortality. Today more than eighty known pyramids lay in Egypt, most originating from these eras. The Egyptian people accepted all the hard work that went into pyramid construction because they believed their fate to be linked with the god reposing in the sarcophagus.

For Egyptians, the pyramids were intimately associated with their king. Here the king rested in the final sleep of death. The pyramid was considered the king himself, not the mortal king, but a being who was to enter eternity.

Once the pharaoh decided to build a pyramid, he appointed officials to oversee the project, and recruited workers for construction. A town soon sprang up around the site.

After completion of the pyramid and the death of the pharaoh, the king was laid to rest in the funerary temple. Priests maintained their residences nearby and observed the royal sites following the king's death. The worship of some Old Kingdom kings went on for several generations and officials continued to maintain the premises. Eventually the financial burden became so great, that the succeeding kings abandoned the monument and it fell into ruins, becoming an object of curiosity. A curse then fell on the tomb, and if the tomb was disturbed, the deceased could punish the culprits by wringing their necks or arousing the anger of the "serpent."

The ancient Egyptians were a comparatively easy people to govern. They were hospitable, fond of good living, and had a good sense of humor. They were attached to their local gods, towns, professions, and priests. Occasionally, they rebelled against the priests, but the revolt was always short-lived, except in the time of Moses.

MOSES

Manetho, the ancient Egyptian historian, wrote an Egyptian version of Moses that differs from the biblical story. Egyptians regarded Moses as a great man, perhaps even divine, and they claimed him as their own.

Moses was a priest of Heliopolis who was dismissed from the order because he had contracted leprosy. He was segregated in a stone quarry east of the Nile, along with 80,000 lepers referred to as the wasted or "polluted" people.

A wise prophet had predicted that certain allies would join the "polluted" people and take possession of Egypt for thirteen years. After writing this prophecy, he committed suicide.

These outcasts in the stone quarries suffered hardships for many years and begged the king to assign them to a refuge in the deserted City of the Shepherds, named Auaris. The king agreed.

The city was used as a base for revolt, and they chose a priest of Heliopolis named Osarseph as their leader. Named after Osiris, he later changed his name to Moses. People took an oath of obedience to him. This new leader outlawed worship of Egyptian gods and permitted sacrifice of animals that had been designated as sacred in Egypt. They should sacrifice all alike. The new law decreed sexual intercourse was allowed only with members of their group. The people were instructed to repair the walls of the city and prepare for war against King Amenophis.

The outcasts sent an embassy to the Shepherds in the city of Jerusalem, who had been expelled from Egypt by King Tethmosis. If the Shepherds joined them, the outcasts promised them supplies. As a result approximately 200,000 Shepherds arrived in Auaris. Aware of the earlier prophecy, King Amenophis retreated with 300,000 troops to Memphis and finally to Ethiopia for thirteen years.

The Solomites, the dwellers from Jerusalem, and the "polluted" Egyptians treated the resident Egyptians savagely and impiously. They set towns on fire, pillaged temples, and mutilated images of gods.

After thirteen years of exile from Egypt, King Amenophis returned with his large army from Ethiopia and battled the Shepherds and "polluted" Egyptians, defeating them. Many escaped from Egypt but were pursued to the frontiers of Syria by the Egyptians. Such is the Egyptian account of the Exodus.

According to Manetho, the Shepherds were a people known as the Hyksos. He called them an ignoble race that had come from an unknown land in the mysterious east. These nomads numbered 280,000, invaded Egypt, and subdued the country without battle. The Hyksos established a dynasty that worshiped "one true god." They eventually left Egypt for a land known as Judea and founded the city of Salem, which became Jerusalem.

THE GODS

Religion and devotion to the gods were the primary life purposes of ancient Egyptians. The gods guarded against illness, protected against enemies, and provided for successful undertakings. They were constant companions of the Egyptians, and the people thought they could never do enough to show their gratitude to them. As in Sumer, the Egyptians believed the gods ruled the earth long before man.

Egyptian traditions, as told in the *Coffins Texts,* claim that a primeval ocean and a Creator-God existed before the creation. In the beginning, the Creator-God Atum was meditating in solitude and set in motion the act of creation. The first stage of creation resulted in the creation of the first pair of divine children. Shu became the first god created, the god of air, and Tefnut the second, the god of water. The texts describe the children coming forth from Atum's own semen or sputum. Immediately thereafter, the second stage was initiated, and the Creator-God began to speak. At that time, the primeval ocean had not become conscious and was not aware of the Creator-God. This process of creation took place without the primeval ocean's awareness. The Creator-God thereby distinguished himself from the primeval ocean, which the Egyptians called Nun.

Shu and Tefnut gave birth to Geb (the god of earth) and Nut (the god of sky), who were closely bound together at birth. Shu split them apart, this separated the sky and earth. Shu occupied the space between the Earth and sky.

The primeval ocean's awakening constituted the third stage of creation. Life developed and gave rise to speech, and speech engendered dialogue. Speech revealed the forces that would animate and guarantee the creation to come. This stage was identified with Shu, the air god, and Maat to whom the Creator-God breathed. Maat was none other than the "norm," which governed the regular occurrence of a cosmic phenomenon. After the world was created, the gods and humans began to live in it.

The gods ruled on earth, one succeeding the next. This was the Golden Age. Geb and Nut gave birth to Osiris, the Elder Horus, Seth, Isis, and Nephthys. These gods in turn created a multitude of beings and inanimate objects.

The epoch of the "First Time" was referred to as *Zep Tepi,* the era following creation. There was an absolute conviction among ancient Egyptians that the "First Time" was an actual historical event. Osiris established a cosmic-kingdom setting in the Memphis region. The kingdom passed down to Osiris's son, Horus, and through the eras it passed on to the subsequent generation of "Horus kings," the living pharaohs on Earth. The Golden Age was an era of perfection, a blissful epoch with no death, disease, or disaster. During this time, Osiris was one of the first gods to sit on the throne of the divine kingdom with Isis, his wife and sister.

The Golden Age came to a disastrous halt when Seth murdered his brother, Osiris. Conspiring to eliminate Osiris, Seth tricked him to lay in a coffin. Immediately thereafter, the conspirators flung themselves upon the coffin, sealed it shut with lead, and threw it into the Nile River. The coffin floated to the sea and came to rest at Byblos, in present day Lebanon. A tree grew around the coffin, and it became incorporated within the trunk.

Upon hearing about the location of Osiris, Isis acquired the sacred tree from the king and queen at Byblos. She summoned Thoth and other gods who helped bring Osiris back to life. Because Osiris and Isis had left no heir to the throne, the pair made love and their union begat Horus. After discovering Osiris was alive, Seth again killed Osiris and this time cut his body into fourteen pieces. Helped by her sister Nephtys, Isis managed to retrieve the pieces, all except the phallus, and put them back together. The mutilated body of Osiris was resurrected to the nether world, which Osiris then ruled.

When Horus was born, Isis hid him in the reeds of the Nile River to keep him away from Seth. A scorpion stung Horus resulting in his death. Isis appealed to Thoth, who descended from heaven and restored the life of Horus.

After reaching adulthood, Horus challenged Seth for the throne of Egypt and vowed to avenge his father's death. Their struggle continued far and wide, including confrontations in the sky. Depictions show Horus in a celestial chariot called a *nar*, a long, cylindrical object with a funnel-like tail. The front of the *nar* had two headlights that changed color from blue to red. Horus shot Seth from out of the *nar* causing Seth to lose a testicle. During the final battle, Seth shot a beam at Horus causing Horus to lose his right eye. Retrieving his lost eye became Horus's mission, as it symbolized the royal power usurped by Seth.

Finally the Council of Great Gods called for a truce. Geb, Lord of Earth, ruled in favor of giving Lower Egypt to Horus, and Seth was made King of Upper Egypt. Shortly thereafter, Geb changed his mind and declared Horus the legitimate heir of Osiris and gave Horus the inheritance of Seth. The ascension of Horus reunited Upper and Lower Egypt. This unification remained throughout most of Egyptian history, and the kingship was given a perpetual divine connection. Each pharaoh was considered a reincarnation of Horus and the occupant of the throne of Osiris.

Seth stubbornly maintained his position, and his constant misdeeds exhausted the patience of his fellow gods. Eventually all misfortunes and accidents that occurred in the divine world would be attributed to Seth. Seth was violent, aggressive, and a drinker known for his excesses and his homosexual inclinations. The gods finally expelled Seth from the divine community. At the end, even Seth's mother, Nut, repudiated him, and some texts say that Seth committed suicide.

Atum was the sun god and creator of the universe and called the "Lord of Heliopolis," the major center of sun worship and learning. The Egyptians named Heliopolis An (the Biblical On), which was built by Ptah to honor An, the god of the heavens. (Is it a coincidence that An is similar to Anu, the major Sumerian god?)

At the beginning of the Pyramid Age, the god Ra had taken over the cult of the earlier god Atum, much like Marduk did in Sumer with Anu and Enlil. Zecharia Sitchin believes Ra and Marduk to be the same. Ra-Atum was now worshiped as the creator of the world, according to the Heliopolitan theology. Ra held unquestionable authority, and the whole divine society of gods found its only real point of anchorage in Ra. The words of Ra as revealed through the god Thoth became the creation of the world. Without exception, all divine writings were considered emanations from Ra.

Ra constantly battled with the serpent who symbolized everything the newly created world rejected. The battle between evil, represented by the serpent, and Ra would go on for eternity. They waged a great battle at Heliopolis, the capital of Ra, where the Creator-God defeated the gigantic serpent, portrayed by Apophis who threatened cosmic order.

Ra, the great god of heaven and Earth, built a special shrine at An to house the Ben Ben, a special object in which Ra had supposedly come down to Earth from heaven.

The god Ptah is Atum fallen to Earth, which Phi symbolizes, the creative power in Atum. Ptah was considered a great scientist, master engineer, and architect. The gods considered him the chief craftsman who helped create and shape man. Egyptian tradition describes his coming to Earth from a celestial disc. When Egypt was inundated with water in the earliest of times, Ptah dammed the Nile and reclaimed the land. Ptah also built Heliopolis before leaving Egypt.

One of the most respected and important Egyptian gods was Thoth, God of Wisdom, who gave speech and writing to humanity. Thoth served as the master god in divine administration. Decisions made by the gods had to be dictated to Thoth to become operational. Thoth wrote down every utterance of the Creator-God. His mastery of the written and spoken word permitted Thoth to give active form to the Creator-God. Known as the messenger of the gods, he served as their spokesman and established their rules of conduct.

Thoth is quoted: "I am Thoth, master of the divine words (hieroglyphics) which put things in their (proper) place . . . Everything that comes out of my mouth takes in existence as if I were Ra . . . I am he who cannot be driven from the sky or the Earth because I know what is concealed in the sky, inaccessible to Earth, and hidden in the Primeval Ocean . . . I am the creator of the sky, he who is at the origin of the mountains . . . I make the gods and men live . . . It is Thoth who created the structure of Egypt, and the organization of the province."

Thoth ensured the permanence of knowledge. He was the memory of the gods, the one who knew everything. Thoth advocated giving writing to man, but Atum, the creator, was concerned that man would come to distrust his memory. Thoth also created speech and the different languages.

The writings of Thoth were recopied for generations. Thoth left a considerable number of texts in secret hiding places, and the *Book of the Dead* was specifically composed by Thoth. The gods themselves did not hesitate to pass some of their secrets to man by letting "manuscripts fall from the sky."

Thoth, an ancient ruler of Egypt, ruled for 7,726 years, according to the *Royal Canon* in the Museum of Turin, which lists all reigning kings from the beginning to the 18th Human Dynasty around the first century B.C. Thoth also claimed to be an Atlantean king.

Some gods did not trust Thoth, as they accused him of retaining their temple offerings. His set speeches would get on the nerves of some gods, and Isis accused him of being slow in making decisions. Accused of being pretentious and pedantic did not bother him, as he knew he was a sage among the gods. The gods knew he was very wise but also boring.

Thoth, the judge of the dead and the lord of truth, revealed to humanity the will of God. He gave magic and alchemy to humans. Some believe he was never born but self-created and considered him interdimensional.

The Ennead of Egypt, the family group of nine gods, included the first three generations of the Creator-God's descendants: Shu, Tefnut, Geb, Nut, Nephthys, Seth, Isis, Osiris, and Horus the Elder. Atum, the creator, was not counted as one of the Ennead's members.

The term *neter* (netjer) meant god, or any entity that could transcend ordinary human reality. Each *neter* symbolized a principle represented by a god.

Khnum, called the potter god, conceived the forms of the gods, people, and animals. Tradition has him molding them on his potter's wheel, relying on the force of his breath.

Some gods were quite large in stature. Osiris's height was said to be fifteen feet three inches, and Horus was more than thirteen feet tall. Gods did not have a fixed height, as their height varied according to the aspect assumed. The gods also emitted a distinctive body odor. The scent preceded the god, announcing his presence. It allowed other gods to recognize one of their own. Old age did not usually affect gods, especially Thoth and Seth. However, Isis and her sister Nephthys did reach an advanced age. Pregnancies of the gods lasted ten months.

In early Egypt, the gods and humans mingled freely with one another. Gods normally dwelt in the sky but took their meals on Earth. They easily transitioned from sky to Earth. The heavenly domain was much calmer, compared to the turmoil found on earth, and the two worlds maintained a permanent relationship with each other. Each reigning god resided in his palace. The Creator-God's palace was supposed to have been located inside the great castle at Heliopolis, the god's seat of government.

Gods kept their real names secret from all the others. To reveal their names was to renounce their god status and allowed others to gain control over them. For greater security, a god's full name virtually comprised an infinite series of names, nearly impossible to remember.

Individual knowledge of the gods oscillated between the two extremes of omniscience and learning. Usually gods had a difficult time grasping matters that they had not created or participated in. Only the Creator comprehended all knowledge. Thoth was considered the most knowledgeable of the gods, and through Thoth's efforts man received knowledge.

Many gods had close affinities with the animal kingdom. Through their animal forms, a god served notice that he possessed the powers of that animal. Thoth was identified with the ibis, Horus with the falcon, and Isis with the swallow. Hieroglyphics often depicted gods in their animal-human forms. Gods were prohibited from harming certain species but also reserved the right to kill certain animals.

Similarities exist between the Greek gods and Egyptian gods. The classical writers gave the Egyptian gods their Greek names. Atum, the Creator-God, was Zeus; Horus was Hercules; Thoth was Hermes; Min was Pan; Khonsu was Hercules; and Hathor was Aphrodite. The Greeks lived in Egypt throughout all eras, but were more numerous during the 26th Dynasty and the Ptolemics. The gods of Egypt, Greece, Sumer, and Atlantis were also similar, strongly suggesting they may have been the same gods but with different names in different civilizations.

THE AFTERLIFE

When one understands the ancient Egyptian's belief in the afterlife, the many mysteries of Egypt become clear. The Egyptians did as much for their dead as they did for their gods. Worship of the dead and the importance given to the tombs were prominent features of ancient Egypt. Osiris, ruler of the nether world, provided Egyptians with a means of salvation. The people believed good works and pious deeds brought remission of sins.

For the people of Egypt, the priests of the pharaoh maintained the cult of Osiris, based on the principle of renewal and reincarnation. However, the elite of the temple received knowledge regarding the Christlike principles of Horus the Redeemer about how to free oneself from the karma of reincarnation, enabling one to return to the source, Atum-Ra.

Horus is the divine man of nature, who must do battle against Seth, the Satan of Christianity, and Horus ultimately defeats Seth. Horus is the direct path to God, the path that subdues the enemy within oneself by one's own efforts. Egypt began with the concept of divine attributes abiding within each man. It was man's destiny to be raised to the gods and go back to the source of Atum-Ra, either through a longer process of reincarnation or directly on the path of Horus. The religion of Egypt was based on initiation to guide humans from a natural state of consciousness to a higher state, which is humanity's destiny and birthright. This higher state was unnatural in the context of natural will.

Two religions prevailed in early Egypt: the Hermopolitan that worshiped Osiris and the Heliopolitan that worshiped the sun god Ra. The death of Osiris cost him his earthly kingdom, but it made him the monarch of the nether world, which was neither Earth nor heaven, but a middle region. When Seth cut Osiris into fourteen pieces, he was pieced back together into a mummy by Osiris's son, Anubis, whose mother was Nephthys, Seth's wife. This act enabled the gods to reassemble the bones of Osiris and allowed Isis and Osiris to engender Horus. Osiris perfected the hidden nether world for his mummy.

Once a person died, Egyptians prepared the deceased to make a journey consisting of varying and unpleasant trials. Those dead who were satisfied with their lot and who passed the judgment of the divine tribunal, took up residence in a world described as a paradise. They enjoyed a state of well being similar to that of an earthly dignitary. Both gods and humans went to this paradise after dying a seeming or real death, and here they discovered the road to rebirth. To reach this judgment tribunal, the dead had to make a journey. They hoped eventually to secure Ra's permission to climb aboard his barque (barge) so they could join him and eliminate the cycle of rebirth.

Written guidelines were available for the journey. Those who knew the spell or secret words could journey to any part of heaven they desired. Having knowledge prior to the journey was important. Evil demons lay in wait for the ignorant dead who set out to serve Osiris. The dead needed to pass through a series of seven gates to reach Osiris's kingdom. To pass through the gates, the deceased needed to impersonate Egyptian gods. Funerary texts explained to the dead the knowledge required for the journey, but access to this knowledge was restricted. If the dead possessed this knowledge, they were not in fear. Their salvation depended on the goodwill of those who remained on Earth and who could read out the appropriate spell.

Once the deceased reached the great Hall of Osiris, they were greeted by Anubis who said, "May your weighing take place in our midst." Before entering the Great Hall, the deceased had to restate the name of the gate through which they wished to pass.

The time came for the dreaded trial to weigh their hearts, the core of the deceased's innermost thoughts and depository of their good and evil deeds. Scales were placed in front of Osiris, and the heart of the deceased was placed on one of the scale's pans. It had to be as light as the feather placed in the other pan. Anubis proceeded to weigh it, and Thoth recorded it to eliminate all possible grounds for contesting the judgment.

The deceased then recited two long lists of sins he or she had never committed, such as, "I have not acted sinfully toward men, and I have not obstructed the god in his coming forth," followed by "I am purified," repeated four times. The deceased then declared what they had done that pleased the gods such as, "I have given bread to the hungry, water to the thirsty, and clothed the naked." They then saluted the god of the dead. Next an exam was given to the deceased, designed to test their knowledge of conditions in the afterlife. Forty-two judges asked them to state their new identity as a divine human being.

They then entered the last new gate which became the abode of the deceased, only if they knew the secret names of all its constituent parts. Thoth then asked his own set of questions. If the newly arrived failed one of the tests, an animal called the "eater" would eliminate them. Fortunately, not all punishment was deadly. They could also be imprisoned, chained, or mutilated.

Osiris usually displayed a certain passivity, but occasionally he was despotic. Usually, he conceded some freedom of will to everyone. The dead had a choice of either serving him or, with the help of their souls, they could attempt access to the celestial domain of Ra.

Osiris's bodyguards controlled the *ba* (soul) of the dead. If the *ba* could be liberated, it meant escaping the uncertainties of the dead, which were an extension of the living world. The dead desired to board the solar barque and ascend to the sky and join Ra. This journey to the sky again meant encountering untold obstacles. They needed to know the path, and if successful, they would be in heaven with Ra.

The Heliopolitan god, Ra-Atum, was the god of light and life. Only the king's soul, after facing Osiris's tribunal, could ascend to heaven and join the solar barque of his father Ra.

The king's person was composed of two elements, the body *(tchet)* and the spirit. The latter was composed of three principles, the *ka*, the *ba*, and the *akh*. *Ka* is part of the divine *ka*, the divine omniscience of the universal mana. *Ba* is the immortal soul, the being's personification. *Akh* is described as the power that generates and receives waves, the energy and spirit connected to the life of the perishable body *(khet)*.

Two things were essential upon the king's death. Keeping the body latently alive was necessary so that his akh might allow him to remain in contact with his soul *(ba)*, which had joined the solar barque. The divine *ka* must also remain connected to the earth by forcing it to pass magically into the body of the king's successor. These were the goals of the royal *Isial* funerary rites.

The mummification of the royal body followed the magical operation of the transferral of the *ka*. The deification of the pharaoh began with mummification (embalmment) so that the dead king would resemble Osiris with all his members tied together. A statue or double was placed in a special chamber, and as did the mummy itself, the statue had to undergo the rites of the opening of the mouth and eye. After undergoing these animation rites, it was placed in the cella of the funerary temple adjoining the temple.

Alive once more, the royal mummy and its double would then become the receptacle of the deceased king's *akh* (the power that generates and receives). This permitted communication with the soul sailing in the solar barque.

Heaven was the ultimate goal of the soul, but it first had to descend into Hades and appear before the tribunal of Osiris. Here it conformed to requirements of all souls. Once declared "justified," the soul could attempt the ultimate test, ascension into heaven to join the solar barque. Egyptians believed the sky was an immense basin of water upon which the barque sails. For that reason, barques were placed near the pyramids.

To ascend to heaven and join the gods, the dead king underwent a hazardous journey. His goal was to reach a place called *Neter-Khert,* but first he had to cross a long, winding lake of reeds. Beyond it lay the Duat, which was a magical abode for rising to the stars. To reach the Duat he had to go through subterranean labyrinths. Here he met certain gods who opened secret gates that led to the Eye of Horus. From there he was led to a celestial ladder that allowed him to soar skyward to the eternal afterlife.

The Duat was perceived as a completely enclosed circle of gods divided into twelve divisions. It took the king twelve hours to journey through this realm on the magical barque. Each division of the Duat required the king to pass through trials and tribulations. At the twelfth division, the king reached an object called "ascender to the sky," which was necessary for eternal life. This object, a divine ladder bound together by copper cables, led him to the Eye of Horus.

Once the king emerged triumphantly from the Duat, his barque floated to the celestial waters where the doors of heaven opened for him. This was the stairway to heaven. The journey to the celestial abode lasted eight days.

Heavens was the home of Ra, the Imperishable Star, signified by the winged disk. According to Sitchin this is the twelfth planet symbolized by the winged disk. Sitchin suggests this journey as described in the ancient writings was symbolic of an actual journey to the planet Nibiru. Once the king joined the gods on the Imperishable Star, he achieved immortality.

The soul needed sufficient energy to accomplish ascension. The pyramid shape of the tomb provided this energy and magically represented the divine triad. The sacred Egyptian triangle, with the proportion three, four, and five, represented Osiris, Isis, and

Horus. Starting with the Fourth Dynasty, all the Egyptian pyramids followed this pattern. Only the Great Pyramid of Giza did not have this *isial* slope.

The king's body underwent the mummification process in the temple for seventy days, having been subjected to the last rite of the opening of the mouth and eyes. It was placed within three coffins, one inside the other. When the coffin was slid down the descending passage to the subterranean chamber, the high priest announced that the royal soul had happily boarded Ra's divine barque.

Fifteen hundred years after the Menes reign, the people revolted by defiling and sacking the royal pyramid tombs. They demanded the chance to ascend to heaven as the pharaoh did. As a result, the Heliopolitan rites became democratized, and every Egyptian could build himself a pyramid tomb.

During the 18th Dynasty, a new trend developed at Thebes on the west bank of the Nile. An entire mountain was carved into a pyramid and used by the kings and their families for burial. Descending passages entered deep into the bedrock toward the center of the pyramid mountain, which led to the burial chambers of many pharaohs in the Valley of the Kings.

INITIATION AND THE NAME

Egyptians believed nothing existed before it had a name. By giving a creature a name, a personality was created. The name is an aspect of *ka* (soul) that animates the body it penetrates. That which no longer has a name no longer exists.

A mother would mysteriously confer a secret name upon a child immediately after birth. Generally not even the child knew the name. The primary goal of the *Isial* initiation was to "know thyself," for whoever did not know his secret name, the name of *ka*, could not claim to be his own master.

Knowing the *ka* name of a god allowed one to become master of that god. The Kabbalah attributes God with seventy-two known names and one ineffable name, unknown to man, which only seven archangels can pronounce. To keep gods' names among humans forever, Isis initiated the *Isial* mysteries. These rites provided the means to reach immortality, according to the writings of Diodorus Siculus, and were partially transmitted by certain initiating sects.

The Catholic Church, Druids, Essenes, and Freemasons have preserved part of these magical rites.

Isis, wanting to discover Ra's secret name, caused a magic serpent to bite Ra. While Ra was made vulnerable with so much pain, Isis asked him for his secret name. He gave Isis seventy-two divine names successively before divulging his real name, the secret of his power.

Before a pharaoh possessed the secret name, he was required to attain the seventy-two initiatory degrees. He received the secret name upon the death of his predecessor.

The importance of the name was demonstrated in the *Book of the Dead,* attributed to Thoth. To enter Amenti, the divine domain, one needed to know the name of the gods, the goddesses, and forty-two Followers of Horus. They also needed to know the guardians of the seven doors and ten portals. Doors to Amenti would not open unless the soul of the deceased pronounced these guardian names correctly.

The names, constituted seventy passwords, indispensable to the soul in order to reach the abode of Osiris in Amenti. To ensure remembering of these names, one recited them in a ritual and placed the names on the mummy's body. The ineffable name handed down to humans by Isis, which allowed humanity to ascend, seems to be permanently lost. Masonic lodges partially transmit the *Isiac* ritual, but the complete ritual seems to have vanished forever.

Thoth said one needed to die a second time before a third birth. Initiations prepared a select few for the tribulations of death and to raise consciousness. During the first degree of initiation following a preparatory period, a neophyte was placed in the depth of a subterranean pit, which symbolized the female reproductive tract. Here one was supposed to die and then come back to life. Only the pharaoh could attain the highest degree of initiation in the Old Kingdom. The king assumed the personality of Osiris and then like him was assassinated, and his body laid out in the central chamber. Mysterious rites allowed him to be in contact with his divine *ka,* and the pharaoh was then brought back to life. The layout of the Great Pyramid was similar to the crypt of the Temple at Dendera, used in the major *Isial* initiation. This suggested the Great Pyramid was also used for initiation. Many scholars concur that the pharaohs built the pyramids as initiatory monuments that allowed a select few to achieve immortality.

Author A. Puncheon believes the three known chambers of the Great Pyramid had esoteric meaning. Initiated scholars refer to the three pyramids as the tombs of Osiris. The subterranean chamber was the site of the second symbolic birth. The Queen's Chamber was the *serdab,* which contained the statue of the royal double. The King's Chamber was where the magical transference of the divine *ka* took place. The divine *ka* transferred from the not-yet-mummified royal cadaver to the body of Kephren, Cheop's successor, who lay stretched out in the sarcophagus in a drugged sleep. Once the miracle happened, the chamber became a sacred place. Access was forbidden to mortals, and a granite block was lowered to close the entrance to the empty tomb.

The initiates learned esoteric wisdom through acts of concentrated intelligence and will. This prepared them for the moment of physical death so they might be equipped spiritually to move as they wished through heaven and Earth.

There is no evidence that the Great Pyramids were built as tombs. The numerous small pyramids built in the Middle and Late Kingdoms of Egypt were however designed as tombs. But the eight Great Pyramids, assigned to the Third and Fourth Dynasties of the Old Kingdom, had no sign of coffins or mummies

Chapter Seven

LOST CIVILIZATIONS OF CENTRAL AMERICA
A Refuge for Atlantis and Mediterranean Civilizations?

The ruins of Mesoamerica marveled archaeologists who again came upon evidence of an advanced civilization that had completely disappeared. The Olmecs, first to leave behind their legacy centuries before the birth of Christ, were followed by seven centuries of the Classic Maya civilization. The Toltecs replaced the Mayans, and finally came the Aztecs who encountered the Spaniards during the 16th century. Arriving with the Spanish conquistadors, the priests of the Catholic Church proceeded to burn and destroy invaluable manuscripts in their determination to eliminate pagan doctrines. Flames consumed the written history of the indigenous people. Luckily, several important manuscripts survived the insensitive actions of the church and provide insight into these ancient civilizations.

These ancients developed hieroglyphic writings that told their story about creation, the Flood, and the gods. They, too, built pyramids with similarities to the pyramids of Egypt, suggesting a possible connection. One of the most intriguing aspects of the Indians was the highly sophisticated calendar system they developed, and fortunately for the historians and archaeologists, the ancients dated most of their stelae and monuments. Astronomy was quite well developed in these ancient cultures, and numerous observatories have been located in the ruins. Venus was their most cherished star.

Gods of Mesoamerica functioned similarly to other gods around the world, but of course their names differed. Their most important god, Quetzalcoatl, was depicted as the feathered serpent, a god-man that myths claim helped create humanity, and who was ruler of the Toltecs. He possessed Christlike attributes, characteristics of the Egyptian god Thoth, and similarities to the Sumer god Enki.

The Olmecs established their culture in central Mexico, the Pacific Piedmont of Mexico, and coastal zones of Guatemala. Maya civilization ranged from Yucatan in Mexico, to the highlands of Guatemala, to the western region of Belize, and covered an area of 125,000 square miles. The Toltecs inhabited Teotihuacan, the "City of Gods," located thirty miles from Mexico City. This magnificent city was thought to have been built by the Toltecs, the master craftsmen. Departing Teotihuacan, the Toltecs later overcame the Maya civilization, occupying much of their land including Chichen Itza. The Aztec migrated to the Valley of Mexico and established their great capital Tenochtitlan, on the shores of Lake Texcoco.

THE ATLANTEAN LEGACY

Peter Tompkins, in his book *Mysteries of Mexican Pyramids,* describes the research of Charles Brasseur de Bourboura who came to Central America in 1845. Brasseur had discovered two very important documents, The *Annals of Cakchiquel* and the *Popol Vuh.* Determined to translate the documents, he mastered the local dialects.

The *Popol Vuh* was a collection of myths, history, and customs of the Indians that Brasseur published in French. His research impressed the Spanish academicians so much that they opened their archives in Spain to Brasseur. Here Brasseur discovered Bishop Diego de Landa's manuscript *Relacion de las Cosas de Yucatan,* which today remains the greatest source of information about the ancient Maya culture of Yucatan.

Brasseur also became proficient in deciphering the Maya hieroglyphics, and while in Madrid he became acquainted with a Maya book of divination known as the *Troano Codex.* These myths supported the myths still found among Central American natives that a great terrestrial convulsion sank an island in the Atlantic Ocean, which had extended in a crescent shape as far as the Canary Islands. The codex placed the sinking of the Atlantic continent in the year 9937 B.C.

Brasseur also came across a Nahuatl manuscript regarding the early history of the Kingdom of Calhacan and Mexico that he called *Codex Chimoalpopoa.* He concluded that civilization had originated in the West and not in the Middle East, as maintained by European historians. Civilization had spread to Europe and Egypt across a large continent that stretched from America across the Atlantic.

Brasseur could now explain the interesting similarities he found between the Maya Quiche languages of Mesoamerica and the languages of Greece, Latin, French, English, and German. It appeared they had derived their languages from the Maya Quiche.

The Nahuatl texts recorded how mighty cataclysms submerged the cradle of civilization, millennium before the arrival of the Spanish. A continent, originally occuping the Gulf of Mexico and Caribbean Sea, was engulfed by a tremendous convulsion of nature. Much of Yucatan, Honduras, and Guatemala had also been submerged, but subsequent upheavals brought parts of this area back to the surface. Brasseur also traced the myths of Quetzalcoatl to Plato's Atlantis and concluded that the Toltecs could have been descendants of the survivors of Atlantis. He believed that the inhabitants of Central America had anticipated many truths of modern science centuries before. With his belief system, contemporary scholars did not take him seriously.

The Carinas of Central America, asserts Brasseur, were the oldest known civilization. This industrious and commercial people worked with metal and precious stones. Being great sailors and astronomers, they traveled the world colonizing Atlantis, the Mediterranean, and ancient Egypt. As mentioned in an earlier chapter, the Greek Herodotus, known as the father of history, claimed to be a Carina descendant. The physics, astronomy, and religious practices of Mesoamerica were similar to the Old World. Both included a strong cult of Sirius, the Dog star, and deified the crocodile. Brasseur concluded that Egypt had been a Mesoamerican colony or vice versa.

The *Codex Chimoalpopoa* was written in code, said Brasseur, so that each word had two or more meanings. It enabled the priestly scribes to conceal the history of the cataclysms and their cycles within a more harmless text. His translation concluded that instead of one cataclysm as described by Plato, a series of them shaped the present-day world. The writings tell of four periods of cataclysms around 10,000 B.C. caused by a shifting of the earth's axis. He also suggested that some of these earth changes originated extraterrestrially, such as a meteor or comet, and that primitive cultures were the "debris" of higher civilizations left after natural catastrophes. American historian Hubert Howe Bancroft described Brasseure as,

"In actual knowledge pertaining to his chosen subject, no man equaled or approached him."

Augustus Le Plongeon came to the Yucatan in 1873, learned the native language, and spent twelve years researching the ancient culture and ruins associated with Chichan Itza. He concluded that the Maya were connected to Atlantis. He also asserted that the Phoenicians crossed the Atlantic long before Columbus, and Le Plongeon found similarities between the architecture, sculpture, and artifacts of Central America and those of Asia, Europe, and Africa. His research suggested that Mayan colonists sailed westward to Polynesia, Burma, India, Babylonia, and Egypt millennia before Christ. Maya legends about adepts known as Naacal, the exalted ones, supported his conclusions. They had set out across the world to teach others their language, architecture and astronomy.

Le Plongeon quotes the Chaldean historian Beorsu, who claimed civilization was brought to Mesopotamia by Oannes, who came from the Persian Gulf. In Mayan, "Oaana" means "he who has residence in the water." Many Akkadian words of Mesopotamia are similar to Maya words. Le Plongeon claims that one third of the Egyptian words he has deciphered were the same as Mayan words, a claim supported by other scholars.

Mayan sculpture, according to Le Plongeon, provided evidence that the Masonic rites of sacred mysteries were practiced in Mayaland 11,500 years before modern Masonry. The meaning of several initiation rite symbols were similar in all countries. This similarity gives a better understanding of the laws that govern the material and spiritual world.

Le Plongeon first realized that the buildings at Chichen Itza were used as astronomical observatories. He thought the Mayas, as did the Egyptians, embodied their cosmology and religious conceptions into their sacred buildings and pyramids.

The *Traono* manuscript describes the collapse of a landmass referred to as "the ten countries of Mu." Le Plongeon assumed the texts were describing Atlantis, and not Lemuria as James Churchword claimed. Le Plongeon asserted as a result of this catastrophe, the Maya started computing their calendar on a base thirteen with weeks of thirteen days, centuries of four times thirteen years, and a great cycle of thirteen times twenty, or two-hundred sixty years. The date for the inception of the Maya calendar coincided precisely with the Platonic date of 9500 B.C. according to Le Plongeon.

Le Plongeon claimed he found ancient Maya books written by the wise men of Yucatan, which had been buried before the advent of the Spaniards. He tried to work out a deal with the U.S. government to disinter them if the government agreed to protect this treasure against arbitrary seizure. The State Department refused.

He had shown James Churchward his unpublished work on the Yucatan and eventually bequeathed his literary estate to him. As Tompkins aptly describes, both became fair game for the academics.

In 1908, Le Plongeon died before doing anything about the hidden books. Realizing he would soon die, his wife, Alice, entrusted a map of the ancient books location in the ruins of Uxmal and Chichen Itza to Mrs. Henry Blackwell. The chronicles of Le Plongeon fill the gap between 9500 B.C., regarding the destruction of Atlantis, and the historical records of Sumer and Egypt, five thousand years later.

William Niven, a mining engineer for a Mexican corporation, provided evidence that a very ancient civilization occupied the Valley of Mexico near Mexico City. As mentioned in an earlier chapter, between 1910 and 1930, Niven came across ruins of two separate prehistoric civilizations buried at depths of six to thirty feet. The civilizations appeared to have been overwhelmed by a series of cataclysmic tidal waves, perhaps at several thousand-year intervals. By their depths beneath the surface, Niven estimated the oldest remains to be 50,000 years old. One of the stratum layers,containing two to three feet of volcanic ash, covered a vast city and contained many artifacts and human bones. Three miles away from this dig, Niven found thousands of terra cotta and clay figures with faces representing "all the races of southern Asia," buried in the sand and gravel.

In 1921, five miles northwest of Mexico City, Niven unearthed a series of stone tablets with unusual pictographs buried beneath twelve feet of soil. Within an area of twenty square miles, he found more than twenty-six hundred tablets. From the depths they were buried, he estimated they were between 12,000 and 50,000 years old.

No scholarly archaeologist could decipher the tablets. Niven proceeded to trace each of the tablets and forwarded them to James Churchward for his analysis. Coincidently, the symbols and design of the tablets resembled those Churchward saw on tablets in monasteries in Tibet and India. They were the Naacal tablets, which contained sacred inspired writings originating from Mu. Churchward claimed that Niven's tablets confirmed data found on the Tibetan's Naacal tablets, filling in missing gaps. He concluded they were written by a colony of Mu established in the Valley of Mexico. Mu sank into the Pacific Ocean about 12,000 years ago, about the same time that the last remnants of Atlantis went down in the Atlantic.

The tablets described an extended history of Atlantis. They tell of Osiris's birth in Atlantis around 20,000 B.C. Osiris traveled to Mu, but was forced to return to Atlantis to eliminate the extravagance, superstitions, and misconceptions that had infiltrated the Atlantean religion. He reinstated an original religion of love and simplicity and became a high priest. The Osirian religion came to Egypt about 16,000 years ago. Churchward asserts the religion was identical to the teachings of Jesus, and had the same monotheistic principle of Moses.

The *Troano Manuscript* tells of Queen Moo who lived during the first period of Egyptian history. Of the last dynasty, she visited the Maga Nile colony at Sais, Egypt, and met Thoth 16,000 years ago.

Churchward also believed that many Yucatan ruins were standing 11,500 years ago. Many Mayan buildings were adorned with the heads and trunks of mastodons. He claims the buildings with carvings of feathered serpents were erected 15,000 years ago during the Can (Serpent) Dynasty. He also believed that Quetzalcoatl reigned between 16,000 and 34,000 years ago.

American clairvoyant Edgar Cayce had insights about the Yucatan and its connection to Atlantis. Cayce said Lemuria sank beneath the sea before the end of Atlantis, and fleeing Lemurians arrived on the Yucatan peninsula. They played a role in changing the civilization already established by the Atlanteans, but the Atlanteans maintained the most powerful influence in shaping the earliest culture of Yucatan. Before the first destruction, a few Atlanteans went to South America, Central America, Egypt, Spain, and Portugal. During the final destruction of Atlantis, much of Yucatan also sank.

He gave no date for the first destruction period, but in 50,722 B.C., Cayce said Atlanteans held a meeting to discuss ridding the Earth of hordes of prehistoric beasts. The first destruction of

Atlantis occurred shortly afterward. During the first destruction, the land area of the Sargasso Sea submerged.

The second period of destruction occurred around 28,000 B.C., and many Atlanteans fled and settled in the Yucatan. Considerable temple construction took place by the Atlantean refuges. They propagated the original faith and preserved the knowledge that unified the understanding of the relationship with man to the creative force.

An Atlantean leader named Lltar, according to Cayce, developed a civilization on the Yucatan as it had been on Atlantis. Atlantean temples of Yucatan were rediscovered in the 1930s, said Cayce, and many of the temples still standing contain secrets of the Atlantean occult.

The two type of ruins with Atlantean characteristics were the circular ruins and the ceremonial altars used for cleansing. The altars were not used for human sacrifice but to cleanse undesirable traits such as hate, malice, and self-indulgence.

Ancient texts suggest that the Yucatan civilization originated in the east. *The Books of Chilam Balam* claim the Yucatan inhabitants came from the east across the water with their leader Zamna, known as Itzamna. They were the people of the serpent. The *Popol Vuh* states, "Then they came, they pulled up stakes and left the east." The *History of Zodzil* by Juan Darreygosa tells of a legend, "The most ancient people who came to this land were those who populated Chichen Itza . . . and were the first after the Flood." Bishop Landa reports, "Some of the people of the Yucatan say they heard from their ancestors that a race of people occupied this land who came from the east, and whom the god had delivered by opening twelve paths through the sea."

THE OLMECS

A most mysterious ancient civilization of Mesoamerica was that of the Olmecs. Scholars agree they were the mother culture of the Central American civilizations who gave birth to hieroglyphics, the calendar, and the pyramids. All the Mesoamerica civilizations copied and adapted their culture. Originating on the Gulf of Mexico about 2000 B.C., the Olmecs had a strong influence in Mesoamerica for well over a millennium, reaching their zenith around 1200 B.C.

with forty sites established. By the time of Christ, all the sites were mysteriously abandoned. They were named Olmeca, meaning "rubber people," because of their association with rubber trees. Olmecs were considered strangers who had come from across the sea. Three important ruins provide the majority of information about the Olmecs: at San Lorenzo (1200 B.C.), at LaVenta (800 B.C.), and at Tres Zapotes. The Olmec influence spread from the Valley of Mexico to El Salvador.

One of the remarkable discoveries associated with the Olmecs has been the gigantic stone heads, which now number eighteen. Sculptured from basalt stone with great skill by unknown tools, they are thought to portray Olmec rulers. One head weighs twenty-four tons, is eight feet high, and measures twenty-one feet in circumference. The sculpture depicts a Negroid African wearing a distinct helmet. Radiocarbon dating has placed the stone heads at 1200 to 1500 B.C. The basalt used in the monolithic heads and other statues was quarried some eighty miles away. Some sculptures weigh more than fifty tons

The Olmecs left behind hundreds of depictions of themselves, most are tall, stocky, and muscular. Many of these African faces were found carved on jade artifacts discovered in sacred wells throughout Mexico. Olmec sculpture was the first major art style to evolve in the area, and many considered them the finest sculptors in Mesoamerica. Their exquisite jade carvings rivaled the best jade carvings of ancient China.

Studies by Dr. Leo Wiener of Harvard University concluded that the Olmecs were Negroid based not only on the racial features, but mostly on linguistic analysis. The Olmec tongue belonged to the Mande group who originated in West Africa between the Niger and Congo Rivers.

Fifty years later, an academic study by Alexander von Wuthenau also concluded the Olmecs were Negroid. He believed the first link between the Old and New Worlds occurred during the rule of Egyptian Pharaoh Ramses III in the 20th century B.C. He surmised the Olmecs were Kushites from Nubia, which happened to be Egypt's principal source of gold. Von Wuthenau also hypothesized other black Africans may have come over on Phoenician and Jewish ships between 500 B.C. and 200 A.D. He investigated thousands of pre-Columbian terra cotta heads and figures. Von Wuthenau discovered portraits of five different racial types including Mongoloid, Chinese, Japanese, Negroid, and all types of white people.

The stone heads also had Mongoloid epicanthal folds, round faces, thick lips, and flat Negroid noses. The Oceanic Negroid of Polynesia are a mixture of Negroid and Mongoloid types from India and Indonesia. Some scholars have speculated they may have come from the islands of Polynesia.

Zecharia Sitchin hypothesizes that the Olmecs went to Mesoamerica to find gold. Stelae depict the Olmecs emerging from altars representing entrances into the depths of the earth, and inside these caves held a mysterious array of tools. Legends of the Voltans tell of the Olmecs tunneling through mountains. One depicts a flame-thrower cutting through stone.

Sitchin believes the African Olmecs lived in Mesoamerica before the bearded ones. The roots of their arrival may link to the mysterious beginning of the Long Count, 3113 B.C., found in the Mayan calendar. Sitchin hypothesizes a decision by the pantheon of gods sent the Olmecs to Central America. The gods had come to Earth for gold, their primary mission. He speculates that under the leadership of Thoth, the Olmecs and bearded Near Easterners came to Mesoamerica to mine gold. Sitchin asserts that the god-man Thoth and the god-man Quetzalcoatl were one and the same.

The Olmecs had an obsessive concern with the jaguar, a symbol of the forces of earth and night. Figures and symbols of the jaguar appeared in all forms of jade, mosaics, tools and stone. Their deity symbol was the jaguar and not a humanized form. The Olmec jaguar cult diffused throughout much of Central America.

Another ancient group of ancient Mesoamericans, the Zapotecs, occupied the central Valley Oaxaca south of the Mexican plateaus. Small groups began to occupy the hills and valleys as early as 1500 B.C., and by 600 B.C. the Zapotecs began to occupy the hills of Monte Alban. One of the earliest stelae is dated 644 B.C., the earliest American date transcribed in writing. Some scholars claim the Zapotecs of Monte Albans were the first large city dwellers in Mesoamerica and invented writing and hieroglyphics. Others disagree and believe their culture was influenced by the Olmecs, Mayas, and Toltecs, who surrounded Monte Albans. The Zapotecs are known for their preoccupation with death as numerous tombs have been discovered. In the 10th century A.D., the Zapotecs abandoned the city of Monte Albans after the Mixtec Indians invaded from the mountainous Mixteca-Alta region to the north.

THE MAYA

The most brilliant civilization of the New World, the Maya, flourished during the third to 16th century A.D. Their pyramids, calendars, and hieroglyphics remain an enigma to scholars today. They lived on the Yucatan peninsula of Mexico, in the highlands of Guatemala, and the western region of Belize. Maya history is divided into three stages, with the Pre-Classic stage beginning around 2000 B.C. and ending around 100 A.D. The Classic era began around 250 A.D. and ended 900 A.D., followed by the Post Classic period, 900 A.D. to 1200 A.D. Scholars referring to Maya civilization only refer to the culture of the Classic era.

Shortly after the Spanish arrival in the New World, the Catholic clergy destroyed most of the Maya writings. In the century following the conquest, Maya natives recorded in Spanish a number of prophecies, myths, rituals, and current events in the *Books of Chilam Balam*. Also included were five chronicles briefly describing the leading events of Maya history. A similar type of manuscript came from the Quiche Maya in Guatemala, who wrote the *Popol Vuh* (Book of Quiche). It preserved fragments of their cosmogony, religion, mythology, and history. The Quiche were the most powerful Maya people of the southern highlands, in present-day Guatemala.

Only three known pre-Columbian Maya hieroglyphic manuscripts survived the mass destruction. The Maya native books include the seventy-eight-page *Codex Dresdensis,* a treaty on astronomy; the one-hundred-twelve-page *Codex Tro-Cortesianus,* a textbook on horoscopes and mythology; and the twenty-two-page *Codex Peresianus,* a ritualistic text. The codices were made from the bark of a tree called the *copo,* pounded into a pulp and bonded by a natural gum.

The earliest date in Maya hieroglyphic writing is 8.14.3.1.12, which corresponds to the year 320 A.D. of the Christian calendar, and the oldest large stone monument or stele was carved in 328 A.D. These dates fell at the close of Baktun eight of the Maya era to be explained later.

Scholars do not know the exact origins of the Maya civilization, but know the earlier Olmecs influenced them. They know the Maya economy was based largely upon maize agriculture, which originated from the Guatemalan highlands and spread to the surrounding Maya regions. Nearly all the Maya corn farmers used the calendar to regulate their ceremonies and sacrifices, considered necessary for the production of crops.

The Maya people were short, men averaged five feet one inch and the women four feet eight inches. They had broad heads and relatively thick bodies with little body hair since they held little esteem for beards and mustaches. An epicanthal fold at the inner corner of the eye suggested an eastern Asia influence. A small bluish Mongolian spot at the base of the spine, present at birth, disappeared before the age of ten. Many of today's Maya resemble the figures on the monuments.

Depressed foreheads were considered a mark of beauty among ancient Maya. They achieved the deformity by binding the heads of the babies between a pair of flat boards that were left in place for several days. Upon removal, the head remained flattened for life. Crossed eyes were also a mark of distinction. They attached a ball of resin to their hair and let it fall between their eyes, causing them to cross.

Mayan parents brought their young children to a priest, who cast the child's horoscope and gave the child a name to be used during childhood. Several other names were given to the individual throughout life. When a child reached puberty, a ceremony was held and the priest cast out evil spirits. At that time, the girls were ready for marriage, and matchmakers or families would arrange marriages. To divorce, all one had to do was repudiate the spouse.

The Mayans were devoted to personal cleanliness, but their homes were often less than orderly. A sociable people who were considered just, they were good natured, trusting, and unselfish.

The Maya language has been likened to the Romance languages of the Old World, which developed from a common tongue approximately two thousand years ago. There is no indication what the original Maya language was.

Many scholars believe there was a connection between the Maya and Phoenician people of the Near East. They shared similar hieroglyphics, the customs of deforming heads, infant sacrifice, the use of incense, phallic worship, pyramidal temples, worship of the sun and moon, and the use of gnomons (sundials) to measure the sun's shadow. A white man with a handlebar mustache holding a thunderbolt was the symbol of the Mayan rain god Tlaloc. Both the Maya and Babylonians measured the year in 360 and 365 days. A fourteen-foot stele, which depicted a Hittite or Phoenician, was unearthed twenty miles inland from the Gulf of Mexico. Other carvings in Mexico bear a resemblance to Phoenicians.

The archaeological sites of the Classic Maya were primarily religious, with little evidence of city ruins. Tikal, located in the Peten area of Guatemala, was the largest and probably the oldest center of the Maya civilization. It's six great pyramidal temples range in height from 143 feet to 229 feet and spread over one square mile. Located in Copan, Honduras was the second largest center of the Maya civilization. It was the principle scientific and learning center of the Classic Stage. The acropolis contains a complex of pyramids, terraces, and temples covering twelve acres. Archaeological ruins at Chichen Itza are some of the best preserved.

A most significant intellectual achievement, the Maya invented a calendrical system with a fixed zero date, known as the Long Count. Long Count dates were often sculptured on stone stelae that served as durable memorials to rulers and other elite people. The Mayas were the first to establish a fixed point from which chronological records could be counted. Their calendar began 3113 B.C. and would end 2012 A.D.; it is unknown why the Maya began their calendar at that date. The ancient Maya could fix any date in their chronology so exactly that it would not recur before a cycle of 374,440 years passed.

The Maya, also known for their skill as astronomers, used fixed lines of sight, crossed sticks, and buildings for alignment to provide observation points. They meticulously plotted the movements of the sun, moon, and Venus, and were thought to have probed Mars, Jupiter, Mercury, and Saturn. The Maya undertook intensive studies of lunar eclipses and could accurately predict them.

For some unknown reason, the Maya civilization declined rapidly. Professor Sylvanus Morley, the Maya's most renowned researcher, speculated on possible reasons for the fall. His theories included earthquakes, climatic changes, epidemics, foreign conquest, civil war, intellectual exhaustion, social decay, government decline, or economic collapse.

Legend regarding Chichen Itza describes three ruling lords who had come from the West. They were devout, pious brothers who built beautiful temples and lived chaste lives without wives. The Maya people held one brother, Kukulcan, in such great respect because of his piety. They willingly labored hard to build the religious construction at Chichen Itza and they promoted their new religion. Kukulcan went away, and the remaining two brothers behaved so indecently that they were put to death, and Chichen Itza went into decline. After the fall, Kukulcan founded the city of Mayapan, meaning the "standard of the Mayas," which replaced Chichen Itza as the capital. Kukulcan was also known as Quetzalcoatl.

The Toltecs conquered the Yucatan Maya and changed the Maya way of life more than the Spanish ever did. They left their capital of Tula and proceeded to Yucatan. Kukulcan became the culture hero of the Toltecs, and he was symbolized as the feathered serpent, Quetzalcoatl, the exiled King of Tula. The Toltecs introduced their religion at Chichen Itza, which also was practiced at Mayapan, but the essential framework of the Maya religion survived.

THE TOLTECS

A third great civilization, the Toltecs, blossomed within the confines of Mesoamerica. The capital, Teotihuacan, lay approximately thirty miles northwest of Mexico City. Being the foremost civilization of Central America, its influence spread from both coasts south to El Salvador, Costa Rica, Peru, and Colombia. Teotihuacan was known as the "City of Gods," and scholars today describe it as a well-integrated cosmic vision. Here the first Tollan city of a fully integrated society of 200,000 people operated under the authority of supernatural forces and cosmic magical formulas. It reached its peak in 500 A.D. as a great cosmopolitan city. Religious pilgrims traveled from distant cities to receive blessings, revelations, and inspiration at Teotihuacan.

Several centuries before Christ, the Toltecs built this magnificent city whose civilization was almost completely religious. The empire has been compared with Tibet, to the Holy Empires of Rome and Mecca, to the Hellenistic empire of Greece, and to the intellectual and religious empire of Alexandria, Egypt. Known as the "City of Gods," it was the birthplace of the recorded myths and religion of Quetzalcoatl.

Legend holds the Toltecs left their old kingdom of Tollan in Asia and came to Mexico. The race is reported to be nearly six thousand years old. Various codices describe Toltec kings reigning from 510 to 1519 A.D.

Author Frank Waters describes the ruins of Teotihuacan as laid out with geometric precision that still exists in a space-time continuum beyond worldly comprehension. The ancient city was dominated by a 217-foot-high Sun Pyramid with a 750-foot square base. At one end of the 2000-foot Street of the Dead, the Pyramid of the Moon rises 149 feet in a square courtyard surrounded by thirteen temples. Toward the other end of the street lies the Citadel, enclosed by a 1300 foot long wall with fifteen pyramid temple foundations. Along the Street of the Dead lay other temples and palaces that housed priests and their helpers. The East-West Avenue intersected the Avenue of the Dead at right angles, dividing the urban space into four great quarters. In the center lies the Temple of Quetzalcoatl, embodied within a temple that was built later. The facade is decorated with sculptured heads of Quetzalcoatl, the feathered serpent, and alternating with sculptures of Tlaloc, the rain god. The Temple of Quetzalcoatl formed the meeting point of heaven, earth, and hell.

The great residential palaces of the elite and rulers lay further away from the ceremonial precinct. In the periphery were the homes of citizens. The urban layout included grid streets interlaced with canals and sewers, market places, and hostels for traveling merchants. It was the first metropolis of the New World.

Teotihuacan began in a cave at the mouth of a well, now located under the Sun Pyramid, and became the greatest classic city. A natural tunnel, over three hundred feet long, led to a series of seven chambers arranged in the shape of a lotus flower that served as a sacred ritual center. Throughout ancient Mexican history, caves were considered sacred places where the creation of gods, humans, and celestial bodies took place. They served as a place of communication with the underworld.

During the 1960s, René Millon mapped the ruins of Teotihuacan, and researchers discovered it was laid out as an image of the cosmos. Many temples lay in similar relationship to one another as the planets did to the sun. The Toltecs knew the heavens and its twelve divisions. The ceremonial city was planned to reflect precise astronomical patterns that guided the general activities during the year. The Pleiades, an important star cluster to the people of Central America, appeared before the sun rose on the day of the sun's zenith. The great stairway of the Pyramid of the Sun faced a westerly point, where the sun would set on that important day.

Builders of Teotihuacan were master craftsmen of all arts. The people were known as Toltecs, the Nahuatl name for a "master craftsman." The city was originally called Tollan, which means "a great city" in Nahuatl, and Teotihuacan was thought to be the first great Tollan of Mesoamerica. No inscriptions have been found to reveal the language of the builders, and nothing is known of their physical appearance. The great Pyramids of the Sun and Moon were built between 200 B.C. and 150 A.D., followed by the erection of the Temple of Quetzalcoatl.

By the third and fourth century A.D., corresponding to the eighth Baktun (to be explained in the following chapter) of the Maya calendar, the influence of Teotihuacan had begun to spread throughout Mesoamerica. The presence of the Toltecs and the imagery of the god Quetzalcoatl became synonymous. In the jungles of Peten, the Toltec religion of Quetzalcoatl encountered the Maya tribes, and at Tikal, the marriage of Teotihuacan and the Mayan presence occurred. Inspired by the spiritual influence of Quetzalcoatl, whom the Maya called Kukulcan, the Maya civilization began to rise. A major difference between the civilizations, the Maya pyramids of Tikal were nine levels compared with five levels at Teotihuacan.

After inhabiting Teotihuacan for a millennium, the Toltecs for some mysterious reason packed up and left, around 700 A.D. No one knows why they completely abandoned the "City of Gods," but they established a new capital at Tula (also called Tollan) fifty miles northwest of Mexico City, patterned after Teotihuacan. A dynasty of priest-kings who claimed to be descendants of the god Quetzalcoatl ruled Tollan. Before the fall of Teotihuacan, barbaric nomads began entering the Valley of Mexico from the north. The first immigrants were the Chichimecas followed by a second wave of seven tribes, which included the Aztec (Mexicas). The migration began in 720 A.D., and the seventh tribe arrived in 1022 A.D. A religious conflict arose among the Toltecs during the 10th century when some of the priests introduced human sacrifice to pacify the war gods.

Legend tells that Mixacoatl, a great Chichimeca chief, fathered a son just before his assassination. His son, CeAcatl Topiltzin, adopted the teachings of Quetzalcoatl, and as the King of Tula he became known as Topiltzin-Quetzalcoatl. After avenging his father's murder, he moved the capital to Tula. The ancient Quetzalcoatl religion opposed human sacrifice, but many barbarians under Topiltzin's rule began to worship the war god Tezcatlipoca. Gaining influence, they forced Topiltzin to abdicate the throne and to leave Tula, which became a desolate city by 1168 A.D. The fall of Tula ended the third sun. The Toltec-Tula culture had become a militaristic society built upon the highly religious culture of Teotihuacan but had failed to assimilate it.

The Toltecs left Tula in 987 A.D. under their leader Topiltzun-Quetzalcoatl and sought a place where they could worship as in the past. They came to the Yucatan, reaching Chichen Itza, already abandoned by the Maya (the Itzas had inhabited Chichen Itza after the Maya). The Toltecs rebuilt the city in the image of their capital, Tula, building a nine-step pyramid, 185 feet high, dedicated to Quetzalcoatl and called the Temple of Warriors.

Some scholars believe Kukulcan of Chichen Itza was the same Quetzalcoatl who was cast out of Tula. The conqueror of Chichen Itza, referred to as a chaste man, taught new rituals, including fasting and confessions. Other scholars disagree they were the same, because this Quetzalcoatl believed in human sacrifice.

Quetzalcoatl contributed to the organization of six capitals and served as the patron deity of Teotihuacan, Cholollan, Tula, Xochicalo, Chichen Itza, and Tenochtitlan. Quetzalcoatl and Tollan were two symbols that revealed a vision of the cosmos that integrated the city, king, and gods and helped many cultures achieve stability. A sacred history, taught in Mesoamerica, told about the sacred being, the heroic and inspirational Quetzalcoatl, who incarnated in the city of Tollan. He became the first ruler of Tollan, due to his military achievements and religious piety.

Tollan was a name given to many Toltec cities. It had a material, spiritual, and political meaning, symbolizing a social and cosmological integration. Portrayed as the original earthly city, it derived its power from celestial forces that set the example for human existence. Tollan symbolized sacred space, while Quetzalcoatl symbolized sacred authority. The cities symbolized the interaction between terrestrial space and celestial design. Tollan was the great capital, serving both as a historical capital and a symbol of a mystical city.

The Toltec Kingdom was a kingdom abundant in food, goods and technology. The *Florentine Codex* states that the wealth of the Tollans resided in their fields. Their squash and corn were gigantic. The cotton fields grew multicolored cotton: burnt red, yellow, rose, violet, green, and so on. There was no need to dye cotton. Ancient texts describe the Toltec technology as the original technology of an ancient culture. The Aztecs remember Tollan as the original city-state where farming, crafts, and religions were effectively integrated with cosmological forces. They invented divination and calendrical calculations, and they understood the influence of stars based on their movement.

THE AZTECS

The Aztecs were one of seven tribes that migrated from Aztlan by boat and arrived in Central America. No one knows where Aztlan was located but some scholars speculate it may have been Atlantis, and others think it was Wisconsin.

Legends from the *Codex Boturini* describe Aztlan as the ancestral home of the Aztec tribe. It was the home of the first patriarchal couple, Itzac-Mixcoatl (white cloud serpent) and his spouse Ilan-Cul (old woman). They gave birth to sons from who the Nahuatl-speaking tribes originated, including the Aztec. All seven tribes migrated from Chicomozto in the legendary Aztlan. The Aztec were the last of the seven tribes to leave.

Being a nomadic tribe, they forced their way into the Valley of Mexico on the heels of the Chichimeca invasion and inhabited the city of Teotihuacan. The tribes arriving from Aztlan had four wise men to guide and lead them, who carried ritual manuscripts and knowledge of the calendar secrets. Historians describe the early Aztecs as a miserable band of savages dressed only in the skins of animals. Other legends claim they left Aztlan in 1160 A.D. and arrived in the Valley of Mexico around 1196 A.D. For nearly two centuries they lived on the central lakes' marshy edges. They called themselves Mexica and considered themselves a chosen people destined to rule over other tribes. In time, they overthrew the neighboring tribes and borrowed their culture and art.

One of the great archaeological finds in Mesoamerica was the great Aztec Calendar Stone, believed to be a record in stone of the five ages. The first inner ring of the calendar depicts twenty signs representing the twenty days of the Aztec month. Four rectangular panels on the calendar symbolize the past four eras and the catastrophes that ended each: water, wind, quakes and storms, and the jaguar.

The first sun, the age of white haired giants, ended by a deluge. The second era, the Golden Age, succumbed to the wind serpent. The third sun was known as the age of the red-haired people and presided over by the fire serpent. They were survivors of the second age who came by ship from the east. They came to the New World to an area called Botonchan. Here they encountered giants who enslaved them. The fourth sun was the era of the black-headed people (a term that also describes the Sumerians), an era when Quetzalcoatl appeared in Mexico. He was a tall, bearded man wearing a long tunic and carrying a staff shaped like a serpent, painted black, white, and red. He was the master of knowledge and wisdom. During this time they built Tollan. Toward the end of the fourth sun, wars between the gods broke out, and Quetzalcoatl returned East abandoning Tollan. Shortly thereafter, the Aztecs arrived on the scene to begin the fifth sun, the Aztec era.

The *Codex Vaticano Lationo* states the first sun lasted 4,008 years; the second sun, 4010 years; the third sun, 4081 years; and the fourth sun began 5,042 years ago, totaling 17,141 years. By dating the fourth age to 5042 years before their own time, the Aztecs would date from around 3500 B.C. The Sumerian civilization began about 3800 B.C.

In 1325 A.D., the Aztecs founded what was to become the great capital of their nation, Tenochtitlan. They rose to power through their fanatic dedication to war. They made alliances with their neighbors to defeat other tribes, and over time the bounties built up. In 1376, they chose their first ruler, King Acamapichtli, a descendant of the Toltec ruler of Culhuacan, which they destroyed. Thereafter, they claimed rights to the Toltec heritage.

In 1427 the fourth king, Itzcoatl, was elected. He established a cultural and religious basis for Aztec military domination by first destroying the Toltec records. The priests rewrote the ancient prayers and hymns to Quetzalcoatl, and declared Huitzipochtli their supreme god. The Aztec people believed their divine mission was to dominate all the nations of the Earth in order to nourish, with sacrificial blood, their god Huitzipochtli, the sun. The rule of Itzcoatl spread well beyond the confines of the Valley of Mexico.

Upon the death of Itzcoatl, Moctezuma I ascended to the throne and reigned from 1440 to 1469. He built the Lake Texcoco island capital of Tenochtitlan into a magnificent metropolis, as large as most European cities. Three broad causeways connected the city to the surrounding land. In the middle of the city's great plaza he erected a circular temple of Quetzalcoatl symbolizing god of the wind. A 100-foot high Great Temple Pyramid with a 150-foot square base dominated Tenochtitlan.

To dedicate the Great Pyramid of Tenochtitlan, the Aztecs needed an appropriate number of sacrificial victims. To acquire victims, they declared a perpetual war with neighboring cities, a war in which neither side would endeavor to destroy the other. Their objective was to capture prisoners for sacrifice. The city Tlaxacala kept its independence as long as it provided Tenochtitlan with new supplies of captives. Thus began the "Flowery Wars" between Tenochtitlan and its neighbors. In 1487, when the temple was completed, King Ahuizot sacrificed hordes of victims at its dedication. The reported Aztec sacrifices ranged from 20,000 to 80,000.

In 1502 A.D.,Moctezuma II became the ninth hereditary ruler and a high priest ascribed with divinity. Cortes landed on the eastern coast of America in 1519. Moctezuma believed the Spaniards were descendants of Quetzalcoatl and that Cortes was the spokesman of the god himself. Quetzalcoatl had vowed to return on the year of his birth, One Reed. In the Aztec calendar, the cycle of years completed itself every fifty-two years, and the year Cortes landed was One Reed. The Aztecs literally poured gold at the Spaniard's feet, believing they represented the returning Quetzalcoatl. Moctezuma welcomed the Spaniards in his magnificent gold-adorned palace. The Spaniards later kidnaped Moctezuma and demanded a ransom of enough gold that would fill a ship. After the ransom was paid, the French captured the Spanish ship, causing a war. The Spaniards lost patience with the Aztecs and ordered a massacre of the Aztec noblemen and commanders, and in the turmoil they killed Moctezuma.

THE PYRAMIDS

The ruins of Mesoamerica are known for their stepped pyramids that served as religious monuments and astronomical observatories, based on knowledge of sacred geometry and advanced mathematics. Hanub Ku, the Maya supreme deity, was considered the sole dispenser of movement and measure in the world. His symbol was the circle and square identical to that of the Great Architect of modern masonry. They considered every element in nature to be in cosmic harmony and bound by its own vibration, determining its geometric form. As the vibration changed, the formed changed in type and quality.

They believed that Earth was a living entity connected to the existence of man. Great civilizations appeared and disappeared according to rhythmic astronomical cycles. The priests maintained they could understand these cycles through mathematics, astronomy, and astrology. Everything could be foreseen if one understood the numbers which lay beneath their manifestations. The Mayas knew the math of addition, subtraction, division, and multiplication. Their zero was not a symbol for nothing, but it represented completion and the seed from which all could be derived.

Their very simple checkerboard system of math could handle high numbers with little effort. It had been written that a child of four could multiply, divide, and do square roots without having to memorize. Several thousand years before Christ, a simple system was devised using grains of two colors to represent the numbers of one and five. Mayas placed these grains in various positions on a checkerboard, drawn on any flat surface. With these boards, the Maya were able to handle their chronology, astronomy, engineering, and architecture, all so important to pyramid construction.

The ancient city of Dzibilchatun, discovered in the Yucatan, was considered to be the earliest large city of the Maya in Central America. It was built sometime between 2000 and 1000 B.C. For many centuries afterward, the Maya migrated from one place to another throughout Mesoamerica. Suddenly, in the third century A.D., the Maya changed abruptly, perhaps invigorated by religion. They began erecting great stone monuments, pyramids, and temples that recorded the passage of twenty-year katun periods, which marked the founding of their cities and the general course of history.

This began the era of the Classic Period of architectural splendor from which came nineteen Mayan cities and numerous towns of lesser importance.

They built pyramids of stupendous size from cut stone. Majestic temples and palaces were adorned with beautifully carved facades, and they constructed solar observatories, water reservoirs, and irrigation systems.

Maya tradition tells that the city of Palenque, the birthplace of the gods and mankind, lay at the center of the geographical landmass of the Americas. The Great Palace of Palenque corresponded to the Parthenon of Athens, as its architecture exemplified Pythagorean art. Palenque exerted universal appeal, considered to be the loveliest Mayan city.

The earliest major city of the Classic Mayan period was located at Tikal in the heart of Peten, Guatemala. Within a six-square-mile area lay three thousand structures, with the oldest stele dated to 292 A.D.

The Great Pyramid of Cholua, Mexico, is a step pyramid composed of four superimposed truncated pyramids. It covers forty-five acres and by cubic content is considered the largest pyramid in the world, being one-half the height of the Great Pyramid Cheops, which covers thirteen acres. According to the *Codex of Cholua,* it was built shortly before the Flood so men could climb upon it to escape destruction. Some of the oldest mural paintings are found on the inner walls of the pyramid. Author Frank Waters compares one motif, a mythological insect, to the insect painted on the mask of the Mastop Kachina. The mask worn during the contemporary Hopi Ceremonial of Soyal, symbolizes the appearance of man on Earth after the Deluge.

The great four-stepped Pyramid of the Sun at Teotithuacan has a base one yard shorter than the Cheops Pyramid of Egypt. It faces the exact position the sun sets on the day it reaches its zenith, and it also marks the solstices and equinoxes.

The Temple of Kukulcan at Chichen Itza is a nine-stepped pyramid, seventy-five feet high, with stairways on each of the four sides. Each stairway has ninety-one steps adding up to 364, with the upper platform making a total of 365, coinciding with the number of days in the year. Fifty-two panels on the nine steps symbolize the fifty-two-year cycle.

The Pyramid of Xochicalo contains a vertical shaft on which the sun shines one day a year without casting a shadow. In Uaxactun, the relationship of three temples and two stelae give the precise orientation of the sun's position at the solstices and equinoxes.

The Mayan pyramids may be more practical than the Egyptian pyramids. For access to the temple, Mayan pyramids provided a stairway up one side. Mesoamerican pyramids did not entomb their rulers as did the later Egyptian pyramids.

The Teotihucan builders used a unit equivalent to 1.059 meters. Calculations by astronomer William Haleston suggested that the Pyramid of Quetzalcoatl, like the Pyramid of Cheops and the stepped pyramids of Mesopotamia, were scale models of Earth. Haleston also discovered that the Mesoamerican builders knew both Pi and Phi, as did the Egyptian builders.

In the mid-18th century, Johann David Titius discovered a numerical connection between the planetary orbital distances of the solar system known as Bode's Law. The formula derives the mean distances of the planetary orbits by multiplying a series of numbers by three and adding four to each result. The numbers obtained corresponds approximately to the positions of the planets.

In 1787, Harleston discovered that by starting with the center of the Teotihuacan Quetzalcoatl Pyramid, which represented the sun, and measuring northward up the processional, all the known planets fell on definite temple markers, which were symmetrically spaced. Encouraged by these processional markers, he came upon two typical temple mounds that had not yet been reconstructed. His calculations represented planets not yet discovered, which accurately mark the orbital distance of Neptune and Pluto, both planets discovered long after Harleston's predictions.

Harleston came across the remains of another ancient temple in the ruins known as the Temple of Xochitl, which appeared to represent another unknown planet. This planet would be located at twice the distance of Pluto and calculated to be three and one-half times the size of Earth. Harleston gave this planet X the name of Xiknalkan. Astronomers have long predicted another planet beyond Pluto because of perturbation in the orbits of both Uranus and Neptune.. One can only speculate that this was the Sumerian's twelfth planet called Nibiru.

Chapter Eight

THE LEGENDS AND GODS OF MESOAMERICA

A Look into our Past and Future

Through legends a history of ancient civilizations can be reconstructed. These legends were often metaphors for a higher message. Historians benefited because the Middle America culture developed the art of hieroglyphics to record their legends, and because the calendar was important in their life and religion it provided a chronology of their monuments and history.

Quetzalcoatl was a god and god-man similar to the gods found in Sumer and Egypt. Similarities occur between Quetzalcoatl and Thoth of Egypt, Enki of Sumer, Buddha, and Christ. Civilization was based upon Quetzalcoatl and he formed the nucleus of religion in Mesoamerica. As in other parts of the world, Mesoamerica was provided a great spiritual leader to help in its evolvement.

The obsession with the calendar and its influence on life became a major part of the Mesoamerican religion. A god governed each day, year, and cycle. The priests knew these cycles and acted as intermediaries between the people and the gods.

The ancient Mesoamericans knew of the previous worlds. Each of these four or five prior creations had been destroyed by a cataclysm of natural origin, such as a flood, earthquake, wind, or fire. Ancients taught that disobeying the gods brought on these catastrophes. They knew the present era would come to an end as well. With the end of the Mayan calendar being December 21, 2012 A.D., the Mayans acknowledged that this date marked the end of the fifth sun that was to be destroyed by earthquakes. The sixth sun would begin. They believed each new creation improved over the previous one.

On a microcosmic scale, the life, death, and resurrection of a soul reflects the grander earth cycles. The message, we are all in a

161

state of evolvement, and we are entering into attunement with the galactic forces beyond our solar system.

COSMOLOGY OF MESOAMERICA

The natives of Central America had their legends about creation, as did other ancient civilizations, and part of their legends included tales of mass destruction of the earth. The seeds of ancient civilization would eventually enter a new era, and the cycle of rebirth and death would again occur. Many of the creation stories show similarity to other ancient cultures, with only the names changing. The *Popol Vuh* of the Maya Quiche describes the Maya creation story and all the great cosmogonic myths of the Maya. Scholars have discovered the mythologies of other cultures in Central Mexico to be almost identical to the Maya Quiche.

A word began the initial creation similar to the biblical account, and Earth suddenly rose from a mist, formed, and unfolded. The word of the creator god Tonacatecuhtli, then created the first humans named Qxomoco and Capactonac. This supreme couple begat four sons named Tlatlauhgui Tezcatlipoca (Red Smoking Mirror); Yayaauchgui (Black Smoking Mirror); Quetzalcoatl (Feathered Serpent); and Omitecuhtli (Bracelet Serpent), called Huitzilopochtli by the Aztecs.

The four sons met and decided that Quetzalcoatl and Huitzilopochtli should become creators. They created Tlalteotl (Lady of Earth), and Earth was formed. They also created Tlalocantecuhtli, the god of water known as Tlalocan. The creator god Tonacatecuhtli blew and separated the water from the heaven and earth. The gods then made the days and divisions of time, after which Quetzalcoatl created fire. Qxomoco and Capactonac were ordered to cultivate the earth and begin the human race. The gods next created a place of the dead called Mictlan, ruled by Mictlantecuhtli. They created two heavens along with divine beings, and the four ages of the cosmos began at this point of history. Legend then asserts that natural disasters destroyed the planet, and the Earth needed to be created again.

In an original paradise called Xochitlicacan, breaking of a prohibition had disastrous ramifications. Oxomoco and Cipacvtonal had given birth to a son, Piltzintecuhtli. For him, the gods created a woman out of human hair. The gods who lived in this paradise of Xochitlicacan violated a prohibition by cutting flowers and branches from a forbidden tree. Likewise, Ixnextli, a counterpart of Eve, sinned by picking flowers from the garden which upset the creator god Tonacatecuhtli who banished her and the disobeying gods to Earth and the underworld. The god Xochiquetzal also sinned by eating fruit from the tree before the Flood, and the legend claims this caused all the world's misfortunes and afflictions. Other gods banished from the paradise were Quetzalcoatl, Tezcatlipoca, and Huitzilopochtli. Comparison of this ancient legend to the biblical story of creation found in Genesis cannot be dismissed.

Xochiquotzal gave birth to Cinteotle, the maize god whom Piltzintecuhtli fathered. Picking flowers, according to scholars, was a metaphor for sexual transgressions. The gods transgressed by cutting the flowers and eating the forbidden fruit, the symbol for procreating. To procreate was to deny immortality, as procreation was a compensation for the loss of immortality.

Tezcatlipoca and Quetzalcoatl were then transformed into serpents, the fire serpent and feathered serpent respectively. In order to dismantle Tlalteotl (Earth) and support the firmaments, and to maintain space between both parts, Tlalteotl became dismembered, becoming the Earth, moon, and heavenly bodies.

Both the *Pinturas* and *Legenda de los Soles* legends tell of successive foundations of the universe with varying durations that ended in terrible cataclysms. Cosmic regeneration balanced these cosmic destructions. The god Tezcatlipoca headed the first foundation, known as the Sun "Four Tiger." After a period of 676 years, the giants who inhabited this age were devoured by jaguars. A terrific wind swept away Quetzalcoatl and all humanity, while some survivors were turned into monkeys.

The second era, the Sun "Four Winds," lasted 1725 years. During this era, ordinary humans populated the earth. To protect themselves from a new flood, they built an enormous tower in Cholula. A confusion of languages transpired, causing the people to scatter in all directions. Lightening destroyed the tower. Again, a legend resembles that found in the Bible, as well as the myths found in Sumer. A great hurricane brought the second foundation to an end.

The god Tlaloc presided over the third age, the Sun "Four Rain." This was during the time the Olmec arrived from the East to the coast of Yucatan. It was also the time of Quetzalcoatl, who taught virtue. The era ended when Quetzalcoatl departed to the East, predicting he would return in the year One Reed. A mighty rain of fire destroyed these people.

The god Chalchiuhtlicue ruled over the fourth great age, the Sun "Four Water." This era ended with a great Flood that swept the people away. There was darkness when the sky fell, and flatness existed between heaven and Earth. A consensus among scholars describes four suns or eras that the universe passed through, and all their durations were multiples of fifty-two-year cycles ending in cataclysms.

The successive creations and destructions listed in the *Popol Vuh* were caused by the failure of men to acknowledge their creator, the ultimate transgression. The number of suns varied among all Indian tribes. Mexican Indian myths describe four suns, while the Maya, Mixtec, and Aztec legends tell of five suns. Earth, water, wind, air, and fire each corresponded to a Mesoamerican sun, and each era corresponded to an element.

According to legend, eight years after the Flood of the fourth sun, Tezcatlipoca, Quetzalcoatl, and other gods met at Teotihucan to decide who should inhabit the Earth. They decided they needed humans to repopulate the Earth. Quetzalcoatl descended to the underworld and asked Mictlantecuhtli to give him the bones of the dead. He gathered up the bones and took them to Tamoanchan, where the goddess Cihuacoatl, the goddess of magic, ground them up. Quetzalcoatl drew blood from his penis and sprinkled it over the ground-up bones, as did the other gods. Cihuacoatl mixed the ground bones with the god's blood and a male was born, followed in four more days by a female child. From these children, humanity descended. A Nahuatl depiction shows a god and goddess mixing an element that flows into a huge flask with the blood of a god that drips into the flask. From the mixture a human emerges. This legend is very similar to the Sumerian creation tale of humans by Enki and Ninti.

The *Popol Vuh* states the preceding three creations had failed, and the last creation brought the Maya Quiche into the world whose fathers were made by the creator from corn. In this last creation, humans not only worshiped the gods, but they understood their relationship to them, and realized the necessity to make sacrifice to sustain the gods. This belief system mirrored the life purpose of serving gods held by the Sumerians.

The legends tell that cataclysmic floods destroyed the world because the people committed sins against the gods. The *Popol Vuh* credits people who did not acknowledge their creator. Mexican myths describe three or four destructions of humanity, but always survivors seed the next world. Each time, the world's renewal is accompanied by a new transgression, which results in another catastrophe. The metaphor of these legends appears to be life, death, resurrection, and triumph over death. Light is restored to the world, resulting in reestablishment with the creator (supreme couple) and the lost paradise.

Venus symbolizes much of this metaphor, so important in the Mesoamerican legends and their astronomy. Its voyage across the night, its disappearance, and reappearance as the Morning Star ushering in the sun, symbolizes life. The legends are of a rebirth, and the Mayan calendar records these various cycles of time. Each new creation or sun progresses over the last, with each creation less imperfect than the previous.

QUETZALCOATL

Quetzalcoatl has been referred to as the Christ and Buddha of ancient Central America. Scholars still debate whether he was myth or real, but he is considered both a god and god-man. Most religions of the native Central Americans evolved around Quetzalcoatl.

The myths of Quetzalcoatl describe him as an active deity, one of four sons of the creator. Along with his brother Huitzilopochtli, he generated the world, and the two created humanity. Quetzalcoatl ruled over one of the cosmological eras and created the sun of the fifth age. He assisted in the discovery of corn, and also created fire. Quetzalcoatl participated in the sacrifice to the gods, but he did not play a role in the creation of human sacrifice.

Quetzalcoatl became the symbol of sovereignty and sanctified authority. He represented a principle of creative order and the ordering of time, space, and culture. Being a lawgiver, his laws diffused into the kingdom. All art and knowledge flowed through Quetzacoatl, and he was considered master of wisdom.

The model of priesthood, Quetzalcoatl ordained and applied the laws and practiced the rituals and customs established in Mexico. He taught men how to properly evoke the gods, to erect temples, and to institute rituals. Being the incarnation of the creator god, he penetrated the levels of heavens and communicated with the high god. Quetzalcoatl was the standard for the essential relationship between kingship and divinity.

Numerous city-states in Mesoamerica strived to achieve stability in an unstable world, and to achieve this they revitalized the Quetzalcoatl tradition in their ceremonial center. He became patron deity of many capitals, and the Quetzalcoatl religion appeared in many cities over the space of history. Over time, Quetzalcoatl as god and god-man changed significantly.

A plumed serpent symbolized Quetzalcoatl. The plumes referred to the exquisite green tail feathers of the once common quetzal, now nearly extinct. Quetzal came to mean "precious whose plumes were prized." Coatl means "snake" and also "twin." He was depicted as a multiple god: a flying dragon, called the plumed serpent; the wind god, Ehecatl; the morning star called Ceacatl, One Reed; and the Toltec priest ruler, the god-man Topiltzin. His heavenly residence was Omeyocan, associated with the high gods. The Aztecs believed Quetzalcoatl was the only god who cared for humans and had a special relationship with them.

Scholars believe the Toltecs inherited Quetzalcoatl from precedent cultures. They took this prestigious god and changed him into a patron of warriors. They gave him the date name Ceacatl, One Reed, claiming that he had been the first ruler of Tula (Tollan). He was their hero god, and their symbol of sanctified authority.

The second Quetzalcoatl was Topiltzin-Quetzalcoatl of Tula, who was a religious personality who directed social life in Mesoamerican society. An exemplary human, he represented the deity's power and authority on Earth, and provided the model for ritual and political life in Tula. His religious structures permeated throughout all Toltec derived dynasties. The creative acts of Topiltzin-Quetzalcoatl in founding the primordial city of Tollan reflect a prior foundation of the cosmos order, demonstrated in the creation myths of the Toltecs and Aztecs.

Tollan was the center of the world then and an archetypal city of power and authority for subsequent city-states. Other Tollans which organized in central Mesoamerica were ruled by an elite. They used this paradigm of primordial order to sanctify their own authority. For the Valley of Mexico, it remained a model of rulership until the time of Spanish conquest.

Being of divine parents, Quetzalcoatl's birth was considered a miracle. He grew up in a sheltered penitent life before becoming a ruler-priest of Tollan. His birth followed the creation of the fifth age. Another legend describes Quetzalcoatl as born into a world of warfare, where he became a warrior and conqueror. He underwent seven years of penance, seeking divine aid to become a great warrior. He displayed extraordinary skill as a warrior and advanced to the rulership of Tula. His wise rule created a utopian kingdom similar to the golden age of Old World tales. Ideal harmony existed throughout his reign and was reflected in its beautiful art.

Quetzalcoatl descended from an ideal divine life to a human life by the actions of his creative brother, Tezcatlipoca who was a complimentary part of Quetzalcoatl in the unity that formed Ometeotl. Tezcatlipoca could take the shape of sorcerers. He was an Aztec supreme god and a patron god of sorcery, warriors, and ruling dynasties. His magic mirror allowed him to look into the hearts of men.

After looking into the magic mirror of Tezcatlipoca, Quetzalcoatl saw for the first time his physical being and own mortality. He appeared gross and disfigured. His response was to cover his body with plumed feathers and his face with a wondrous mask. This was the first initiation into the depths of the physical world of nature.

The sorcerer next induced Quetzalcoatl to become intoxicated by drinking pulgue, which helped relieve his pain. For the first time, Quetzalcoatl thought about death and where he was to go after death. This metaphor symbolized the cyclic nature of life where death is not an end but a prelude to rebirth. The drunken Quetzalcoatl then enticed his sister to share his pulgue, and after drinking together, they fell from a divine spiritual state into a grossly physical sexual relationship.

The fall of Topilzin-Quetzalcoatl caused his personal suffering along with suffering of his people and city. As god-man, Quetzalcoatal could not deal with the weakness of his physical body even though he established a kingdom of spirit on Earth. He renounced the physical world in order to return to spirit.

He called for the destruction of Tollan and left the city for his fateful journey to Tlapallan toward the Gulf Coast sunrise. He stepped onto a raft of serpents reserved only for sorcerers and wise men and floated away across the waves to Tlapallan. It is not known where Tlapallan was located, but some scholars speculate it may have been Chichen Itza. His disappearance is a mystery and myths offer various scenarios. Some believe his departure was an allegory of the regenerative waters of the sea after these symbolic episodes.

Quetzalcoatl vanished into the East with the understanding that he would return in a later year, One Reed. For Moctezuma, the arrival of the Spanish was a fateful coincidence. He believed that the cycle had come around again, and Quetzalcoatl had returned from the realm of the spirit to reclaim his earthly kingdom.

One myth describes Quetzalcoatl becoming Venus when he died, symbolized by the Evening Star, which would disappear for four days. Then began the process of resurrection and he was born again as Venus the Morning Star, which heralded the rebirth of the sun. It was a symbol to the people that tragedy and catastrophes are a normal part of everyday affairs, and that rebirth came only after a return to spirit, which was a fundamental truth of Mesoamerican religion. This tale was ancient, perhaps 900 B.C., and carved in stone on an Olmec plumed serpent.

In 987 A.D., Topiltzun-Quetzalcoatl and his followers left Tollan and migrated eastward, emulating the earlier departure of the divine Quetzalcoatl. They settled in the Yucatan, seeking a place where they could worship as in the olden days. They came to the abandoned sacred city of Chichen Itza.

THE MAYAN CALENDAR

One of the great legacies left by the Maya was their calendar system. They had three calendars, not all related to astronomy. One system was the Long Count, which counted the number of days that passed from a starting day to the day of the event recorded on a stele or monument. Day one was August 13, 3113 B.C. Scholars have no idea why this date was chosen, and Sylvanus Morley speculated that it may have been the date the Maya gave to creation. The Maya's could predict the synodic return of the planets and the cyclic phenomena of solstices, equinoxes, and eclipses of the sun and moon.

Mayans observed three distinct year measurements: the 260-day year or *tzolkin,* also known as the Sacred Year Calendar; the 360-day year or *tun;* and the *haab* or vague year, which included 365 days divided into eighteen months of twenty days with an addition of an extra five day month called the *uayeb.* The *haab* calendar was identical to the Egyptian calendar. The *haab* year was used in secular events; the *tzolkin* determined dates for ceremonies and prophecies; and the *tun* was employed in computing Long Day counts.

Great ritualistic importance was placed on the Calendar Round, which was the meshing of the *haab* year with the *tzolkin*, much like the meshing of two gears. This was accomplished by synchronizing the days and months of the 365-day *haab* year with the repeated sequence of twenty days and the number's one to thirteen. This comprised the 260-day *tzolkin* calendar. There were a total of 18,890 possible combinations of days, months, and numbers involved in the synthesis of the two calendars making the Calendar Round. The interval required for a particular day to repeat its original position in the round was 18,890 days or fifty-two years. It was widely used for recording time and as a divinatory almanac.

The time period of *tzolkin* determined the pattern of ceremonial life for each individual. The birthday of a Mayan was determined by the day of the *tzolkin* upon which he was born, and the god of that day was his patron saint. The sacred year was a succession of 260 days, each prefixed by a number from one to thirteen, to one of the twenty Maya day names.

The *tzolkin* had no day name without an accompanying number. The calendar ran 1 *Ik*, 2 *Akhac*, 3 *Kan*, 4 *Chiccan*, and so on. The fourteenth name, *Men*, had the one again, followed by 2 *Cib*, and so on. Since thirteen and twenty had no common factor, 260 days had to elapse before 1 *Ik* recurred and a new *tzolkin* began. Not until every one of the thirteen numbers had been attached to the 20-day name, was a *tzolkin* complete.

To give any day in the Maya Calendar Round its complete description, it was necessary to add a corresponding position in the 365-day haab year calendar to the *tzolkin* designation. The 365-day calendar was composed of nineteen months. There were eighteen months of twenty days and a closing month of five days.

Copan, considered the astronomical capital of the Maya, lay fourteen degrees forty-two minutes north latitude. Perhaps it was a coincidence that the interval between the two zenith days of the sun was 260 days, and perhaps not. The sun reached its zenith when it passed directly overhead at midday. The Indians suggest this was the basis for the calendar year.

To escape calendar chaos, the Maya priests devised a simple

numerical system involving the conception and use of the mathematical quantity of zero. Morley believed this was one of the most brilliant achievements of the human mind.

There were nine orders of time. The unit of the Maya calendar was the day or *kin*. The next unit of order was the *uinal,* consisting of twenty kins. *Tun,* was the third order of the Maya calendrical system. It was composed of 360 *kins* or eighteen *uinals.* The fifth order, the *baktun,* was called the cycle by scholars. The Great Cycle of the Maya consisted of 1,872,000 *kin* (days) or thirteen *baktun* (one *baktun* is 144,000 days). The Great Cycle began August 13, 3113 B.C. and will end December 21, 2012 A.D.

1 kin	= 1 day
20 kins	= 1 uinal or 20 days
18 uinals	= 1 tun or 360 days
20 tuns	= 1 katun or 7200 days
20 katuns	= 1 baktun or 144,000 days
20 baktuns	= 1 pictun or 2,880,000 days
20 pictuns	= 1 calabtun or 57,600,000 days
20 calabtuns	= 1 kinchiltun or 1,152,000,000 days
20 kinchiltuns	= 1 alautun or 23,040,000,000 days

The Long Count was based on the "vigesimal" mathematical system of the Maya that evolved around the number twenty. The Maya Long Count dating system was the most accurate calendar ever devised in the ancient world. It was complex in structure and consisted of nine interrelated periods, which made it possible to keep track of very large time spans. Every Long Count inscription on the stele and monuments included only the first five divisions or *kins* through the *baktuns,* plus the position of the Calendar Round on which the date terminated. Numerical coefficients accompanying the glyphs indicated the number of times each cycle had occurred since the beginning of Maya chronology. In 1887, Ernst Forstemann discovered every Long Count inscription was calculated from a base of 13.0.0.0.0 or 3113 B.C. called the Zero Date.

The Maya Long Count dating system used vertical columns where values were lowest at the bottom. A date on the stele twenty-four, the earliest date of a royal monument, read 8.12.14.8.15, written in the vertical. This date, 292 A.D., occurred 3404 years and

304 days after the mysterious day one (August 13, 3113 B.C.). The date would be:

8 baktuns	– 8x400x360	=	1,152,000 days
12 katun	– 12x20x360	=	86,400 days
14 tun	– 14x360	=	5,040 days
8 uinal	– 8x20	=	160 days
15 kin	– 15x1	=	15 days
		Total	1,243,615 days

THE MAYAN FACTOR

College professor Dr. Jose Arguelles believed the Maya were trying to pass on to humanity a hidden message. His research into their writings and ruins produced some startling conclusions as recorded in his book *The Mayan Factor.*

He found in the Chinese *I Ching,* the binary triplet configuration of a hexagram, symbols that possibly represent the DNA genetic code. The *I Ching,* the Chinese Book of Divination, dates back to 1000 B.C. Confucius, and the Taoist sages valued it highly. The *I Ching* is said to gauge the flow of yin and yang energies. It offers the seeker an appropriate course of future action based on the interplay of positive or negative forces that shape our destinies. He believed there was a relationship between the Mayan sacred calendar matrix, the 260 unit *tzolkin,* and the *I Ching.*

By 1985, Arguelles was certain that the code behind the Great Cycle was a key to unlocking our own history. The *tzolkin* was a means of tracking information through knowledge of the sunspot cycles, asserted Arguelles, and at least two star systems communicated the information. This created a binary communication system through the sunspots. He hypothesized that the two star systems were the Pleiades and Arcturus.

Arguelles said there was little evidence to support a formative stage of trial and error for the Maya mathematics, astronomical, and calendrical calculations. They were complete and accompanied by a highly developed hieroglyphic code. With the rise of Maya over two thousand years ago, began the proliferation of the great Toltec pyramids at Teotihuacan. The Toltecs shared with the Maya the 260-day calendar and the ritual ball game, but the Maya remained artistically and intellectually distinct. Around 300 A.D., the Mayans built their harmoniously proportioned stepped pyramids at Peten and left behind many stone markers called stelae with recorded dates. With the transition from *Baktun* nine to *Baktun* ten came the abrupt disappearance of the Classic Maya.

Baktun nine was the Classic Maya era, and according to Arguelles, the Classic Maya possessed a distinct mission and message: to place the Earth and its solar system in synchronization with a large galactic community. Once they accomplished this purpose, the Maya departed. A few remained behind as caretakers of the cryptic code language, the language of the Zuvuya, significant of the different cycles of time. According to ancient texts such as the *Popol Vuh,* the Yugis were the first of the Mayan tribes to separate from the rest of the clans. Their purpose was to keep the original teachings pure in a remote place.

Their purpose and science, according to the Maya, were embedded in the simple system of thirteen numbers and twenty symbols called the *tzolkin.* Mayan science operated in a galactic framework that could not be separated from myth, art, and religion.

Two Mayan terms, *Hunab Ku* and *Kuxan Suum,* were essential in providing a galactic view of synthesizing science and myth. *Hanub Ku* means "one giver of movement and measure" and describes purpose and activity. Movement refers to rhythm, periodicity, and form. *Kuxan Suum* means "the road to the sky leading to the umbilical cord of the universe." It defines the invisible galactic life thread that connects both the individual and planet, through the sun, to the galactic core, the *Hunab Ku.*

The Mayan factor brought a world of coherence and unity into focus. The civilization was based on harmonic resonance. Mayan science based itself on mind as the foundation of the universe. They believed the universe was mental rather than material in nature, and reality was saturated with purpose. The form of things was the shape of consciousness at a particular resonant frequency junction. This meant a synchronization of two or more tonal spectrums which join momentary needs with universal purpose.

The galaxy consisted of complex star systems coordinated by the galactic core, *Hunab Ku.* So that all systems attain the same level of harmonic coordination, information would have to be systemized into the simplest code, for common use. The systemization and transmission of this code were the responsibility of the Maya. The code is found in the *tzolkin*, the harmonic module, the periodic table of galactic frequencies. The Maya acted as mediators between *Hanub Ku*, the galactic core, and the evolving intelligence of a local star system.

Once a particular planetary consciousness was placed in alignment with the whole, through the parent star (sun), which is the harmonic module, they could establish communication with another star system. The code language of the *tzolkin* describes the passage of the *Kuxan Suum* to the Earth.

The *tzolkin* condenses overtones and levels of meaning. Its thirteen numbers occupy a possible twenty positions for a total of 260 permutations. Harmonic cycles called *uinal, tun, katuns,* and *baktuns* are created by the sequence of days *(kin)*. The *tzolkin* is a keyboard or table of universally applicable periodic frequencies.

The Mayan calendar describes a galactic pattern or synchronization beam in a harmonic calibration. The Earth passes through this galactic synchronization beam, which has a diameter of 5200 tuns and lasts for 5125 Earth years. Passage began August 13, 3113 B.C.

Being 5200 *tun* in duration, the galactic harmonic pattern belongs to the fractal series based on fifty-two. The fractal principle describes the capacity of a number to remain proportionally constant. As a fractal, 260 is actually an overtone of twenty-six or two times thirteen, and 360 is an overtone of thirty-six or two times eighteen and four times nine. The 260 unit is the galactic constant and 360 is the harmonic calibration. The number 260 defines the least possible set of changes accommodating the greatest number of galactic possibilities from wave frequency to archetypes.

The purpose of the Maya, according to Arguelles, was to make present and record the galactic harmonic. It had not yet been perceivable to humanity in their evolutionary position in the galaxy. The Mayas were galactic masters who brought the entire galactic information matrix to us.

The midpoint of the current Great Cycle, 3113 B.C. to 2012 A.D., corresponded to 550 B.C. This represented the approximate time of the Danzante sculpture of Monte Alban in the Oaxaca highlands, dated between 500 and 600 B.C. The midpoint refered to the coming of the Nine Lords of Time, and it brought galactic measures to the planet. It was the first wave of the galactic Maya in

Mesoamerica. Arguelles believed that key Mayan emissaries were assimilated into the high cultures of the Olmecs.

The great Mayan Number of Synthesis was recorded in the *Dresden Codex* as 13 66 560. It was a phenomenal number capable of being factored by all the key numbers corresponding to all the harmonic cycles, 13, 20, 52, and 260. It corresponded to the year 631 A.D., the year Pacal Votan of Palenque was incarnated. His tomb was the only one of Mesoamerica comparable to the Great Pyramid tomb of Egypt and was dated 683 A.D., fifty-two years later than 631 A.D. Pacal Votan, a galactic master, declared himself to be a serpent, an initiate, and a possessor of knowledge.

By a decree from above, he left his homeland (the mysterious Valum Chivim) and went to the Yucatan. Valum Chivim referred to one of the Mayan star bases, perhaps the Pleiades. The star bases, according to Arguelles, had monitored the Mayan mission since the first wave of galactic masters. This included the Nine Lords of Time, who helped seed the planet Earth. Pacal Votan oversaw the final phase of the Mayan Earth project. He traveled by the "dwelling of the thirteenth serpent," which referred to the intergalactic passage via *Kuxan Suum. Baktun* nine came to a close in 830 A.D., and by that time the galactic masters had already gone.

Like the *I Ching,* the *tzozlkin* is an information system relating to a larger purpose. *I Ching* is synchronized with the genetic code, and the *tzolkin* is synchronized with the galactic code. The galactic code is the primary source that informs and vitalizes the code of life, DNA, represented by the *I Ching*. The *tzolkin* is to *I Ching* what light is to life.

The thirteen numbers of the *tzolkin* represent primary patterns of radiant energy pulses, and the twenty symbols represent the cycle of frequencies. The latter give the range of possibilities for transformation or evolution that each radiant energy pulse may undergo. The 260 symbolic pulses of the *tzolkin* create the entire resonant field that we experience as reality. A symbol is a resonant structure that Plato and Carl Jung called the archetypes. It is an archetype that forms constants which define a field of consciousness that transcends both time and the individual. A resonant code informs the light body. The light body is the electromagnetic galactic code that informs the genetic code.

The Great Cycle consists of thirteen *baktuns* or 144,000 *kin* (days). The thirteen *baktuns* are represented by the thirteen vertical columns of the *tzolkin.* The calendar of the Great Cycle can be over-laid on the time period of 3113 B.C. to 2012 A.D.

During the passage through this beam of 5200 *tun,* the advanced DNA life-forms on this planet undergo an acceleration. We are presently in the last *baktun,* the thirteenth harmonic cycle. Everything from the initiation point in 3113 B.C. is a buildup of the cycle of transformation and of synchronization.

Arguelles believed the Mayan sages were prepared for a return on August 16-17, 1987. This was the global event, Harmonic Convergence, that so many people participated in through prayer and meditation on those dates. It was the first Mayan return entry point. Harmonic Convergence signaled the return of Quetzalcoatl and the elimination of Armageddon as well. To some, it was like a second coming of Christ energy. It was the awakening of 144,000 people predicted by prophecy of the Zuvuya. By 1992, the plan initiated on Harmonic Convergence was to have stabilized the world.

The 5200 *tun* cycle goes through five Great Cycles, and is roughly equivalent to the Platonic Great Year, the precession of the equinoxes. The Maya prophecies indicated that earthquakes would end the fifth world on December 21, 2012. (Others have placed the Mayan date on December 24, 2011.)

THE SPIRITUAL INFLUENCE

Mesoamerica's spiritual world bore many similarities to that of the ancient world across the sea. They, too, believed in a life after death and in the immortality of the soul, and they also believed their purpose was to placate the gods. The Mesoamericans worshiped a pantheon of gods, with each god having a responsibility to oversee a certain aspect of the material world. The priesthood was the liaison between the physical and spiritual worlds. They believed in a duality of good and evil, where souls would enter the realm of heaven or the underworld. Many of their myths had a theme of life, death, resurrection, and rebirth. As in many parts of the world, the spirituality of Mesoamerica played an important role in everyday life.

Similar to most indigenous cultures around the world, the natives believed in three levels of existence. Above Earth, heaven consists of different levels, and below Earth lays a multi-layered underworld, a land of the dead.

Lord of the underworld, Mictanlecuhtli, ruled over Mictlan, the Aztec name for the lowest level of the underworld. The lord of death was known as Ah Puch. Both the Maya and Aztec believed the underworld consisted of nine levels. Most of the dead went to the underworld. Aztecs believed the spiritual journey lasted for approximately four years after death, a venture where they met many painful obstacles and underwent a series of difficult trials. The underworld was characterized as cold, putrefied, and in perpetual discontent. Not all the dead went to Mictlan, as it depended on the way one died. The most coveted fates were death in battle, by human sacrifice, suicide by hanging, and death by childbirth. All these went directly to the Mayan paradise.

The Aztecs believed their behavior in this world resulted in neither rewards nor punishments in the afterlife. The Maya believed the evil descended into the lower region they called Mictnal, the Maya hell. Here they were tortured with hunger, cold, weariness, and grief. Mayans called their lord of death Hanau, and he presided over hell. They believed paradise and hell would never end. Some myths suggested that the dead returned to life in a cycle of reincarnation.

The *Codex Vaticanus* describes heaven as having thirteen levels, with Omeycon being the highest, the place of duality. Mayan's believed the supreme deity functioned through a principle of dynamic dualism or polarity, such as masculine and feminine, active and passive, and so on. Each heaven was associated with a variety of gods, goddesses, and heavenly bodies. Closest to the Earth was the paradise of Tlalocan, the rain god. Mayan paradise was described as a place of delight with no pain or suffering.

Priests were the most powerful group in the state. They usually inherited their position, and most came from nobility. The high priests were able administrators, outstanding scholars, astronomers, and mathematicians. Their ability to predict eclipses, and their ability to penetrate into every phase of life made them feared and respected. Through the priests, people made offerings and built ceremonial centers.

The *chilane's* (diviner-priest) responsibility was to give the reply of the god to the people. In later times, the *nacom* priest, elected for life, cut open the sacrificed victim and plucked out the heart. He then handed it to the *ahkin* priest who offered it to the idol of a Mayan god. He was also the medicine man.

The seers of Central America saw their rulers as avatars of the gods who entered and exited the world of time and space at regularly intervals. The rulers mysteriously served as the shelters for gods, and from within them, the gods spoke. Through ritual, the god entered the body of each successive king, providing spiritual order to his people's lives. The ruler was one of the multiple incarnations of Tezcatlipoca, the first ancestor through the cycle of time. Tezcatlipoca was seen as a creative force himself and a manifestation of Ometeotl.

The moment of enthronement or divinization was the ascension moment, when the ruler became the god. It was the moment at which spiritual reality manifested itself anew in material form in the world of space and time. The Maya believed that when the ruler died, kingship did not. Their emphasis was on the office, not the person.

The *Books of Chilam Balam* suggest that the calendrical cycle of the twenty-year *katun* was used to rotate the seat of rule from one heaven-born capital to another every twenty years. They virtually abandoned the previous capital in favor of a new capital and a new ruler. Some scholars suggest that the so-called collapse of the Maya Classic Period was a similar response to the ending of a cycle.

The Maya considered time a supernatural phenomenon that involved omnipotent forces of creation and destruction. Gods who were believed to be either benevolent or evil directly influenced time. No other period was so obsessed with the passing of time. They labored tirelessly, trying to understand time's mysteries and to control its great influences. Their efforts led them to evolve a calendrical lore that extended millions of years into the past, and produced a profoundly complex philosophy.

Deities were associated with specific numbers and took form in hieroglyphic inscriptions. Each division of the Maya calendar was ruled by a god who fulfilled his responsibility in that time period before a successor god assumed the responsibility for the following time period. There were gods in charge of days, months, years, decades, and centuries. Maya viewed time as cyclical, rather than linear. They believed events associated with specific calendrical cycles would likely repeat themselves when the cycles recurred.

They believed strongly in divination and astrology. Only those with esoteric knowledge could recognize the attributes of gods, and they alone could determine when beneficial and harmful deities ruled a specific period. With this knowledge one could forewarn of future events. The priest who possessed this esoteric knowledge, could correctly interpret the will of the gods and knew how to placate them.

With the strong dualistic tendency in religion, the power of good and evil struggled eternally over the destiny of man. Benevolent gods brought bring rain and ensured bountiful corn harvests, while malevolent deities brought forth war and drought. Foremost, religion procured life, ensured health, and provided sustenance.

The people made sacrifices to ensure the gods would provide enough food to eat. They invoked and placated the gods through ceremonies, fasts, and abstinences. Sacrifices ranged from simple offerings such as food, ornaments, and valuables during classic times to human sacrifices in post-classic. Blood-letting was a common ritual in which blood was drawn from an ear and sprinkled over an idol. Incense burning and dancing were common in the religious ceremony.

As in many of the ancient civilizations, the Maya had a pantheon of gods. Itzamna, the Lord of the Heavens, stood at the head of the Maya pantheon. He served as lord of day and night, and patron of the day Ahau, the most important of the twenty Maya days. Itzamna divided the lands of the Yucatan and invented writing and books. A benevolent deity, he was always a friend of man. Chac was the rain god, a universal deity of major importance. He was god of one of the four cardinal points. The god of corn did not have a specific name, and scholars referred to him as God E. Ah Puch, the god of death, was associated with war and human sacrifice. Xamen Ek was god of the North star, a benevolent deity who guided merchants. Ek Chuak was god of war, a malevolent deity. Kukulcan was the god of wind, also known as Quetzalcoatl to the later Maya. Ixchel was goddess of floods, pregnancy, and perhaps the moon. She destroyed the world by flood and was the consort of Itzamna. Ixtab was the goddess of suicide, as the ancient Maya believed that suicides went directly to paradise.

The Oxlahuntiku, the thirteen gods of the upper world, formed collectively a single deity. Collectively the nine gods of the underworld were called Bolontiku. Each of the nine Bolontiku served as a patron of a day of the Maya calendar.

Each of the thirteen *katuns* of twenty years had a patron deity. Chac was patron of the *Ik* days, corn god of *Kan* days, Ah Puh of Cimi days, Itzamna of *Ahau* days, and so forth. The patrons of the fourteen variant numerals were another important series of Gods. Each member of the pantheon was a deity of a particular number.

The ancient Maya made no distinction between the supernatural and natural worlds, and the supernatural guided all aspects of their life. History for the Maya recorded the workings of the spirit world as manifested on the earthly plane. Invisible powers governed all aspects of the Maya's visible world, and they feared the ultimate sanction, the threat of supernatural retaliation. If one deviated from a task or failed to fulfill an obligation, one could be punished with misfortune, illness, or even death. The earliest supernatural intermediaries were the village shamans; however the Maya ruler was the supreme shaman for his society. The king served as both a political leader and priest.

HUMAN SACRIFICE

Human sacrifice became common during the post-classic era of Mesoamerica but the Quetzalcoatl religion prohibited it during classic times. In all sacrifices, human or animal, the victim's blood was smeared on the idol of the god being honored. Sacrifice placated and honored the gods who would in return honor the people. Several sources claim that human sacrifice was necessary to keep the cosmos in working order. To die by sacrifice took the victim directly to paradise in the afterlife.

Human sacrifice was performed in several ways, the most common and most ancient being to remove the heart. They stripped the victims of clothing and painted them blue, which was the sacrificial color. The victim wore a special peaked headdress as they led him to the site of sacrifice, usually a temple courtyard or summit of the pyramid supporting the temple. The priest then expelled evil spirits from the intended victim.

They smeared the altar, a convex stone, with the sacred blue paint. The four chacs, the assistants in the sacrifice, grasped the victims by arms and legs and stretched the victim on his or her back over the altar. The *nacom* priest advanced toward the victim holding the sacrificial flint knife. He plunged the knife into the victim below the left rib cage. Thrusting his hand into the opening, he pulled out the still-beating heart and handed it to the *chilan* or officiating priest.

If the sacrifice was on the pyramid summit, the *chacs* threw the corpse to the courtyard below. Priests of lower rank skinned the body, except for the hands and feet. The *chilan* removed the sacrificial vestments and proceeded to arrange himself in the skin of the victim, followed by dancing solemnly with the spectators. If the victim had been a brave soldier, the body was sometimes divided and eaten by the nobles and select spectators. However, victims were often enslaved prisoners of war. They sacrificed prisoners of high rank immediately, but those of lower rank became the property of the soldiers who had captured them.

Another type of sacrifice was practiced in the Well of Sacrifice at Chichen Itza. A great pocket of water lay in a large depression of limestone. The oval well measured 150 feet by 190 feet and was 65 feet from the ground level to the surface water, which reached a depth of 70 feet. Sacrifices often took place during times of famine, epidemics, and prolonged drought. The victims were thrown alive into the well. Often they were children of slaves thrown in by their masters at daybreak. If any survived the plunge, a rope was lowered into the well to rescue them. Their masters then asked the survivors what type of year the gods had in store for them. Other offerings such as precious personal belongings were often thrown into the well.

In 1885, Edward Thompson purchased one hundred square miles of jungle for seventy-five dollars, which included the ruins of Chichen Itza. Thompson was best known for writing the book *Atlantis, Not a Myth.* He organized dives into the well for the Peabody Museum of the Harvard Museum. The divers retrieved numerous sacred offerings, but found only forty skeletons. They retrieved thirty-four hundred artful objects made of jade and hundreds of metal objects made of gold, silver, copper, and bronze. Many of the objects came from distant lands and depicted bearded men. Some believe the depictions were of Phoenicians.

Chapter Nine

MYSTERIES IN THE ANDES
A Golden Age

When the Spanish Conquistadors arrived in South America during the early part of the 16th century, they were surprised to find a civilization so evolved, but so unlike the Old World. Centered in Peru, the Inca Empire spread north from Ecuador to central Chile in the south, from the Andes in the east to the Pacific. The Incas were in midst of a civil war when the foreigner's arrived, providing an advantage to the Spanish invaders. Inca temples adorned with much gold delighted the greedy Spaniards. They marveled at the ancient ruins constructed of monumental-size stones. The Spaniards were received as the returning ancient gods whom legend and prophecy had anticipated. The Incas based their religion on the creator god, Viracocha, who had once inhabited the land. Upon his departure he promised to return. Unfortunately for historians, the Incas had not developed writing to record their legends as had the Mesoamericans, but fortunately, the Spanish padres who followed the invaders did chronicle legends, history, and myths of the native inhabitants.

The Incas, the last custodians of the religious heritage of Peru, had preserved strong memories of their past civilization, said to have been founded by the Viracochas. Being expert farmers, they grew maize, potatoes, and quinoa. Viracocha had taught them how to terrace the land and build irrigation systems in the steep valley walls, often at elevations between 10,000 and 13,000 feet. Even today, the Andean peasantry believe their ancestors had been taught agriculture by Viracocha, whose age dawned around 200 B.C.

For the Incas, gold symbolically expressed the sorrow that the creator might abandon his creation. Gold, known as "tears of the sun" by the Incas, served as a symbol for unrighteous actions of humanity. Silver was known as "tears of the moon." These metals were so sacred to the Inca that no object fashioned from them and brought to Cuzco (the capital of the Inca Empire) could ever be removed, under penalty of death. The land of the Inca had no monetary system, and they valued gold only for its inherent beauty.

To the Incas, gold belonged to the gods, and they gave it to them in the form of sacrifices. They gathered gold from the surface and in streambeds when the Spaniards arrived, not from working mines. For many centuries following the invasion, the Spaniards and mining engineers spoke of prehistoric mines, especially the various sites in Mexico. Legends say Quetzalcoatl instructed the Toltecs on the secrets of mining. In the Andes, modern mines overlay indigenous operations, where some ancient shafts still contain remnants of primitive tools. Zecharia Sitchin writes the Annunaki were responsible for ancient mining around 4000 B.C. According to Sumerian texts, they wanted gold to ensure protection of Nibiru's atmosphere. Many petroglyphs found in the Andean gold centers resemble Sumerian cuneiform script, including symbols that the Sumerians used to represent Nibiru.

Sitchin writes that Quetzalcoatl arrived in Central America around 3113 B.C. at the beginning of the Long Count Calendar, and introduced the calendar to these lands. At that time Marduk/Ra reclaimed lordship over Egypt, replacing his brother Thoth. Thoth found himself a god without a people, and Sitchin hypothesizes that Thoth and Quetzalcoatl were one and the same.

When the Spaniards arrived in South America, they found the ruler Lord Inca had recently died. His first-born son by Lord Inca's secondary wife was challenging the legitimacy of the succession by a son born to Inca's first wife. A civil war broke out between the rulers who were vying for the kingship. The Spaniards captured one contending ruler, Atahualpa, and demanded ransom of a large roomful of solid gold. Inca goldsmiths subsequently hurried to melt down artful objects to meet the ransom demand. They gave about 200,000 ounces of gold hoping to exchange it for Atahualpa. However, as with Moctezuma in Mexico, the Spaniards reneged and sentenced Atahualpo to death. Pizarro and his men divided the wealth.

When they entered the capital Cuzco, amazed Spaniards saw temples and palaces literally covered and filled with gold. In the royal palace, they found a hoard of 100,000 gold ingots, weighing nearly five pounds each, waiting to be created into artful objects. They came upon a courtyard measuring 300 feet by 600 feet covered with a field of maize. Every stalk was made of silver, and each ear of corn made of gold. At the peak of their plundering, the Spaniards extracted 6 million ounces of gold and 20 million ounces of silver annually. Unfortunately for the Spaniards, this created hyperinflationary devastation for the Spanish economy, but it did finance the war against the Ottoman Empire.

The Incas were not the first to inhabit the land. Legends told of gods, giants, and kings living there centuries before the Inca. The coastal natives had legends of gods who instructed their ancestors to migrate to these promised lands. They told of giants who despoiled crops and raped the women.

The Incas, the dominant highland people, claimed they had been given divine guidance in all matters involving their activities including crafts, agriculture and the building of cities. However, much of their heritage was acquired from other native peoples of Peru. At the time of the conquest, Huayna Capac was the fourteenth Inca (Inca, meaning "lord") of a dynasty that began in Cuzco about 1020 A.D. Several centuries before, the Incas had conquered the coastal regions. They superimposed their rule over societies that had thrived for millennium prior. The Chimu people were the last culture to fall within the Inca Empire. Their capital was located at Chan-Chan on the northwest coast Peru. The sacred precinct of this metropolis covered eight square miles and included stepped pyramids, palaces, temples, aquaducts, reservoirs, tombs, and dwelling compounds. Many similarities were found between this ancient capital and Egypt and Sumer. The great pyramids were built of sun dried mud brick similar to pyramids of Mesopotamia. The Chimu civilization flourished from 1000 to 1400 A.D. They mastered goldsmithing, which the Incas did not until the conquest. The Incas were astonished at the amount of gold from the highlands that the Chimus possessed.

Farther south on the north central Peruvian coast lay the ruins of Mochia, dating back to 400 B.C. Their artifacts depicted winged gods, threatening giants, and symbols suggesting a pantheon headed by a moon god called Si-An. This lost society mastered the art of casting gold, centuries before Chimu. At Pacatnamu, excavators found a buried sacred city and unearthed thirty-one pyramids during the 1930s. The smallest pyramids were a thousand years older than the largest pyramid which measured forty feet high with a two-hundred-foot square base.

The highlands, south of the Rimac River where Lima is located, were occupied by the Aymara-speaking people. The Aymara gave the Inca their tales of creation. The Chincha Indians lived on the coastal zone south of the Rimac River, and the Incas obtained their pantheon from them.

LAKE TITICACA

Lying high in the Andes is Lake Titicaca, where most Indian legends say creation began. It is on the border between Peru and Bolivia at an elevation of 12,500 feet. It covers 3200 square miles, 130 miles long by 70 miles wide. It measures 1000 feet deep. Twelve miles south of Lake Titicaca lay the ruins of Tiahuanaco, which some scholars believe may be the remnants of the oldest city in the world. Mysteries abound in this sacred city of the Andes.

James Churchward studied an ancient Nacaal map in Tibet that showed a seaport at Tiahuanaco. The port lay on a water route connecting the Pacific Ocean to the Amazon Sea located in present-day Brazil. At that time, the Andes Mountains had not risen. The Lemurians used this ancient route to sail to Atlantis. Scholars believed this was an outlandish assertion and put no credence in it, still believing the Andes had been formed 100 million years ago. They totally discredited Churchward, but evidence now suggests they should have heeded him.

Millions of fossilized sea shells are scattered throughout Lake Titicaca, proving that at some point in time, the area was forced upward from the seabed. A great number of marine creatures remained behind, suspended among the ranges of the Andes. Lake Titicaca contains many ocean-type fish and crustacea, such as sea horses. Geologic evidence indicates that the water forming Lake Titicaca came from the sea and was dammed by the rising Andes. The lake was much saltier in earlier periods than today.

Lake levels have fluctuated enormously over the years. Geologists have discovered an ancient sloping shoreline. The shoreline was 295 feet higher to the north of present day Lake Titicaca, and 400 miles south, it was 274 feet lower. This suggested the Andes rose unevenly. The city of Tiahuanaco at one time was a port on Lake Titicaca, but now lies twelve miles to the south. It is one hundred feet higher than the present shoreline.

Indian legends tell of foreigners that came to Tiahuanaco ages ago, and with their godlike powers built the city. Natives at the time of the Spanish conquest acknowledge the city was built long before the Inca reign. Their legends claim the city appeared suddenly in the course of a night. A Spanish chronicle states, the Indian legends tell of gigantic stones being miraculously lifted off the ground and carried through the air to the sound of a trumpet.

Archaeologists discovered that Tiahuanaco was a principal harbor. Excavations revealed two artificially dredged docks on both sides of a magnificent pier that could have handled hundreds of ships. One construction block comprising the pier weighed 440 tons, with others weighing from 100 to 150 tons. Many of these monoliths had been fastened together with I-shaped metal clamps, similar to the notched stone depressions found on Elaphantine Island in the Nile River. Bronze clamps that were made for the notches have been found.

Located among the ruins of Tiahuanaco, an artificial hill rises 50 feet with sides measuring 690 feet. Known as the Akapana Pyramid, the dominant structure of Tiahuanaco, it is orientated very precisely toward the cardinal points. Deep within the confines of the pyramid, scientists found a network of zigzagging stone channels, lined with ashlar stones. The sluice's precision angular joints allowed water to be channeled down from a reservoir on top of the structure. Sitchin hypothesizes that the sluices may have been used in processing ore.

A large stone gateway known as the Gate of the Sun also lies among the ruins of Tiahuanaco. Weighing more than one hundred tons, it was cut from a single block of stone measuring ten feet by twenty feet. Truly a work of art, it contains many intricate carvings, including a central figure depicting Viracocha holding a scepter in his right hand and forked lightning in the other. Three rows of winged attendants flank him. A twelve-month calendar also carved upon it, begins at the spring equinox and marks the remaining equinoxes and solstices. Eleven of the months contain thirty days, and a great month has thirty-five days.

Even though no elephants were found in the New World, on the third column from the right, contains a carving of an elephant's head with ears, tusks, and a trunk. A similar species called *cuviero-nius* existed in the Andes until around 10,000 B.C.

Also carved on the Gateway of the Sun was a Toxodon, a three-toed amphibious mammal reaching a length of nine feet and height of five feet. It resembled a cross between a hippopotamus and a rhinoceros and flourished during the late Pliocene epoch (1.6 million years) ago and became extinct almost 12,000 years ago at the end of the Pleistocene epoch. Forty-six Toxodon heads had been carved on the frieze. The frieze contained other extinct species including a shelidoterium, a diurnal quadruped, and a macrauchenia, a three-toed horselike animal.

A series of vertical stone pillars called the Kalasasaya were found among the ruins that comprised a rectangular enclosure measuring 450 feet by 400 feet, with the axis running east-west. The Gate of the Sun stood at the north edge of the west wall. Various stones situated on the east-west axis permitted astronomical observations. The position of eleven pillars convinced Arthur Posnansky that people with an advanced knowledge for the precise fixing of the the equinoxes and solstices built the structure. Posnansky, a European engineer who moved to Bolivia in the early 1900s, was considered the greatest researcher of the Tiahuanaco ruins.

He measured the distances and angles between the solstice points and realized the obliquity of the earth with the sun, on which the astronomical aspects of Kalasasaya were based, did not conform to the angle of our present era. The angle between the plane of the earth's orbit and that of the celestial equator is presently 23 degrees and 27 minutes. During a cycle of 41,000 years the obliquity varies between 22.1 degrees and 24.5 degrees. The sequence of all previous angles can be easily calculated. His calculations showed that the angle was 23 degrees 8 minutes and 48 seconds, meaning the structure was built around 15,000 B.C. He announced that Tiahuanaco was the oldest city in the world, which upset the scientific community. In 1926 and 1928, the German Astronomical Commission set an expedition to confirm the findings of Posnansky, and their study verified Posnansky's, concluding that it was constructed in 15,000 or 9,300 B.C.

Posnansky believed that two natural catastrophes befell Tiahuanaco during the 11th millennium B.C., one caused by a great deluge and the other by earthquakes. Archaeologists unearthed prehistoric lake flora mixed with human skeletons in the alluvia. Alluvium layers cover the ruins along with lacustrine sand mixed with shells from Lake Titicaca. Volcanic ash and decomposed feldspar had also accumulated and covered the ruins. Posnansky believes when the flood water subsided, the culture of the Andes did not return to its former height but fell into total decadence. Following the cataclysms, the Andean people migrated toward compatible elements.

The tortora-reed boats of Suriqui found today on Lake Titicaca are identical to the papyrus-reed boats the pharaohs sailed on thousands of years ago. They are also similar in construction and finished appearance to the Sumerian reed boats. Local Indians claim the Viracocha people gave them the original design. Both the boats of Titicaca and Egypt were designed for long-distance transport of heavy building materials such as obelisks and building stone. Thor Heyerdahl replicated the boat and made his famous voyage on the Kon Tiki to prove that the ancient Sumerians could have crossed the ocean. The Aymara Indians claim they learned how to make the boats from the Urus.

Local Aymara Indians spoke a language considered by some scholars to be the oldest in the world. It had an artificial syntax character (words arranged in a sentence), which was rigidly structured and unambiguous to an extent, considered inconceivable in normal organic speech. Its synthetic and highly organized structure meant that the Aymara language could be transformed into a computer algorithm that could be used to translate one language into another. The language, skillfully and deliberately designed, appeared to be a made-up language. The Aymara algorithm is used as a bridge language, meaning the language of an original document is translated into Aymara and then into any number of other languages.

Some scholars claim that the Quechua and Aymara language's of indigenous Peru had a Sumerian-Assyrian origin. The native Aymara or Kholla Indians who now comprise most of the region's inhabitants state that their ancestors came from another land called Uru meaning "olden ones." They were the pre-Inca occupants of Tiahuanaco. Sitchin believes they may be referring to the Sumerian capital, Ur. The Indians of Titicaca are called Urus, whose myths say, "the people of the lake are the oldest on this Earth, a long time before the time when the sun was hidden, the day of darkness," which was around 1400 B.C. Uru means "day" in the Andean language and "daylight" in Sumer. Posnansky concluded that two races originally settled Tiahuanaco: the first, the Mongoloid people and then Middle Eastern Caucasians. Serious researchers of this area accept his research of Titicaca.

Local Indians carried away many stone ruins of Tiahuanaco, quarrying them for personal use. Scholars believe there is far more of Tiahuanaco below the soil than above it. In 1610, Spanish chronicler Father Cobo said it was possible to dig within a mile and one-half of the ruins in any direction, and at a depth of five to six feet, one would hit wrought stones, some very large and beautifully finished. He believed a great city was buried there. Tiahuanaco is surrounded by a ditch, surveyed by Posnansky in 1904 and 1912. It measured 3280 feet by 1470 feet.

Copacabana on Lake Titicaca is one of the great holy places of the Inca. Copacabana refers to two islands in the lake, one called Titicaca and the other Coata (moon), located five miles apart. The Shrine of the Sun, found on the island of Titicaca, is a large crag. Ancients tell of being without light from the heavens for many days. Finally the sun came out with extraordinary radiance, causing the ancients to believe the crag was the dwelling place of the sun. After the Incas arrived, they enhanced the shrine. Legends say the sun failed to rise and the night was endless. Chapter ten in the book of Joshua states that on the other side of the world, "the sun stood still and the moon stayed until the people avenged themselves of their enemies." Scholars estimate the sun did not set for twenty hours. The Bible says this happened when great stones fell from the sky. According to Sitchin, this occurred about 1400 B.C., possibly caused by a comet that may have disrupted the earth's rotation on its axis.

Myths of the local Indians claim that creation happened at Lake Titicaca. When all was still and dark, the creator Tici Viracocha emerged from the lake and killed the shadowy beings who had offended him, and they were turned into stone. Then he rose from the lake once more and created the sun and moon and fashioned new people out of stone. He went to Tiahuanaco and there dispatched the people to different places, directing some to Cuzco.

Spanish chronicler Sarmiento de Gamboa writes about the Indian legend of a world inhabited by giants who were ultimately destroyed by a flood. In the second age of the world, Viracocha created the present Indian race in the region of Lake Titicaca.

Garcilasco de la Vega was taught creation legends by sages

who survived from pre-conquest time. He was told that "our father the sun" took pity on mankind's ignorance and sent two sons to Earth. They emerged from Lake Titicaca and proceeded to the Cuzco region.

Chronicler Lopez de Gomara wrote in 1512 of two primordial gods, Con and Pachacama, who created humanity. A flood destroyed the new race of humans. Another legend tells of Con and Pachacama forming earth, sun, moon, and sky. They engendered all living things before leaving Earth for the sky. Centuries later Pachacama came back and destroyed everything, making humans into monkeys.

The Inca myth of human origin comprised a kind of double creation and at times involved two successive worlds, peopled by two successive races. Other legends tell of the creation of four or five worlds, and some tell of inhabitants being transformed into animals after a series of cataclysms. Most Andean legends mirror the other indigenous creation legends around the world, which end in natural disaster with the process of humanity then starting again. Scholars believe the events of the basic Inca legends all take place around Lake Titicaca.

At Lake Titicaca, Viracocha performed his creation feats. Here humanity reappeared after the deluge, and ancestors of the Incas were given a golden wand to establish an Andean civilization.

CUZCU, THE SACRED CITY

The greatest Spanish chronicler, Inca Garcilaso de la Vega, tells of the creation of man and woman by the creator sun who had placed them on an island in Lake Titicaca following the destruction of the world by a flood. The creator gave them a staff of gold and instructed them to settle wherever the staff sank into the ground and disappeared after thrusting it into the earth. The pair journeyed northward and came to the valley of Cuzco. Proceeding to the hill of Huanacauti, they thrust the golden staff into the ground, it disappeared, and the city of Cuzco was founded.

The city was divided into two parts. In Hanan Cuzco or upper Cuzco, the prince's (Inca Manco Capac) followers settled, and in Hurin Cuzco, the followers of the queen Coya Mama Ocllo settled. After they established the city and state of Cuzco, the Inca Manco

Capac taught the Indians agriculture, and Coya Mama Ocllo taught the women weaving and sewing.

Scholars believe that Cuzco was established and planned in accordance with the prehistoric site at Tiahuanaco, under the direction of Manco Capac. Cuzco was a grand and stately city with fine narrow streets and houses built of beautifully joined stone. The twelve city wards emulated the twelve signs of the zodiac, and the stream that bordered the city emulated the serpentine Milky Way. People brought gold and silver into the city to pay homage to the gods but could not remove it under penalty of death.

The oldest structures of Cuzco were built of perfectly cut and shaped stones. Some stones called ashlars, of great size and unusual shapes, were fitted together with great precision and without mortar. The polygonal stones were joined so closely that a needle could not be passed between the two joints. How they shaped the stones remains a mystery, no tool marks provide clues.

Located above Cuzco on a promontory sits the citadel Sacsahuaman with its massive wall constructed of monolithic stones. The terraced wall measures 1500 feet long and 54 feet wide. It reaches 60 feet high, and the lower part of the wall contains colossal boulders weighing ten to twenty tons. One block is twenty-eight feet high and weighs 361 tons. Another structure, one-half mile away, has one stone estimated to weigh 20,000 tons. These stones also are polygonal shaped and fit precisely together without mortar, similar to the cyclopean construction of Cuzco. The mammoth blocks were quarried ten miles away and transported over mountains, valleys, and rivers. The Incas said their predecessors who possessed supernatural powers constructed the walls. Catholic priests assert the construction was done by diabolical means, and some say that magic and demons were used. Author Erich von Daniken suspects ancient astronauts constructed them, while author Bryford Jones speculates giants from another world moved the blocks. The Indians claim the gods built them. Legends of the Andes claim the giants and gods built them in an Old Empire where kingship began with a divine golden staff. Other traditions tell of the megaliths being built before the flood.

One tale describes an Inca king, during historical times, trying to emulate the achievement of his predecessors. To add to the fortifications, he tried to transport a colossal boulder from several miles away. Twenty thousand Indians hauled it across a mountain, but it slipped out of their grasp over a precipice and crushed more than three thousand men.

Spanish chronicler Fernando Montesinos arrived in Peru in 1628 and compiled a comprehensive history and prehistory of Peru. This resulted in his masterful publication of *Memorias Antiquas Histoiales de Peru* following twenty years of research. He concluded that the people originated from the biblical land before the kingdom of Israel. He was told by the natives that long before the Inca dynasty, an ancient empire existed there. After an era of growth and prosperity, the civilization was destroyed by upheaval, earthquakes, and wars, during which comets appeared in the sky.

Prior to the abandonment of Cuzco, there had been sixty-two kings who ruled the land, which included forty-six priest-kings and sixteen semidivine rulers. Before that, the gods themselves ruled, which correlated with legends found in Egypt and Mesopotamia. Scholars believe that chronicler Montesinos had come across the *Blas Valera* manuscript in LaPaz, Bolivia, and was allowed to copy from it. Blas Valera was a Spanish padre and one of the first to record the native prehistory tales. Other versions of his manuscript suggest that the true ancestors of the Inca were immigrants who arrived in Peru by ship.

The chronicles of Peru's kingship began with the journey of four Ayar brothers and their four sisters, whom were sent to find Cuzco with the aid of a golden staff. Chosen to be the first leader, Pirua Manco whose namesake is Peru, led the people to the Andes and founded the sacred Cuzco site. His son, Manco Capac, built a temple to the great god Viracocha. From that time on, the chronicles of the dynasties began, and Manco Capac was considered the son of the sun and the first of the sixteen rulers.

While in the reign of the fifth Capac, the calendar and chronology of time were renewed. Astrology was the principal science at that time. The people wrote on processed leaves of the plantain tree. The worship of the great god Ticci Viracocha was introduced.

During the reign of the twelfth Capac, according to Montesinus, giants settled on the entire coast, despoiling the land. The great God became upset, and destroyed the giants with heavenly fire. Relieved from the threat of giants, the people became complacent and abandoned the commandments and rites of worship.

They were then punished by the creator god with the twenty-hour disappearance of the sun.

In the reign of the fortieth Capac of Cuzco, an academy for the study of astronomy and astrology was established to determine the equinoxes. The fifth year of this reign, which was twenty-five hundred years from point zero, marked the Deluge. During the rule of the fifty-eighth monarch, Jesus Christ was born twenty-nine hundred years after the Deluge.

In the sixty-second monarch's reign, the first Cuzco Empire ended bitterly. Earthquakes, wars, and comets destroyed the civilization. Survivors moved to Tampu-Tocco where the dynasty lasted almost one thousand years, from the second century to the 16th century.

During the ninetieth monarchy, the fourth millennium from point zero, the monarch Ciboca became corrupted. Mama Ciboca proclaimed her young son, Rocca, was destined to rule the throne at the old capital, Cuzco. The ruler Inca disappeared and returned in golden robes. He asserted the sun god had taken him aloft and instructed him with secret knowledge, telling him to lead the people back to Cuzco. He became the first of fourteen of the Inca dynasty, which eventually ended with the Spanish conquest.

This began the Fifth Age, the age of human kings. The First Age was that of Viracocha, the gods who were white and bearded. The Second Age was that of giants who were in conflict with the gods, and a Third Age was that of primitive man of uncultured humans. An Age of Heros was the Fourth Age, when men were demigods.

Montesinos claimed the Peruvian monarchies began five hundred years after Point Zero, in 2400 B.C. Scholars had difficulty believing that kingship and urban civilization began at Cuzco thirty-five hundred years before the Incas. Sitchin suggests they may have been a third offshoot of the Sumerian civilization as were Egypt and the Indus in India.

An ancient tradition says a reigning king, who left Cuzco, led his followers to a refuge in the mountains called Tampu-Tocco. During that time, the art of writing was lost. Centuries passed, and periodically the kings went from Tampu-Tocco to Cuzco to consult divine oracles. After the abandonment of Cuzco by the king, twenty-eight successors reigned from the mountain refuge Tampu-

Tocco. Scholars were mystified about the location of Tampu-Tocco. In 1911 when Hiram Bingham of Yale University discovered the ruins of Machu Picchu, he believed he had found Tampu-Tocco. The writings of Montesinos left clues to its location. Inca Rocca had ordered the construction of a masonry wall with three windows that was to be the emblem of his father from whom he had descended. The wall represented the haven to which the royalty fled after Cuzco's destruction by earth changes. From here the tribes emerged, and the ancient empire of Peru began.

Only in Machu Picchu was there a structure with three windows as described in legend. Machu Picchu, the Quichua name, is a sharp peak that rises 10,000 feet above sea level and four hundred feet above the Urubamba River. Located seventy-five miles from Cuzco as the crow flies, it consists of twelve wards, as did Cuzco. The Sacred Plaza of Machu Piccchu faces the Great Terraced Plaza to the east. On two sides of the Sacred Plaza lay the two largest temples, made of cyclopean polygonal stones. One block has thirty-two angles. Finding the Temple of Three Windows led Bingham to believe he had found Tampu-Tocco.

Confirming the ancient construction of these cities, astronomy professor Rolf Muller of Potsdam concluded that the perfect ashlar structures of Machu Picchu and Cuzco were at least four thousand years old. His calculations centered on the Earth's wobble every seven thousand years. The archaeological sites were positioned for an era between 4000 and 2000 B.C. Structures from the pre-Inca age were built over two zodiac ages and the megalith structures belonged to the age of Taurus.

Cuzco, considered the universal sanctuary of the entire kingdom, contained the principal temples and shrines. When Manco Capac arrived at Cuzco, he built the Coricancha Temple in honor of the sun and it became the Inca's most sacred site and one of the most magnificent temples. Coricancha means the "house of gold," and gold was embedded in its chapel walls, ceilings, and altars. The Coricancha Temple, known as the Temple of the Sun, housed an ample contingency of priests who needed a large income to sustain them.

South of Lima, Peru, stood the largest temple dedicated to the deity, Pachacamal, the creator of the world who headed the pantheon. The pantheon included Vis (lord Earth) and Mama Pacha

(Lady Earth), a divine couple. Other members were Kon (hero god), Si (moon god), and Illa-Ra (sun god). Many names were similar to the deities' names of the Near East.

The temple of Pachacamal was a mecca for the ancient people living on the southern coasts. Over the years they made large offerings of gold to the gods. When the Spaniards arrived, they looted much of the gold. However, the priests hid most of it and refused to divulge its location. Rumor's claim it is still hidden somewhere between Lima and Lurin. The men under the command of Hernandez Pizarro pulled silver nails that held the gold and silver plates in place from out of the wall. The nails themselves weighed 32,000 ounces. Native tradition says giants built the temple, and the Incas later enlarged it. The temple, located on a mountainside overlooking the Pacific Ocean, stood on top of four platforms that supported a terrace five hundred feet above ground level.

When the Spaniards arrived in Cuzco, it was a thriving metropolis of 100,000 dwellings, and a city of magnificent temples, palaces, gardens, plazas, and roads. A sophisticated network of roads, 15,000 miles in length and extending along the Pacific Coast and Andean highlands, connected Cuzco to the Inca Empire. The roads ran from the northern border of Ecuador through the whole of Peru to central Chile. Two parallel roads ran north and south, each running for nearly six thousand miles. Both roads were paved and connected by frequent links. Suspension bridges crossed rivers, and tunnels bored through solid rock. These roads eventually led to the downfall of the Incas, when the Spanish used them to accelerate their advance.

VIRACOCHA AND ANDEAN SPIRITUALITY

The most important deity of the Andean Indians was Viracocha, the creator god in human form. Considered the great god from heaven, he came to Earth in an age of antiquity and chose the Andes as his creative arena. Native tradition placed the creation of the world at Lake Titicaca. Here, Viracocha created the sun, moon, and stars, along with all the tribes of the Andes, their languages, and customs. Father Acosta writes that after the Flood, ". . . the Indians report that out of the great Lake Titicaca came one Viracocha, which stayed in Tiahuanaco, where at this day there is to be seen the ruins of ancient and very strange buildings, and from there came to Cuzco and so mankind began to multiply." Other traditions emphasize Viracocha came at the same time a terrible deluge overcame the Earth and destroyed most of humanity. Some myths claim the Viracochas were white-skinned strangers and the original builders.

All the native nations of Peru have legends of a universal flood that followed humanity's beginning, with waters covering the highest peaks. Everyone perished in the Deluge except for a few, saved by the creator's divine providence to repopulate the world. The creator saved three or four people in each province by guiding them to a safe place. Each Indian nation claimed for itself the honor of having been the first people from whom all others originated. The Incas worshiped the cave of Pacaritampu because here their ancestors had escaped the destruction of the world. They claimed that all people originated from the cave. For that reason, all people were their vassals and obliged to serve them. Most of the tribes did not distinguish the creation of the world from the restoration after the Flood subsided. Along with Lake Titicaca, other sites have been claimed to be the centers of creation by Indian nations: Pachacama, Tiahuanaco, and a hill called Huanacauri outside Cuzco. Other legends say the will of Viracocha caused the Flood, and the first land to appear after the Flood was the Island of Titicaca.

Viracocha was the most holy of the deities. The Indians thought of him as a universal god and the sovereign lord and governor of all things. They did not give a proper name to the god but gave him a title, Ticci Viracocha, meaning divine origin. Accounts of Viracocha were handed down from person to person.

He had come in a time of chaos to right the world. The Earth was inundated by a great flood and plunged into darkness by the disappearance of the sun. Society, in great disorder, suffered much hardship. Tradition says a white man of large stature suddenly appeared from the south. This man had great power and made hills into valleys. He caused terraces and fields to be formed on the steep sides of ravines, and he instructed the Indians about agriculture and irrigation. He traveled along the highland route to the north, working marvels never before seen by the Indians, as he was a master of magic. He gave men instruction on how they should live and admonished them to be good and not to damage or injure one another. This man taught kindness and asked them to love one another and to show charity to all. He was a teacher, healer, scientist, architect, and engineer. Natives were taught writing by him. In most places this man was called Ticci Viracocha but was also known as Con, Thunupa, and Kon Tikki. Credited with initiating the long lost Golden Age, he carried out his civilizing mission with great kindness.

Viracocha was not an Indian but had a bushy beard with a pale complexion, suggesting he was Caucasian. An idol of Viracocha stood in the Holy of Holies in the Temple of Coricancha before the Spanish plundered it. It depicted him as lean, bearded, past middle age, white, wearing sandals, and dressed in a long, flowing cloak. One tradition describes his blue eyes and long gray hair. The Spanish likened him to Saint Thomas.

If threatened, according to Sitchin, Viracocha had at his disposal weapons of heavenly fire. One anecdote describes a group of Indians about to stone him when he sank to his knees and raised his hands to heaven, asking for help in his peril. The Indians observed fire in the sky all around them. Fire consumed their stones, and they also reported large blocks being lifted as if made of cork. They immediately asked for forgiveness. His command extinguished the fire.Viracocha proceeded to the coast, and holding his mantle, he disappeared amidst the waves and was seen no more. The Indians then gave him the name Viracocha, that means "foam of the sea."

Another legend says Viracocha carved great stone figures of giants, which he brought to life. The giants fought among themselves and refused to work. After deciding they must be destroyed, he turned some back into stone and others he overwhelmed with a great Flood.

The Spanish conquistadors came upon the tales of Viracocha everywhere. They heard of gigantic white men who had come from the sky, a race of sons of the sun who instructed humanity in all kinds of art and science.

Many similarities existed between Quetzalcoatl and Viracocha. Both were Christlike figures, fair-skinned, bearded, and dressed in a long, white robe. They were both itinerate deities who departed by sea, and promised to return.

Next to Viracocha, the god most highly honored was the sun. The Incas believed they were children of the sun and made every effort to enhance sun worship. The most magnificent temple of all was Coricancha, the Temple of the Sun. It housed a most venerated image called Panchau, shaped like a human face looking east, surrounded by sun rays. It too was plundered by the Spanish.

The worship of Chuqui Illa was ranked third in the hierarchy of worship. This god had power to make it rain or hail and was the deity in charge of providing water to the Indians.

The natives thought a patron lived in heaven for each of the animals and birds, and provided for the preservation and proliferation of each specie. They believed that all these patron deities came from the Pleiades, which they called Colla, and the power given these animals and birds flowed from this group of stars. They called the Pleiades Mother and kept tract of its course all year long, more than any other star system. All the native nations sacrificed to the Pleiades. They identified many other stars with species of animals, and for that reason they worshiped many stars. The stars represented the animals and planets represented the gods. Andean myths told that the helical rise of the Pleiades was a harbinger of the Deluge itself when the rise occurred thirty days before the June solstice.

Researcher William Sullivan in *The Secret of the Incas* describes the Deluge date as May 20, 650 A.D., based upon the myth of the Celestial Llama. At the time of the Flood, the Llama star formation was setting. The flood of 650 A.D. paralleled the helical rise of the Milky Way's cessation at June solstice. It was an event of exceptional importance to the priest astronomers of the Andes.

Andean religion taught that the reality of human obligation was laid out in exactitude in the heavens. The world of the living and of the unknown world was visible in the plane of our galaxy, the Milky Way. The Milky Way, in the pre-Columbian Andes, serves a river or road traveled by the gods and spirits of the dead. It was the ultimate abode of the dead, according to the native people, but the spirits of the dead must travel a long turbulent road to reach this abode.

Capri Raymi, the Inca festival of the dead, culminated at the December solstice. At this time, the dead returned to Earth to reanimate the power of tradition by communicating with the living. During this ritual, the living caroused with their dead ancestors in days of eating and drinking with them as if they were alive. The mummified remains of the Inca kings and all the wakas (representatives of tribe lineage) were brought from various shrines into the main plaza. At dawn, at the moment of the helical rise of the Milky

Way on the solstice, the souls of the dead ancestors returned. At this moment, the entrance to this other world's realm lay open. The ritual use of the concha trumpet kept open the routes between the physical world and the home of the dead. It was sounded on the eve of the December solstice. When the dead ancestors returned to Earth, they were returning from the abode of their lineage, the Celestial Llama: Alpha Centauri and Hadas are the two stars known as the eye of the Llama. The conch stood for the December solstice, the Milky Way rising, and the entrance to the land of the dead.

All the native nations believed the soul was immortal, that good people were rewarded in the afterlife, and that bad people were punished. A good person could become a star, and bad people would suffer eternally. Some native nations believed souls that left human bodies in one life would be reborn in another life, the principle of reincarnation. Some nations believed afflicted souls remained in the world, wandering around alone, suffering from hunger, thirst, chill, heat, and fatigue. These soul apparitions visited members of their family, and today they would be called ghosts. Families were always careful to celebrate birthdays of the deceased.

The Incas worshiped the dead body as if it were a god. They embalmed the body with great skill and care, preserving it for many years so it would not deteriorate or give off a foul odor. They kept none of the personal property of their dead, placing part with the deceased, and buried some in locations where the deceased had enjoyed themselves. Relatives looked after the bodies, wrapped them in cotton and often kept them in their house. However, the bodies of Inca kings were placed in the Temple of the Sun. Attendants often sustained themselves on farmland that the deceased had designated for that purpose. During major festivals, they brought out the bodies.

Often an important man or woman was assigned to a body, and whatever the man or woman wanted became the will of the deceased. If they felt like a drink, they said the deceased was making a request. Many natives devoted themselves to caring for dead bodies. Descendants made large offerings to ensure proper care of the bodies. As the deceased's children or grandchildren died, the deceased were often forgotten.

The Spanish priests described the Incas as so idolatrous that they worshiped almost every thing created. Peruvian kings required all conquered people to give up their religion if it differed with the Inca religion and to adopt the Inca theology. The Incas accepted the gods of the conquered people and restored them to honor and gave sacrifice to them. The Indians used two names to describe their gods, *vilca* and *quaca*.

During their lifetime, the king and lords made statues depicting themselves called *quauque*. The kings gave their *quauque* a house and servants, and assigned farmland to support those in charge of the statue. People treated the *quauque* with the same reverence as they did the king himself. After the king or lord died, the statue was kept with the body and both were equally respected. Occasionally, armies carried the statue thinking it would ensure victory; they believed the *quauque* had the same powers as the bodies of the owners.

From the Temple of the Sun, certain lines radiated out which the Indians called *ceques,* corresponding to the four royal roads leading from Cuzco. On each of these *ceques* were arranged in order the *quacas* and shrines as in Cuzco. They kingship units and families of Cuzco maintained them like stations of holy places.

Sacrifices were often forced rather than made willingly. The first sacrifice was made to each god from the personal property of the Inca. Sacrifices made to Viracocha came from the property of all the gods. Sacrifices were so common and costly that they consumed most of the Inca's income. They made offerings to honor the gods, to support priests and attendants, to pay for medical practitioners and diviners, and to have questions answered.

The most authoritative sacrifice, human blood, was made only to the major gods. When the Inca conquered other nations, they selected many very attractive individuals and brought them back to Cuzco. They sacrificed them in honor of the victory. Human sacrifices were not frequent. Children were also sacrificed, and some were voluntarily offererd by the priests. They killed more females than males, usually under the age of ten, but some older females, fifteen or sixteen, were sacrificed. Maidens were kept in a convent, and only those without a blemish or mole were selected for sacrifice. Before sacrifice, they were given plenty to eat, and the older ones would get drunk. The victims were marched around an idol two or three times before being strangled or having their throats slit. The priests then smeared the faces of the idols with the blood.

From childhood, some girls were consecrated to their idols and lived in a convent. They were virgins called *mamma conas,* meaning esteemed mother. The girls learned religion, rites, ceremonies, and how to serve their gods. If they lost their virginity, they were often buried alive, as would be the accomplice. The maidens were married to their gods and considered to be their wives. People greatly respected the *mamma conas.*

THE NAZCA FIGURES

An enigma on the high Nazca Plateau in southern Peru, are the famous Nazca lines that baffle archaeologists. These lines depict a heron nine hundred feet long, a huge whale, pelicans, a gigantic condor, birds, fish, triangles, and a pair of parallel lines nearly two miles long.

Indian legends tell of demigods, called the Viracochas, who made the figures thousands of years ago. They were not man-made according to the Indian ancestors.

These figures have remained for thousands of years, some speculate due to the extreme dryness of the region. The Nazca Plateau is one of the driest places on Earth, receiving only a trace of moisture each decade, allowing these intriguing figures to remain intact. The dry climate also prevents a populated region. Pottery, dated between 350 B.C. and 600 A.D., has been discovered on the plateau. Scholars have no means of dating the lines, but some place the most recent date as fourteen hundred years old. They could be much older.

Eighteen different birds and numerous animals are depicted on the thirty-seven-mile long plateau. Drawings depict geometric shapes, including straight lines, triangles, rectangles, and trapezoids. The geometric forms intersect the animal drawings, suggesting the drawings were done in two stages. Scholars conjecture primitive tribes called Narzcans who have since vanished drew the figures. The depictions are enormous. The hummingbird is 165 feet long, a spider is 150 feet long, the condor measures 400 feet, and a lizard measures 617 feet. Some geometric forms are more than five miles long. Only the condor is indigenous to the region. The spider depiction is of a rare genus found only in an inaccessible part of the rain forest.

Some drawings depict peculiar human forms whose heads are enclosed in radiant halos. Author Graham Hancock describes them as "looking like visitors from another planet."

Astronomer Phillis Pitulga conducted computer-aided research of the stellar alignments at Nazca. Her study concluded that the spider figure depicted a terrestrial diagram of the constellation of Orion. Through the ages, the straight lines linked to the spider appear to have been set out to track declination of the three stars of Orion's Belt.

The Nazca lines were first identified this century with the advent of the airplane. Graham Hancock describes the figures as so perfectly made, that the creator could have checked the progress only with aid of aircraft. No natural elevation lay close enough to provide a proper vantage point.

From ground level, the Nazca lines appear like grazes on the surface made by scraping away thousands of tons of black volcanic pebbles. This exposed the yellow sand and clay of the desert base. Viewed from aloft, the geometric shapes appear as a jumble of runways. This lead Erich von Daniken in *Chariots of the Gods* to speculate that they may have been landing strips for the gods, meaning landing strips for alien spaceships. Hancock states the cleared areas are only a few inches deep and much too soft to permit the landing of wheeled vehicles. No one really knows the purpose or age of the Nazca lines.

On the high desert plateau of Marcahausi at an elevation over 12,500 feet, drawings depict camels and lions which have not existed in South America within the past 10,000 years. A peculiar drawing on the cliffs in the Bay of Pisco is nearly 820 feet high and shaped like a gigantic trident or three branched candlestick. A long rope found on the central column of the depiction suggests it served as a pendulum. Approaching by sea, one can see the colossal figure from a distance of twelve miles.

Chapter Ten

ANCIENT MEDITERRANEAN
AND EUROPEAN CIVILIZATIONS
Remnants of Atlantis?

Megalithic ruins whose origins cannot be accounted for abound in regions of the Mediterranean and Europe. They have been found on the islands of Malta, Sardinia, Corsica, Sicily, Crete, and the Balearic Islands, and discovered in France, Spain, Great Britain, Germany, and Scandinavia. Archaeologists have discovered two hundred known sunken cities in the Mediterranean.

A hallmark characteristic of Atlantean architecture, according to Atlantologists, are Cyclopean megalithic blocks that are polygonal in design, fitted precisely to adjacent blocks without mortar. Because the stones are fitted in a jigsaw manner, Cyclopean architecture can withstand the shock of an earthquake. The blocks may move and jiggle with the shock, but the wall generally does not collapse because the interlocking blocks settle back into place. This polygonal Cyclopean construction is found on mainland Greece, Egypt, Turkey, Spain, Morocco, and Malta; across the ocean in Peru, Bolivia, Ecuador, Mexico; and off the Bahama island of Bimini.

Quarries of these megalithic blocks have been found at Pieria, Greece; Ba'albek in the Middle East; in Wales and Ireland; in the Bolivian Altiplano twenty miles from Tiahuanaco; and Mitla in Mexico. Definite patterns of parallel grooves are found in the quarry walls, meaning that extremely sophisticated machines were used to loosen huge blocks up to forty-five feet long with extreme precision. Thousands of these blocks have been transported to unknown locations, while others still lay in the quarry suggesting the quarry was suddenly abandoned. The parallel grooves had been partially melted away, and small pores were seen over the entire surface. Greek author Konstantine Zissis observed that today's technology does not allow us to drill in that way, and what caused the melting remains a mystery. Zissis believes the quarries were of Atlantean origin. In Greece, the "Quarry of the Gods" is located near Mount Olympus, considered the abode of the Greek gods. Thousands of these megalithic blocks lay in megalithic cities beneath the sea, according to Solon, who heard this from the ancient Egyptian priests. This suggests that the floor of the Mediterranean Sea was once above sea level.

David Hatcher Childress in his book *Lost Cities of Atlantis, Ancient Europe, and the Mediterranean* addresses this dilemma. Archaeologist Childress, through academic and hands-on research, wrote a number of books addressing the prehistoric civilizations in his Lost City Series. His writings tell of an Osirian civilization, 15,000 years ago, highly advanced and contemporary with Atlantis. A parallel civilization existed in India called the Rama civilization. These civilizations, according to esoteric tradition, possessed a high degree of technology. They had magnificent cities, ancient roads, trade routes, and busy seaports. Thriving commercial centers were found in India, China, Peru, Mexico, and Osiris.

Tradition tells that at the time of Atlantis and Rama, the Mediterranean was a large, fertile valley and not a sea. The Nile River flowed out of Africa, and in that era was called the River Styx. After turning westward, it flowed into a series of lakes south of Crete, then flowed between Malta and Sicily south of Sardinis, and finally emptied into the Atlantic Ocean at Gilbralter, referred to as the Pillars of Hercules.

The large, fertile valley of the River Styx was known as the Osirian civilization and included the Sahara, then a vast fertile plain. The Osirian civilization was considered "pre-Dynastic Egypt". In this era the Sphinx and pre-Egyptian megaliths, such as the Osirion at Abydos, were built. During the latter warlike years of Atlantis, it invaded the Osirian Empire and war raged throughout the world. Ancient Greece was closely connected to the Osirian civilization. Before the cataclysmic end, Atlantis invaded Greece, as was told to Solon.

Osiris, according to Egyptian legend, was born of the earth and sky. Being the first king of Egypt, Osiris mentored civilization. He eliminated barbaric ways, taught agriculture, formulated laws, and taught the importance of worshiping the gods. Tradition also tells that Osiris was a king of Atlantis prior to Egypt. Many believe

Poseidonis or Poseidon, the legendary king of Atlantis, was the same person as Osiris.

Megalithic ruins at Abydos in southern Egypt are known as the Osirion ruins of "pre-Dynastic Egypt." They include huge granite blocks, some with a thick knob used for moving the stones. The lack of inscription on the Osirion, similar to the Sphinx, suggests it was built before the use of hieroglyphics. Other megalithic ruins of Egypt lay underwater at Alexandria, Egypt. Childress writes that virtually every Mediterranean island of any size has prehistoric megaliths on it, but most are not polygonal.

Ba'albek is an archaeological site forty-four miles east of Beirut consisting of many ruins and catacombs twenty-five hundred feet long. It has one of the largest stone structures in the world. Ancient Arabic writings tell of the first Ba'al Astarte Temple being built by a tribe of giants shortly after the Flood under orders of the legendary King Nimrod. The ruins are considered by some to be remnants of the Osirian Empire.

Today the ruins of a Roman era temple site are found built upon gigantic stone blocks at Ba'albek. The huge stone blocks, called the "Trilithon," lay beneath the Roman temple and are composed of three blocks of hewn stone, believed to be the largest blocks in the world ever used in construction. By conservative estimates, the largest block weighing one thousand tons and measures thirteen feet by fourteen feet by seventy feet. The perfectly fitted stone had been raised twenty feet to lay on top of smaller blocks, a feat that could not be replicated with today's technology, and the quarry was located one-half mile away.

The pre-Roman temple was dedicated to the ancient god Ba'al and his consort Astarte, while the Roman temple built on top was dedicated to the gods Jupiter and Venus. Pilgrims from ancient Mesopotamia and the Nile valley made journeys to visit the Temple of Ba'al Astarte. Massive blocks similar to those of Ba'albek provide the foundation ashlars of the Wailing Wall in Jerusalem, the site of King Solomon's Temple.

THE HITTITES

In 1905, an unknown civilization came to light in Turkey when German Professor Hugo Winckler, an Assyriologist, discovered some ancient cuneiform texts with a mysterious form of hiero-glyphics. This civilization turned out to be the Hittites, referred to in the Bible. They left behind tens of thousands of inscribed clay tablets. This suggested the Hittites were not indigenous to the area, but were Indo-Europeans who migrated from the north, possibly from the Danube region. Atlantologists believe the Hittites may have descended from the Atlanteans.

Achaeologist James Mellaart excavated an ancient city, Catal Huyak, on the Turkish Anatolian Plateau. It was a Stone Age town nearly nine thousand years old. The Hittite people who dwelled there were considered tall for that time, with the men averaging five feet seven inches and the women five feet two inches. Their dwellings ranged in size from 520 square feet to 120 square feet, intended for no more than eight people. This ancient civilization included farmers who raised barley, wheat, peas, and lentils; the remains of domesticated cattle and dogs were also found. A copper cylinder was unearthed, proving people knew how to smelt copper eight thousand years ago.

Ruins discovered there dated to 5900 B.C. and had effigies of both male and female gods, the latter predominating, and suggest-ing a great respect for the mother goddess. With domesticated ani-mals and crops, women were associated with the importance of fer-tility in agriculture. This civilization worshiped the bull, as the bull cult had survived over seven thousand years. This linked the proto-Haitian Antolis with the Hittite Empire. Plato's writings tell of the strong spiritual connection between Atlanteans and the bull. Mellaart found a total of sixty-three cult buildings and one hundred three dwellings, suggesting an unusual dedication to this religion.

One hundred miles east of Ankara, Turkey, Bogazkoy stands in the central Antolian Plateau at an elevation of three thousand feet. The ruins discovered there are referred to as Hattusa, an ancient Hittite city. On this 420-acre site the cuneiform tablets were uncovered.

The texts related to Mesopotamia, as a few of the Hittite gods were traceable to Mesopotamia, and the texts were written in Babylonia Akkadian cuneiform. Their language was unrelated to any known tongue at that time, and for years it went undeciphered. The language was originally christened Arzawa, because it was found written in a cuneiform script on two clay tablets discovered in 1887 at El Amarna, Egypt. It was later rechristened Hittite after the Hattusa find.

Scholars found a resemblance between Sanskrit and various European languages. Fifteen language groups are similar in respect to vocabulary and grammatical structure, including Celtic, Italic (Latin), Romance languages, Germanic, Baltic, Slavic, Greek, Armenian, Iranian, Indo-Aryan, and Hittite. A linguistic connection between India and European languages led to the Indo-European language family, formerly the Indo-Germanic language family. Bedrich Hozney discovered an Indo-Germanic formation of Hittite, causing a debate over whether the Hittites were ancient Germans. Historians today acknowledge that four thousand years ago, Asia Minor received an influx of Indo-Germanic migrants who imposed their language and politics over a wide area. They became a great power whose influence was felt over all of Asia Minor to Syria. The ancients called the Turkish region Asia Minor, as its outline paralleled the larger continent, even though it is no larger than Spain or California.

By the turn of the century, almost a hundred Hittite-inscribed monuments had been discovered. The hieroglyphics, which existed side by side with the cuneiform texts, still remained a mystery. They were difficult to decipher, and the authors were unknown. A Hittite stele, written in Phoenician and Hittite, provided the key for decipherment. It turned out to be a dialect of Arzawa. Hittite text was read in an ox-plow system, left to right, right to left, and so on, such as the Rondo writings of Easter Island and Doric, Greece.

The Hittites appeared in the Old Testament as a Palestinian tribe before the Israelite conquest. They are one of the ten tribes listed in Genesis 15:19-21. According to the Bible they descended from Cath (Hath), the second son of Canaan. The Bible tells that the Hittites lived somewhere in the tract of land between the Nile and Mesopotamia suggesting they lived south of Jerusalem at Hebron. Abraham's wife Sarah died at Hebron at the age of 127, and Abraham wanted to bury her in a cave. The land and cave belonged to the Hittites who offered the land free to Abraham, but Abraham insisted on paying for the land with a deed of sale. It was in this biblical story of Abraham's acquisition that the Hittites were first mentioned in the Bible. The Old Testament also mentions the Hittites as being forced laborers engaged in the construction of King Solomon's Temple in Jerusalem. Ironically, in Numbers 13:29-30, the Bible credits the Hittites with founding Jerusalem. The Syrians also mentioned them as allies of Israel being on a par with the Egyptians. The Hittites called the area in which they lived the land of Haiti.

Many similarities exist between the Hittites, Mayans, Egyptians, and Atlanteans. Hittites had high-bridged noses that went to the middle of their foreheads, which some described as high domed foreheads that merged directly with their noses. This profile was much like the Maya's profile. Their personal seals were identical to the Mayans, and important political announcements were made on stone stelae. Atlantologists claim the Atlanteans wore pointed shoes and long conical caps. Hittites also wore pointed shoes and long pointed caps. They were credited with inventing the chariot, and much like the Atlanteans, the horse was important to them.

The Hittites used Cyclopean architecture with giant megalithic polygonal blocks fitted perfectly together. Cyclopean walls of Heptose provided fortification with unprecedented splendor, as the city precincts were enclosed by a stone wall nineteen feet high and twenty-five feet thick. The Lion Gate is the best known gate of Hattusa. It is flanked by a pair of lions carved into the huge outer gate stone, their gaping jaws repelling the forces of evil. Scholars conclude that these Cyclopean walls of huge irregular polygonal blocks did not occur at Hattusa before the arrival of the Hittites. Hattusa's great temple with its ancillary buildings occupied an area measuring 550 feet by 440 feet.

Like the Egyptians, the Hittites carved massive granite sphinxes of Cyclopean scale. They also worshiped the sun, with the winged disk being the symbol of their sun god, as it was in Egypt and Sumer. Childress writes that the Hittites and Egyptians were the last holdovers from the civilization who arose immediately after the Flood and the time of Atlantis. He believes they were the survivors of Atlantis who became the early seafarers known as the Atlantean League.

Hittites were great seamen thought to be the first to repopulate the islands of Cyprus and Crete after the Mediterranean flooded, writes Childress. These early sailors of 6000 B.C. ultimately became the Phoenicians, according to some scholars. They sailed to northern Europe and controlled the important tin trade from England. Evidence will be presented in the next chapter that they also sailed across the Atlantic to the Americas. By 3000 B.C., they mined pure copper in northern Michigan, and traded weapons to the Maya and Toltecs, and even made their way to the high Andes.

Frank Edwards writes in *Strange Worlds* that the Hittites were among the many ancient cultures who traveled to America. In 1921, Elwood Hummel was fishing in Pennsylvania where he discovered a small flat stone with strange markings. The markings, translated by scholars at the Field Museum in Chicago, detailed a small loan made by an Assyrian merchant in Cappadocia eighteen hundred years before Christ. The artifact perfectly matched the many cuneiform tablets found at the Hittite site at Hattusa. The Assyrians navigated up the river from Mesopotamia, according to historians, to trade with the Hittites, and recorded business transactions on the cuneiform tablets.

In 1896, two woodsmen clearing land on a farm near Newberry, Michigan, uprooted a tree to find three statues and a clay tablet written in Hittite-Minoan. They sent photos of the tablet and the statues to the Smithsonian Institute where they disappeared. Accusations of a cover-up were made against the Institute. It is improbable that the Hittite tablet was forged, because the Hittites were not discovered until nine years later.

Proto-Indic writings found at Hattusa associated the Hittites with the world of ancient India. The country lying between the Hittites and Mesopotamia, an Indic-Hindu state known as Mittani, maintained its ancient links to India. They held the age-old Hindu Dravidian beliefs in reincarnation, cremation, karma, and avatars. Mittani's most famous citizen was Nefertiti who became wife of the Egyptian Pharaoh Akherraton.

Tolerant of other religions, the Hittites did not impose their own gods on the Anatolian (Turkish) population, nor did they Hittenize their adopted deities, as did the Romans. They held equal respect for a multitude of deities. They viewed the gods as immortal human beings. A king had the ability to become divine and require worship after death, because all that distinguished him from the living was immortality in the realm of the dead. As in Sumer, the gods were masters and humans were servants, and sacrifices bound men and their gods. Once man made a sacrifice to the god, it placed the god under obligation. Each village had its own protective deity, cult center mythology, and festival calendar linked mainly to the agricultural year.

The deities and Hittite pantheon had their roots in Sumer. Deities such as Anu, Enlil, and Ea were introduced to the Hittites through the Hurrian religion. The Hittites also worshiped the goddess Ishtar who aided them in battle and was known as "Lady of the Battlefield." The god Marduk had been exiled among the Hittites before his second return to Babylon when he became ruler around 2024 B.C.

Teshub, the weather god, was the Hittite supreme deity also known as the storm god associated with winds, thunder, and lightening. He was nicknamed Taru (bull) and depicted as the god of thunder and lightening mounted upon a bull. Teshub was the husband of Arinna, the national sun goddess of the Hittites called Queen of Haiti land. The texts describe a great battle by the god Kumarbi against Teshub that ranged in both the sky and sea. Teshub was supported by seventy gods riding in chariots.

Archaeological finds show that the Hittites worshiped gods of both heaven and earth. Gods among the Hittites acted as supreme rulers of the land. They later appointed human kings and gave advice on war, treaties, and foreign affairs. These roles of ancient gods were similar to those found in Sumer and Egypt. Zecharia Sitchin believes Sumerians had a strong influence on the Hittites, because the Hittites used the Sumerian language. They employed Sumerian pictographs, signs, symbols, and even whole words. The Hittite language and several Indo-European dialects were influenced by Akkadian, which was the international language of the second millennium B.C.

The Hittites, like the Egyptians and Sumerians, appeared to arrive on the scene with a fully developed culture that did not rise from a primitive state. It was a world of mighty armies, magic spells, sorcerers, and massive fortresses. Hittites built huge megalithic cities and controlled the early iron industry of the Middle East. Their cities and parts of the capital were destroyed by a devastating war. Many of the ruins were vitrified, indicating intense heat from an unknown weapon.

They were conquered by a mysterious people called the Sea People who used quite sophisticated tactics. During the 12th century B.C., the Sea People captured Cyprus and all of coastal Asia Minor. The ancient Hittite cities of Ugarit on the Syrian coast and Byblos on the Lebanese coast were conquered and occupied by these mysterious seafarers. Ugarit was a major trading site for the Mediterranean and the civilizations on the Tigris and Euphrates Rivers. Ugarit was destroyed by the Sea Peoples about 1170 B.C., and some ruins had been vitrified, which fused brick and stone with a glasslike glaze. Vitrification requires extreme heat such as that of nuclear weapons. A mysterious substance known as "Greek Fire," mainly used in naval warfare and launched by catapults from the ships, could cause vitrification. It set the ships on fire and could not be put out with water; it could burn underwater. The chemical composition that produced this fire remains a mystery.

The Hittites signed a treaty with Egypt following a great battle at Kadesh (in present Lebanon) between the Hittites and Ramses II in 1286 B.C. The god Amon-Ra fought alongside Ramses in the battle and allowed Ramses to make a miraculous escape after being trapped by the Hittites. The battle caused Egypt to retreat but also drained the Hittite resources. A treaty was signed after the death of the Hittite King Muwatallis when the reigning Egyptian pharaoh took a Hittite princess for his wife.

After five hundred years of being a great empire, the Hittites were finally defeated. The Sea People, thought by some scholars to include the Minoans and Myceneans, gained control of the Mediterranean coast of Canaan. They became the biblical Philistines, and the area was later called Phoenicia.

THE MINOAN EMPIRE

The mysterious Sea People, now thought by academicans to have included the Minoans, originated from Crete and the islands of Greece. Some scholars have identified the people of Crete with the culture of Atlantis. The Minoan Empire was identified with Crete, whose empire extended throughout the Aegean Sea, and included a group of islands known as the Cyclades and parts of mainland Greece. Greek professor Angelos Galanopoulos believed that one of the Cycladic islands was as important to the Minoans as Crete was.

He believed that this volcanic island was the site of the lost Atlantis, which had undergone a gigantic volcanic eruption 25,000 years ago and another about 1500 B.C., when much of the island sank. Galanopoulos believed the Atlantis that Plato described was Thera, and that an error in translation, from Egyptian hieroglyphics to Greek, had been made by a factor of ten for every numerical symbol. Oceanographer James Mavor of the Oceanographic

Institution in Massachusetts became a believer of this theory. Mavor designed a miniature submarine that could reach depths to six thousand feet, and this sub retrieved a nuclear bomb from the floor of the Mediterranean Sea. Mavor explored this hypothesis in his book titled *Voyage to Atlantis, The Discovery of a Legendary Land* describing the research conducted on the underwater ruins around Thera. Most Atlantologists disagree Thera was Plato's Atlantis but believe that Atlantis left its legacy of ruins with Thera and Crete.

The Minoan culture on Crete laid the foundation for Greek civilization, flourishing from around 2700   to 1400 B.C. The Minoans had evolved from the Neolithic Period during the third millennium B.C. and developed into a peaceful, metal-using, mercantile society with a sensual love of exquisite art. The Minoans built their culture similar to the Atlantean one as described by Plato.

Today, Crete's most popular tourist attraction is the spreading palace of Knossos, which gives evidence that Crete was a highly developed civilization in ancient times. Excavations showed this prosperous civilization had a great taste for naturalistic art and sculpture. An estimated 30,000 to 82,000 people are thought to have lived at Knossos, a city unfortified, suggesting the people enjoyed a life of peace and tranquility. Nicknamed the labyrinth, Knossos has been described as a city with confusing mass streets and buildings, easy to get lost in.

Like Atlantis, the bull was important in Cretan mythology as demonstrated in a legend regarding Zeus. While looking down from atop the highest mountain of Crete, he observed a beautiful Phoenician princess, Europa, on a distant shore. While she was picking flowers, she saw a huge bull in front of her that approached her in a friendly manner. The bull suddenly turned and ran into the sea with Europa grasping onto his back. The terrified Europa held on as the bull swam to Crete. As they came ashore on the sandy beach of Matala in Crete, the bull suddenly transformed into Zeus. Europa and Zeus spent that night together, and she conceived three sons. Europa eventually married the King of Crete who adopted her children. One son, Minos, for nine years as a youth, went to the cave where Zeus was born, and Zeus instructed him on kingship and the laws of the land. Minos became King of Crete and established sovereignty over the whole Mediterranean, making Crete the master of the sea.

Mycenae was the center of the Mycenaean civilization located on the mainland of southern Greece. Greatly influenced by the Minoan Empire, it reached its height around 1400 to 1200 B.C. The Cyclopean walls in Mycenae are identical to those found in Peru. Both cultures used the trapezoidal doorway that tapered toward the top. The huge columns depicting gods and warriors that held up gigantic temples in Knossos and Karnak were similar to those found in Mitla and Chichen Itza in Mexico. Archaeologist Pierre Honore writes in his book *In Quest of the White God* that the seafaring Minoans influenced both Central and South America. He claimed the white gods came from Crete and other countries in the eastern Mediterranean.

The ruins of Stonehenge show many similarities to those of the Minoan culture. Some pegs used in socket joints at Stonehenge were similar to the joints used in the gateways of Mycenae. The manner in which Stonehenge's stones were shaped and dressed indicated a Minoan influence.

When Professor Cyrus H. Gordon deciphered the earliest Minoan script, he discovered a Semitic dialect from the shores of the eastern Mediterranean countries. He believed the Minoans became the Phoenicians after departing the Aegean.

The Mycenean culture from Greece began to permeate the Minoan culture. They were of European stock and were aggressive individualists with warlike tendencies and great bowman abilities. The end times for the Minoan civilization who remained on Crete were thought to have come about through local earthquakes that lasted over several decades. Nowhere in the world is there such an accumulation of earthquake data as in Greece. (More than two thousand severe earthquakes have been recorded in the past two hundred years, registering 4.75 or more on the Richter scale). Earthquakes destroyed settlements on Crete. In 1500 B.C., the European cultures lost contact with the Minoans. Later many people from mainland Greece settled in great number on Crete, and a Mycenaean colony replaced the Minoan Empire of previous centuries.

The Mycenaen culture began its sudden demise about 1200 B.C. Theories on its collapse range from an invasion by the mysterious Dorians from the north to a prolonged drought to the frequent earthquakes. About this time, the Hittites and Egyptians began their conflict with the Sea People coming from Crete.

PHOENICIANS AND THE ANCIENT MEDITERRANEAN

The Phoenicians developed a reputation for being the best sailors and navigators of the ancient world. Dimitri Baramki, a Phoenician researcher and curator at the University Archaeological Museum in Lebanon, does not believe the Phoenicians developed sea prowess on their own accord. Rather through fusion with foreign invaders, the Phoenicians gained their sea knowledge. The Sea People, Baramki asserts, ravaged part of Lebanon and joined with the Canaanites to become the Phoenicians.

The whole of Palestine was basically Canaanite before the Hebrews arrived after the Egyptian exodus in the 13th century B.C. Canaan lay west of the Jordan River and the Dead Sea, and east of the Mediterranean Sea in present day-Israel. Egypt exercised sovereign control over Canaan during the Middle Bronze Age (1900 to1550 B.C.) . However, the Egyptians spoke of an independent monarch in Tyre (in present Lebanon) who formed a great Mediterranean network that linked Egypt, Syria, and Mesopotamia. The Phoenicians could not be differentiated from the general mass of Canaanites until the latter half of the second millennium B.C. By the 14th century B.C., a group of Semitic inhabitants of Canaan became known as the Kinanu, and this group also became known as the Phoenicians. By 1200 B.C., the only independent Canaanite area was the central coastal area called Phoenicia.

Phoenicia lay between the Lebanon chain of mountains, nine thousand feet high, and the Lervant coast of the Mediterranean. The narrow strip of land was very fertile, but as the population grew, it could not support itself. The people could never prosper by agriculture or export alone, one reason they turned to the sea. The four most important cities of Phoenicia were Aradus, Byblos, Sidon, and Tyre.

Byblos is the only city in the Phoenicia homeland of which there is much knowledge. Twenty-eight miles north of Beirut, its own tradition calls it the oldest city in the world. Founded by the god El, it became the most important center of Astarte worship. Artifacts dated around 1800 B.C. have been unearthed at Byblos, where Isis recovered the body of Osiris.

Tyre, on the Mediterranean coast, was another important city of Phoenicia. King Hiram of Tyre (970 to 940 B.C.) was an ally of

King David and King Solomon of Israel. He provided materials and labor to help build King Solomon's Temple in Jerusalem. Many rites of Freemasonry are based on the legend of King Hiram and the building of the temple. Thirteen years after the Babylonian King Nebuchadnezzar captured Jerusalem and enslaved the Jews in 587 B.C., Tyre was defeated following a long siege. In 539 B.C., the Babylonian monarch was overthrown by the Persians. The Phoenician fleets became an important factor in the Persian sea campaign against Greece, even though Phoenicia lost her independence. In 332 B.C. Alexander the Great defeated Tyre.

The Phoenicians always sought advantageous sites for their colonies. They established colonies at some of the best natural fortresses and harbor sites in the Mediterranean Sea. Carthage, on the north coast of Africa in present Tunisia, became the most important and famous colony established in 814 B.C. The circular port was reminiscent of Poseidonis, the Atlantean capital as described by Plato. The port contained docks for up to 220 vessels. Phoenicians living in Carthage were called Punics. During the famous Punic wars, Rome defeated Carthage in 146 B.C.

The Carthaginians went to great extremes not to talk about their profitable sea routes. They exaggerated the dangers and difficulties to frighten sailors of other nations from attempting the dangerous voyages. They talked about the lack of breezes, the dangerous seaweed (the Sargasso Sea), and the great sea monsters. To secure control of the western sea routes, Carthaginian warships were known to stop non-Carthaginian ships and throw their sailors overboard.

The Phoenician sea power dominated from about 1200 B.C., after the Minoan and Mycenean merchants were defeated by northern invaders. The Phoenicians traded cedars from Lebanon, their famous purple dye, fine clothes, metalworks, and agricultural products. Sometimes they acted as middlemen, carrying products from Greece and Egypt. During the fifth century B.C. the earliest coinage was struck.

Carthage developed a western trade route with the African hinterland, and the Phoenicians discovered Great Britain's great tin resources. They established the first trade route to Cornwall, made famous for its tin exports. Colonies were also established in Gades (Cadiz), Spain, in Malta, and Sicily.

Some scholars believe the Carthaginians became the Toltecs of

Mexico, as the Toltecs looked much like the invaders of the Mediterranean. Both had long, thick beards; helmets; spears; and shields. Chichen Itza was originally a Mayan city until the bearded Toltecs invaded it. Remnants of the Toltecs have been found in the American Southwest, and many Phoenician inscriptions have been found all over the Americas. The theory is that after the Punic Wars, Carthaginians and Phoenicians fled across the Atlantic Ocean to the Americas.

The mystery remains of how bearded people settled in Central America, as the native Indians grew no facial hair. Characters in the reliefs carved on walls and columns of Chichen Itza have Semitic facial features, which led various researchers to identify them as Phoenicians or "Seafaring Jews." Some hypothesize they were blown off course and carried by the Atlantic current to the shores of Yucatan. This occurred when King Solomon and King Hiram of Tyre joined forces to send maritime expeditions to Africa in search of gold about 1000 B.C. Spanish chronicler Fernando Montesisnos saw in the name Peru a phonetic rendering of the biblical name Ophir. Ophir was the name of the famous land of gold, which supplied the Phoenicians with gold for the temple in Jerusalem.

Other evidence links Phoenicia to the Americas. The pantheon of the South American Indians was similar to that of the Phoenicians, Hittites, Canaanites, Greeks, and Egyptians. An inscription turned up at a north Brazilian archaeological site in 1872, a message left by the captain of a Phoenician ship. A storm had separated the ship from its sister ships around 534 B.C. when it sailed from the Near East. The name Brazil is similar to the Semitic term Barzel, meaning iron.

Very accurate European maps leading to the "Age of Discovery" were based on Phoenician cartography, especially the maps of Marinus of Tyre. Graham Hancock writes in *Fingerprints of the Gods* about Professor Charles Hapgood. Hapgood claimed that the world had been comprehensively mapped before 4000 B.C. by an unknown and undiscoverable civilization with an advanced level of technology: "It appears (Hapgood concluded) that accurate information has been passed down from people to people. It appears that the charts must have originated with a people unknown and they were passed, perhaps by the Minoans and the Phoenicians, who were for a thousand years and more, the greatest sailors of the world. We have evidence they were collected and studied in the great Library of Alexandria (Egypt) and that compilation of them was made by the geographers who worked there."

Many maps from pre-Columbian times have been discovered. Some include the outline of the Americas and Antarctica, whose coastline is now obscured by ice. The most famous map is the Piri Re'is map belonging to a Turkish admiral dated 1513 A.D. The admiral noted on the map that it was partly based on maps used by Columbus. It correctly depicts the South American Pacific Coast and Andean mountains from Ecuador south to midway Chile. The drawings appear as if they were done at sea.

The Phoenician tongue has been around for a long time. Derived from the old Semitic speech of the Canaanites to which the Phoenicians belonged, it was closely allied to Hebrew, spoken by the Israelites. Phoenician and Hebrew scripts were quite similar and they developed along parallel lines. The Phoenician script in the Ahiram text shows an alphabet consisting of twenty-two consonants. As in Hebrew, vowel letters were never used by the Phoenicians. All Indo-European and Semitic tongues, and all subsequent alphabetic scripts employed the alphabet that the Phoenicians invented.

A series of texts written on clay tablets in cuneiform script was uncovered at Ugarit, shedding light on the Phoenician spiritual philosophy. The supreme god of Phoenicia was El, creator king and father of man. His abode lay at the headwaters of the Tigris and Euphrates Rivers. El's son was Baal, the god of mountains, storms, and rains, whose cult animal was the bull. On the female side, Phoenicia had only one deity throughout the land, and her name was Astarte, the mother and fertility goddess whom was equated with Ishtar and Aphrodite. The goddess of Byblos was identified with Isis, as most Phoenician deities were equated with their Egyptian counterparts.

Elephants comprised part of the war chest of Carthage and were made famous by General Hannibal Barca (born 247 B.C.). Hannibal and the war elephants crossed the Alps as his troops invaded northwest Italy and overran the Po Valley. With no support from Carthage, Hannibal had to withdraw from central Italy. The Punic wars between Rome and Carthage lasted for many years. In 201 B.C., the Roman admiral Scipio Africano (for whom Africa is named) took control of Carthage and allowed Hannibal to be its governor.

THE ANCIENT MEDITERRANEAN

The Mediterranean island of Malta became an early Phoenician colony, and its early history remains a mystery. Megalithic ruins discovered at Malta go back to 3500 B.C. The Malta ruins of Hagar Qim, Mnajdra, and Gqantija Temples are often said to be the world's oldest. In 1930, T. Zammit published an article in *Antiquity* claiming the ruins at Malta predate Mesopotamia, Egypt, and the Hittites. This unknown civilization was destroyed by a cataclysm that deposited three feet of silt. Childress writes that many archaeologists admit that Malta has the oldest stone ruins in the world.

Numerous megalithic buildings are found on the island. A large complex composed of semicircular structures is surrounded by huge upright stones, some being twenty feet hight. Joseph Ellul believes that the gigantic walls of Malta were built to keep wild animals out. Ellul, author of *Malta's Prediluvian Culture,* theorizes that the Mediterranean was a dry valley when the megalithic structures were built. Geologists agree that Malta was once attached to the mainland.

Ellul presents evidence that a huge wave coming from the direction of the Atlantic Ocean destroyed the Malta temples. The walls facing directly westward were completely destroyed, and the huge blocks of the western wall were piled up thirty feet to the east. Sediment shows that Malta was under water for more than three hundred days, and three feet of silt was deposited at the temples of Tarxien and Hagar Qim. Princeton professor Kenneth J. Hsu confirms that the Mediterranean had been dry, and that at some time it was inundated by the Atlantic. His timetable was much earlier than what Atlantologists claim.

Megalithic ruins similar to those on Malta have been found on Gozo, a nearby island off Malta. A German university research team unearthed one hundred skeletons, but were unable to carbon date them because no carbon remained. Carbon dating can only date to 40,000 years ago, proving these skeletons were more than 40,000 years old.

Beneath Malta, a strange cavern system exists. A 1940 National Geographic article mentions a report of "giant men" seen at a closed section of the Hal Saflini catacomb deep beneath the island.

The old city of Rhodes, located in the Aegean Sea, was the largest inhabited city in ancient Europe. Greek mythology describes the island of Rhodes as rising out of the sea. In Rhodes, one of the Seven Wonders of the World, the Colossus of Rhodes, measures 110 feet tall. Taking twelve years to build, it represented the sun god Helios. Rhodes became part of the Dorian Empire at the time of the Sea People's invasion (1200 B.C.). The Dorians were natives of Doris, a division of ancient Greece.

Megalithic ruins are found throughout mainland Greece in Nekrommanteion, Cassope, and Pandosia. Also on the mainland, the ancient city Mycenae, is the city Childress believes may be the ruins of the ancient Greek civilization that did battle with Atlantis in Plato's narrative. According to Greek mythology, the River Archeron was the ancient River Styx, the river of Atlantean time when the Mediterranean was a fertile valley. If Plato, Solon, and the Egyptian priests were right, then ancient Athens would have been a high valley fort, if the Aegean Valley was also dry.

Legends tell of ancient civilizations near Carthage in North Africa. Herodotus (died 425 B.C.) writes of an ancient sea called Triton that has since dried up. Inhabitants around the sea worshiped the gods Triton, Poseidon, and Athena. L. Taylor Hansen writes in *The Ancient Atlantic* that Lake Tritonis was part of a huge inland sea in the Sahara, east of the Atlas Mountains. Lake Chad was the only remnant of the ancient sea. Herodotus tells of a mountain called Atlas, which the natives refer to as the Pillars of Heaven. It is named after a people called the Atlantes, reported not to eat any living thing nor to have any dreams.

According to the natives, the original inhabitants of the Sahara were the Tibesti people who were Dravidians from India. This is somewhat corroborated by James Churchward who wrote that the Ethiopians were of Dravidian lineage. Legends have the Tuareg tribes invading the Triton Sea from the ocean. Hansen believes them to be tribes from Atlantis, who settled in the Ahaggar Mountain region and near the Atlas Mountains. Today megalithic ruins with a great circular wall lay in this region.

The Ahaggar Mountains, in central Algeria, were islands during the time of the Triton Sea. Information from that area has been difficult to come by, writes Childress, as it is very remote and inhabited by a fierce people called the Tuaregs, the veiled people, who guard their secrets and heritage.

Legends tell of many galleries beneath the Ahaggar Mountains. Deep within the ground is an underground lake. Galleries surround it, filled with ancient paintings thousands of years old, and libraries with the oldest books on Earth, and histories that go back before the Flood in the time when the Tuaregs ruled the sea.

The Berbers were another mystery people found in North Africa. Believed to be the descendants from light-skinned invaders of the Middle East, around 10,000 B.C., the Berbers may have been Caspian men named after the archaeological discoveries in Capsa, Tunisia. The well-made artifacts discovered there included large stone axes.

In 1923, Rene-Maurice Gattefosse suggested that the Berbers were descendants from the Atlanteans. He believed that civilization had originated in the northern continent, Hyperborea, and spread to the mid-Atlantic continent of Atlantis. The Hyperboreans migrated south through the Shetlands, Britain, Iberian Peninsula, and to the islands of Atlantis. He attributed the various megaliths such as Stonehenge and Carnac to them and suggested the Cro-Magnon people of paleolithic Europe were pure Hyperborean. Lewis Spence also believes the Basques and Berbers to be direct descendants of Cro-Magnon Atlanteans. He claims their language was the closest to the actual Atlantean language. The Azilians of Atlantis, Spence conjectures, arrived about 10,000 B.C. and founded the civilizations of Egypt, Crete, and later Iberia.

In 1958, Marc Valentine discovered Cyclopean ruins submerged off the coast of Morocco. He found enormous walls with Cyclopean stones measuring more than twenty-five feet long and nineteen feet high lying forty-six feet below the surface. In 1874, French geographer E. F. Berlioux first suggested that Morocco and the Atlas Mountains were Atlantis, claims that others made after seeing the astonishing ruins.

The fabled lost city of Tartessos was thought to be located at the Phoenician colony of Cadiz on the Spanish Mediterranean coast. A legendary city of gold and silver in the western Mediterranean, it was a port city for large ships called Tarshish in the Bible. Hercules is said to have erected two pillars in the Temple of Melgart while at Tartessos. Traditionally, the pillars have been associated with the Rock of Gibraltar. The gigantic ruins, partially submerged at Cadiz, are believed to be ancient Tartessos, and at one time they stood on a large island that closed the mouth of the bay. Childress believes that Tartessos may have been a Hittite-Minoan port where trans-Atlantic voyages originated. (Of course, traditional historians refute this conjecture.) He also thinks the Mediterranean region was flooded around 9000 B.C., and again about 6000 B.C. after which the great sailors of the Atlantean League began to explore the world again.

Charles Hapgood refers to the ancient sea kings as the Atlantean League. The league included sailors from the Hittite Empire, Mittani, Sumer, Egypt, Cyprus, and Crete. Later, the Babylonians, Phoenicians, Minoans, and Egyptians ruled over the ancient trade routes.

Tartessos and Gades coexisted until the rise of the Carthaginian Empire. Historians do not know what happened to Tartessos, as it essentially disappeared from history after the Punic Wars. The legend of Cadiz tells when the Pillars of Hercules opened, the Mediterranean began to flood. After the cataclysm, Cadiz was founded, and new temples were built to honor Ba'al, Astarte, and Melgart (Hercules). In Seville, a megalithic sun temple was discovered twenty-seven feet below street level, leading some archaeologists to speculate that it might be a remnant of Tartessos. Tartessos was reported to have writings dating back to 6000 B.C. Rene Noorbergen writes in *Secrets of the Races* about a 12,000-year-old reindeer bone found in Rochebertur, France that had inscriptions of Tartessos. The script suggests that the Tartessos may be the mother of modern phonetic script predating Phoenicia, writes Childress, and perhaps originating in Atlantis.

The Rio Tinto copper mines in southern Spain are thought to be eight thousand to ten thousand years old. Author E. M. Wisham writes in *Atlantis in Andulucia*, ". . . civilized prehistoric people who in an earlier stage of the history of humanity came to Andulucia (region of southern Spain) from Atlantis to purchase gold, silver, and copper provided by the neolithic mines of Rio Tinto, and in the course of generations . . . welded the Iberian and African cultures so closely together that eventually Tartessos and Africa had a race in common . . ."

The Basques of northwest Spain and southwest France have legends of a cataclysm in which fire and water were at war. Their ancestors hid in caves and survived. One Indian tribe in the Peten district of Guatemala, amid the Mayan ruins, spoke a language resembling Basque. On the Canary Islands, famous for their ancient ruins, lived the now-vanished Guanche people who are said to have spoken a language similar to Basque.

The Etruscans were one of the most mysterious civilizations of Mediterranean Europe. They were the predecessors of the Roman Empire and lived north of Rome in the Po River region. Scholars have a difficult time deciding who these sophisticated people were and why they vanished. In Italy, the Etruscans founded a confederation of twelve city-states united by religious solidarity during the seventh century B.C.

Their culture was obsessed with death and the afterlife. The Etruscan religious philosophy was similar to the Hindus' belief in reincarnation, astral projection, and eternal life of the soul, a philosophy the Atlanteans also possessed. Etruscans followed the advice of their soothsayers almost to an extreme. They divined the will of the gods from the claps of thunder, the flight of birds, and the behavior of birds. They were great believers in magical spells and superstitious rites.

A priestly cult seemed to take control of the people. Elaborate funerary customs were common, including the practices of mummifying, embalming, and entombing the dead. In 1728 A.D., the Etruscan tombs were first unearthed, and since then hundreds of subterranean tombs have been found.

Considered to be sophisticated seafarers and travelers, the Etruscans ambitiously dreamed of a Mediterranean empire. The Romans waged war on the Etruscan lords and rulers, the very people to whom the Romans owed their civilization, and defeated them. By 200 B.C. the Etruscans had completely disappeared. Only one hundred words of their language, similar to Basque, have been deciphered. Childress believes the Etruscans, like the Basques, may be the survivors of the catastrophe that destroyed Atlantis.

Diodorus Siculus (25 B.C.) writes that the Etruscans encouraged the study of science, nature, writing, and theology to a higher degree than any other people. Herodotus (fifth century B.C.) wrote that Etruscans migrated from Asia Minor about 1000 B.C., fleeing a famine. Dionysius of Halicarnassus disagrees and asserts they were a very ancient indigenous people unlike any other in language and custom. A number of Etruscan cities lay totally underwater, while others have reemerged. The Romans inherited the maritime routes of Etrusca and Carthage following their victories over these civilizations.

ANCIENT EUROPEAN CIVILIZATIONS

As one studies the legends of Atlantis, it is amusing to observe the writers and scholars of various countries who claim their country as Plato's Atlantis. This especially holds true for Europe which contains numerous unexplained megalithic ruins.

France has the greatest concentration of megaliths in the world and includes Carnac on the southern coast of Brittany. Scholars conservatively estimate the megaliths of Carnac were erected by 5000 B.C. Carnac of Brittany likens itself to the Egyptian temple of Karnac, which is a huge building with long rows of megaliths supporting an enormous roof. Carnac has hundreds of standing stones, precisely aligned, that scientists have concluded compriseis a huge lunar observatory.

Many Brittany coast megaliths are submerged. The Grand Menhir Brise at Er Grah, said to be the largest mehir (a single upright crude monolith) in the world, now lays broken into four pieces. It was at least sixty-seven feet tall and weighed more than 340 tons.

North of Carnac, megalithic ruins lay in the Bay of Douarnenez where legend tells of the sunken land of Ys (as told in the chapter of Atlantis). Many believe the legend of Ys may be describing Plato's Atlantean capital city of Poseidonis, and the ruins in the bay are believed to be those of Ys.

German archaeologist Jurgen Spanuth claimed he had discovered Atlantis in the North Sea five miles north of the Heligoland Peninsula. The huge sunken city he had come upon had an undamaged wall with a circumference of 3956 feet surrounding the city. He reminds his readers that the citadel of the Atlantean capital was six miles from the coast and surrounded by a wall 3035 feet in circumference.

An ancient book entitled the *Oera Linda* may provide the key to Atlantis. In 1871, a Frisian antiquarian disclosed the existence of an unusual Dutch manuscript held in the family's possession for many generations. Originally thought to have been written in an unknown language, scholars eventually determined it was written in an ancient dialect of Frisian.

The book tells of a lost land, Atlan, that existed in the North Sea. It describes a large semicircular landmass around the north and east of the British Isles that was contemporary with Atlantis. Atlan had survived the cataclysm that destroyed the traditional Atlantis. It was located between Greenland and the Hebrides in a subtropical climate. The Atlanders were a maritime nation who charted the seas of the world, including the Mediterranean. They established colonies in Scandinavia, northern and southern Europe, Africa, and Greece. In the year 2193 B.C., a cosmic calamity struck the earth, and descriptions in the book suggest the Earth tilted on its axis. Within three days, severe climatic changes overwhelmed the planet.

Author Robert Scrutton who studied the book suggests this may have been the cataclysm that sent the Atlantic tidal wave through the Pillars of Hercules and flooded the Middle East, giving rise to the biblical legend of the Deluge. Some believe the *Oera Linda* to be the oldest book in the world.

In the 17th century Dr. Olof Rudbeck announced that Atlantis was located in Sweden. He was a medical professor at Uppsala University and an acknowledged medical genius. He believed that ancient Sweden was the Hyperborea of ancient Greek geography, and also believed that Sweden was the original land of the Druids. Sweden has many megaliths along the coastal region, and more thought to be submerged. The ancient ruins, the cataclysmic ages of their gods, and a legend of Ragnorok all suggest that Sweden was an advanced civilization in the past. Rudbeck and others believed the Scandinavians descended from the survivors of Atland. Evidence also suggests that the Phoenicians established trading settlements in Scandinavia.

Great Britain has many prehistoric ruins that remain a mystery. All along the coast of Wales lay submerged forests, submerged walls, and roads that apparently lead into the ocean. They were submerged within the past few thousand years. Researcher Paul Dunbarin writes that some raised beaches in Britain have been dated to approximately 4400 B.C. He concluded that a great cataclysm occurred around 3000 B.C., during Britain's neolithic age German history professor F. Gidon theorized that based on the distribution of plants in northwest Europe, the Britain landmass separated from mainland Europe around 3000 B.C.

Chapter Eleven

ANCIENT NORTH AMERICA
Columbus was a Latecomer

As one reviews the evidence unearthed in North America during the past centuries, history books about America are obviously in error and need to be rewritten to reflect this accumulating knowledge of ancient America. Pioneer researchers such as Dr. Barry Fell of Harvard University have deciphered many ancient inscriptions found on American archaeological artifacts and petroglyphs. His findings suggest that during the time before Christ, America was inhabited by the Celts, Basques, Libyans, Egyptians, Iberians, Phoenicians, and Jews. They left many clues of their presence: pyramids, temples, grave stones, stele, and cliff inscriptions. Many ancient coins unearthed by farmers provide a key to America's ancient heritage. The paradigm in history needs to change regarding ancient America, as these important discoveries no longer can be ignored by academia.

Contrary to academic dogma, the evidence suggests that the early Native Americans did not cross the Bering Strait to inhabit the North American continent. Many tribes appear to have originated from settlers of the Old World who became founding fathers of Indian nations. Scholars fail to give credence to Indian legends regarding their origin, and not one tribe has a legend describing their voyage across the Bering Strait.

Archaeological findings now suggest that the New World may have seeded Europe and the Old World. American Indians who migrated to Europe may have been the Cro-Magnon man that suddenly appeared and replaced the crude Neanderthal man. One skull from Sunnyvale, California, dated at 70,000 years old, is twice as old as the oldest modern skull from Europe. Native American legends have said all along that they were the earliest of humans.

By studying the archaeological finds of America and understanding ancient world history, one can begin to see the role that

North America played in ancient times. Many mysteries need to be understood, and one of those enigmas regard the ancient copper mines of northern Michigan.

COPPER IN AMERICA

When settlers arrived in northern Michigan, they were astounded to find that extensive mining had occurred in the upper peninsula north of Wisconsin. How was this possible? Archaeologists have now determined that mining in these Michigan mines commenced around 3000 B.C. Before the time of modern civilization, more than 500,000 tons of copper were mined from this remote area. The mining abruptly halted in 1200 B.C., but resumed again twenty-one hundred years later in 900 A.D. and continued until 1320 A.D. An additional two thousand tons were removed, and again operations mysteriously came to a halt. Tools such as mauls, picks, hammers, shovels, and levers were left in place by their unknown owners. The destination of the copper was unknown.

On the northern shore of Lake Superior, the diggings extended for approximately one hundred fifty miles, and mining pit widths varied from four to seven miles. The southern shore has approximately one hundred miles of mines. Overall, more than five thousand open pit mines have been discovered in the Upper Peninsula region. Much of the mining activity took place on Isle Royale, an island in Lake Superior at the Canadian border. Here the contiguous pits were thirty miles long and averaged five miles wide. Every historic Lake Superior mine opened in the past two hundred years has been previously worked by the ancient miners, who tapped into all the productive veins throughout the area.

The prehistoric miners were very effective in extracting the ore from the ground. Atop a copper bearing vein, they created intense fires and heated the rock to a very high temperature. They then doused the fires with water. The rocks subsequently fractured and they used stone tools to extract the copper. Deep within the pits, a vinegar mixture was employed to speed spalling, the breaking of rock into layers, and to reduce the smoke. Crib lifts, used to hoist more than three tons of rock at a time, were more efficient than British mining technology of the late 18th century.

Literally, millions of tools were left behind. In 1840, ten wag-onloads of stone hammers were removed from a single location. Most hammers weighed five to ten pounds and were made of a tough igneous rock. The hammer's workmanship was considered masterful.

Who were these miners? In 1948, bones were found in a grav-el pit, and carbon-14 dating suggested these people, called the Old Copper Culture, lived five thousand years ago. Copper mining at Lake Superior occurred simultaneously with the copper era in Asia and the Middle East. On the shore of Lake Superior a one-half mile long levee was discovered suggesting the miners used large sailing vessels. Scholars think the miners limited their mining operations to the warmer weather and returned to their homes south of the hard frost-line during winter.

Legends of the Menomonie Indians of northern Wisconsin preserved the memory of the old copper mines. They claim the miners were light-skinned "foreign people" who discovered ore-bearing veins by throwing magical stones called "Yuwipi" on the ground. This made the copper-rich rocks ring as brass does. European miners practiced this technique more than three thousand years ago, according to author Frank Joseph. Scholars concur the miners were not native inhabitants.

Between the Upper Peninsula mining area and Rock Lake, Wisconsin lay a number of conical stone pyramids and hive mounds. The region of Rock Lake, also known as Aztlan, lies just below the hard snow line. One Upper Peninsula mound, which measured ten feet by fifteen feet, was virtually identical to the Pyramid of the Moon at Aztlan. The stone pyramids were construct-ed carefully by placing smaller stones inside the larger stones to form a pile. The cone-shaped pyramids that dotted the landscape from the mines to Aztlan appeared to serve as time keepers, sun-dials, and star pointers. The people of Rock Lake-Aztlan and the miners may be the same people.

No evidence has been discovered around the mines of a fur-nace to refine or smelt copper ore, or of equipment to crush the ore into rock and separate it by washing. Rock Lake may have been an ancient mining center that served as a clearing house for the raw copper extracted from the mines of the peninsula. From here it was readied for shipment elsewhere.

In 3000 B.C., the mining operations appeared suddenly fully developed and operational. The miners brought their technology from an outside civilization, and the mining in upper Michigan paralleled precisely the European Bronze Age. Bronze was the most valuable and sought after material at that time. It was used in the production of weapons such as swords, spear points, shields, armor, helmets, and battering rams. In order to make bronze, copper and tin were required. European supplies of copper were quite limited and not sufficient to keep the ancient world in bronze for so many years. Where the mined Michigan copper went was a mystery, and where did the European's get all their copper? Evidence now suggests it may have come from America.

From 2000 to 1000 B.C., the Europeans were in a copper-trading frenzy. Tin came from Britain; Cornwall being the primary port. Once the Bronze Age era came to an end, the American mines shut down. The mystery remains, who were the early miners?

Dr. Eiler L. H. Henrickson of Carelton College in Minnesota believes that most of the copper from the Michigan mines was taken to the ancient Near East around 3000 B.C. These ancient miners, Henrickson believes, were most likely Egyptians and Phoenicians. During the later Copper Age, the mines were used by other cultures including the Norse, Celts, and perhaps the Toltecs. Another theory claims the Aztecs may have been the miners.

Archaeological evidence suggests that around 3000 B.C., the Rock Lake region was transformed by the arrival of a large number of foreigners from across the sea. According to Frank Joseph's writings, they sailed down from the Upper Peninsula and settled around the lakeshore. Here they buried their honored dead beneath great stone monuments, cone-shaped pyramids, and tent-shaped crypts.

About 1200 B.C. the copper trade collapsed. A massive flood deluged Rock Lake, submerging the surrounding city under fifty feet of water. The ruins of nine different structures, inundated by the flood, remain on the bottom of the lake. The most important structure is the Linnatus Pyramid. Another pyramid has walls one hundred feet long that rise eighteen feet above the mud bottom of the lake.

The reopening of the mines in 900 A.D. coincided with the establishment of Cahokia, the greatest ancient city above the Rio Grande. Located in south central Illinois, Cahokia was a megalopolis consisting of pyramids with copper ornaments. Copper armor was also unearthed there. The Cahokian Society collapsed in 1100

A.D., and it is believed the population and culture moved to the Rock Lake region for its copper which had become its chief trade item with the Toltecs and perhaps other tribes in South America. Andean civilizations of the Chimu and other pre-Inca tribes also used copper on a grand scale. The Lake Superior mines were one of a few known workable deposits of native copper in the world. They held pure copper.

The pyramidal ceremonial center of Cahokia's population grew to more than 30,000. Around 1100 A.D., their sacred calendar told them to move on again, and they migrated to Tyranea in southern Wisconsin. Here they built a scaled-down version of Cahokia, a twenty-one-acre city of three pyramids surrounded by a triplicate of stockade walls covered with white plaster. They referred to this city as Aztlan, or water town, for its location on the banks of the Crawfish River. In 1320 A.D., a fire burned the stockade, killing a number of people. Some researchers believe this may have motivated the migration to the Valley of Mexico where they recreated a new city, Tenochitlan. This became the capital of the Aztec nation, and perhaps this scenario explains the mysterious location of Aztlan in Aztec legend.

Aztlan is like a miniature version of Teotihuacan in Mexico. It has a Pyramid of the Sun facing a Pyramid of the Moon. Discovered in 1835, it was given the name Aztlan in 1837 by Nathaniel Hyer. Hyer believed the truncated pyramids on the banks of the Crawfish River described the site in Aztec legend, which said they came from the north, from a land by water. Many of the ruins had been ransacked by pot hunters, and some mounds were leveled and plowed. In 1921, the private land was purchased to become the Aztlan Mound Park and presented to the Wisconsin Archaeological Society. A huge stockade similar to that of Cahokia surrounded the entire city. The stockade was burned in 1300 A.D., the century that the Aztec migrated into the Valley of Mexico.

THE MOUNDS OF AMERICA

The many mounds found throughout the eastern half of America are another enigma that have mystified scholars. Skeletons of great proportion have been discovered in many of the mounds. In Williamson County, Tennessee, a seven-foot skeleton was found in 1821. A nine-foot eight-inch skeleton was discovered in 1879 in a mound near Breusville, Indiana. Giant skeletons were found in mounds located in Rutland and Rodland, New York in the middle 1800's. In Gaslerville, Pennsylvania, a vault contained a seven-foot two-inch giant. Seven skeletons in Minnesota measured seven-foot eight-inches. Twenty skeletons of giants were found in Toledo, Ohio, and beside each lay a bowl with hieroglyphic figures.

Who were these Mound Builders and what happened to them? The valleys of the Mississippi and Ohio Rivers in Wisconsin, Illinois, Indiana, and Iowa were activity centers of this obscure people, the Mound Builders. They built mounds of earth, many shaped like animals, such as lizards or serpents. Conical mounds, huge pyramids, and effigy mounds have been discovered from Oklahoma to New York, and from Louisiana to Minnesota. Some archaeologists believe the last survivors of the Mound Builders were the Natchez Indians of the lower Mississippi River Valley. They were devout worshipers of the sun whose ancestors built gigantic pyramids up and down the Mississippi River to worship the sun.

The Spiro Mounds in Spiro, Oklahoma, have been dated between 850 and 1450 A.D. and include twelve mounds with several large pyramids. The central mound, named the Craig Mound, contained an urn with tens of thousands of pearls. On the floor a large skeleton lay decked out in copper armor, polished beads, and engraved conch shells. Overall, five hundred human burials were eventually discovered at the Spiro Mounds.

Also in Oklahoma is the Heavener Runestone, discovered in the 1830s. It is composed of eight mysterious symbols carved on the face of a huge slab of stone measuring twelve feet by ten feet by sixteen inches thick. The eight runes may be a mixture of the ancient runic alphabets from the oldest (Old Norse) Futhark, which came into being about 300 A.D., and a later Scandinavian Futhark used about 800 A.D. One inscription was translated to read "November 11, 1012," and another read "Valley owned by Glome." At the base of the same mountain where the runestone was located, a coin with a hole in the middle was discovered. The Smithsonian Institute dated the coin to 146 B.C. It had come from North Africa.

The Toltec Mounds State Park is located fifteen miles southwest of Little Rock, Arkansas. Eighteen mounds, nine of them visible, lie here. One is a conical mound similar to a mound at Cuicuilo in the Valley of Mexico.

Near St. Louis, the Cahokia Pyramid, called the Monk's Mound, is considered the largest pyramid in North America. It was named after Trappist monks who farmed the terraces in the early 1800s. The stepped pyramid covers sixteen acres. On the summit the remains of a temple foundation measuring 104 feet by 48 feet are buried. Originally there were 120 pyramids and mounds on the site. Nearly fifty million cubic feet of earth was moved to build the pyramids. Three types of construction are found on the site, including the stepped pyramid, the conical pyramid, and the ridge top.

Pyramids of the Midwest were used as astronomical observatories, burial crypts, and sometimes as ceremonial buildings. Sheets of copper, plates of mica, shells, and turquoise have been found at the burial sites. The evidence, according to David Hatcher Childress in his book *Lost Cities of North and Central America,* suggests the entire Midwest region was a coherent nation. It had a sophisticated network using the extensive river system.

The Koster site, located in southern Illinois, is named after the farmer who found some pottery fragments while plowing his field. In 1969, a test excavation showed there were thirteen layers of habitation going back at least ninety-five hundred years.

Located across the Mississippi River from Memphis in St. Francis County, Arkansas, lies a complex of ancient pyramids, canals, paved lakes, and large mound complexes. It suggests an extensive human population as large as that of Cahokia, Illinois. Early settlers believed an ancient Egyptian city existed there, and these ruins are the apparent namesake of Memphis,Tennessee.

CELTIC AMERICA

When the New Hampshire colonists arrived, they came across numerous one-story stone buildings that were circular or rectangular, several measured thirty feet by ten feet. Some structures were completely sunken beneath the ground, while others were partly buried. All were constructed of large stones with roof slabs that weighed several tons. Many had smoke holes and recesses built into the walls. Being practical, the colonists used these structures as root cellars, and this name for these buildings remains today. The large complex is known as Mystery Hill.

In 1967, carbon-14 dating on charcoal samples at Mystery Hill indicated their period of occupation was in the second millennium B.C. Several inscriptions, written in Iberian Punic, said that one chamber on the site was dedicated to the Phoenician god, Baal. The complex also appeared to be dedicated to other divinities, suggesting the site was a religious center and astronomical observatory. Another slab was dedicated to Ber, the Celtic sun god and considered the same god as the Phoenician Baal. Barry Fell writes in *America B.C.* that the ancient Celts built the New England megaliths and chambers, and the Phoenicians were welcome visitors. From 800 to 600 B.C., the Goidelic Celts were clearly the occupants.

Fell's outstanding research at Harvard provides irrefutable evidence that America was colonized by Europeans and Mediterranean countries before the time of Christ. His specialty is epigraphy, which is the art of reading ancient inscriptions engraved or imprinted on stones or other durable materials. Fell, a multilinguist, was one of the few scholars familiar with the ancient Celtic language. Normally, American archaeologists do not study ancient languages so they are unable to read inscriptions on ancient American ruins. Their lack of knowledge results in dismissing evidence as fortuitous markings made by roots of trees or by plowshares. Fell gave America a history prior to Columbus and wrote several books about his findings. His leadership and scholarship have begun to slowly awaken academics to ancient America. Professor Norman Tolten states that twenty-five hundred years of American prehistory must now be transferred to history, for history begins where writing begins, and we now have the oldest written documents of our nation. However, too many academicians refuse to study the evidence and typically try to preserve the status quo, asserting that no European settled in America before Leif Eriksson or Columbus.

Hundreds of inscriptions have been found among the ruins of New Hampshire and Vermont, written in a forgotten Celtic language called Ogam that few scholars know anything about. The writings tell about a vital European Celtic civilization in pagan times that lived in America during the Bronze Age. About three thousand years ago a number of adventurous Celtic mariners crossed the North Atlantic to discover and colonize North America.

They came from Spain and Portugal by way of the Canary Islands and then caught the trade winds that brought Columbus to the New World. The tropics did not agree with them, so they made their way up the coast to New England, which had a temperate climate. Here they established a new European kingdom which they called *Iargalon*, meaning "land beyond the sunset." They first settled near the mouths of New England rivers in the region of North Salem and on a branch of the Merrimac River in southern New Hampshire. Later, they sailed north to Quechee, Vermont, and eventually they moved westward where they colonized the Hanging Valley of the Green Mountains. In the secluded valleys and hilltops, the Druidic priests erected temples and circles of standing stones. On many of these stones they cut inscriptions using the ancient Celtic alphabet called Ogam. The same thing happened in Europe, but Christian priests had all the pagan inscriptions erased and replaced by Christian Ogam. In America, the old pagan inscriptions remain intact. Fell believes the Ogam in America will shed light on the ancient European Celt.

The name "Ogam" means grooved writing and refers to an ancient Celtic script composed of fifteen consonants and five vowels, along with a few other signs representing double letters. In the 18th century the ancient Celtic language was discovered as contemporary with the Roman occupation of Britain, and evidence suggests that Ogam may be related to Latin. The art of recognizing Ogam was confined to a few scholars in Britain, and Celtic New England Ogam remained unrecognized. Only the Gaelic Celts of Britain had knowledge of the Ogam system, which employed Greek and Latin letters. Gaelic tradition asserts their ancestors came from a land found on the Iberian Peninsula (Portugal and Spain). The oldest Gaelic name for Ireland is Ibheriu, a word that resembles Iberia. Fell believes the American Celts originated somewhere on the Iberian Peninsula during the first millennium B.C., and that they were related to the Gaelics who later settled in Britain and Ireland. The Iberian style of Ogam found in America was discovered also in northern Portugal, suggesting the American Celts were presumably Goidels who had once lived in Spain and Portugal.

The "root cellar" ruins appeared to be the work of megalithic people and resembled corresponding structures in Europe dating back to the Bronze Age, an era that began in the 5th millenium B.C. Many of the ancient Celtic stone buildings were torn down or incorporated into the cellars of the farmhouses. Some stones were incorporated into walls around the fields. The ruins were similar to the

Goidel ruins found in Scotland. The Celtic inscriptions occurring in Spain and Portugal and associated with Iberian Punic inscriptions, were found near megalithic ruins. The Iberian Punic inscriptions identified at sites near Boston were thought to be from the era of 500 to 300 B.C.

The New England Celts used an Ogam alphabet of at least twelve symbols identical to those found in Portugal and Spain during the last Bronze Age, about 800 B.C. Fell says the probability that this happened by chance is less than one in 430 million. The Ogam alphabet of Monhegan, Maine, and Ireland both have seventeen similar letters. Fell concludes that the Celts from the Iberian peninsula settled America and built the ancient stone buildings in New England.

The various temples of the American Celtic ruins were oriented astronomically, eliminating any possibility they were built as root cellars. Numerous monoliths, characteristic of Celtic landscape and similar to those in Europe have been found in New England. The best-known megalithic monuments found in New England are the dolmens, memorials to a chief or important event. A dolmen consists of a huge central boulder sometimes weighing ten tons or more and situated upon three, four, or five smaller vertical stones which act like pegs. The American dolmens of Massachusetts and Maine exactly match those found in Europe and the Middle East.

Rings of stone, common in Celtic land, have been found in Vermont, Connecticut, and Massachusetts. Up to ten feet in diameter, they resemble the ones found in Ireland. Observatories have been found that are inscribed with Celtic identifications of Druid philosophy. Nearly two hundred stone chambers have been discovered that are oriented to serve as astronomical observations to regulate the calendar of festivals. Systems of standing stones have been discovered that suggest a calendar divided into eight seasons, based on the annual cycle of the sun. Some Celtic inscriptions on the stones indicate their function. Druids active in New England still practiced their astronomical craft in the time of Julius Caesar, when they adopted part of the reformed calendar.

In 1885, a thin copper disk, about one-half inch in diameter, was unearthed in Champagne, Illinois, under four feet of undisturbed clay. It was an example of a little known Celtic imitation produced in Britain at the end of Roman occupation. The disk was found along a transcontinental trail that led from New England to the Pacific Northwest coast. Celts leaving New England to settle in British Columbia, Washington, and Oregon followed this trail. Ogam stones with Gaelic inscriptions that used the Iberian alphabet letters have been found along the trail. At the Pacific end of the trail, the inscriptions were painted red.

The first Celtic coins discovered in America came from Illinois and dated approximately from the fourth or fifth century A.D. Dr. Fell believes these coins were minted in Ohio. One coin, dated 200 B.C., was found with an inscription of a town in Portugal from where the Celtic Iberians had come. The inscription read "Odakis Ebiom," with "Odakis" meaning currency and "Ebiom" referring to the Celtic city, Evia. It is the oldest known American coin.

The artwork of the British Columbia Celts resembles that of the New England Celts and that of Europe. The western Celts, a much later vintage than the New England Celts, probably directly descended from them. The Takhehie Indians in the Fraser Lake region of British Columbia have a language that is recognizable Celtic, with much of the same vocabulary.

Later Celtic immigrants came mainly from Ireland and brought Christianity to their pagan brothers. The legendary voyages of the Brendan-era Irish Celts actually did occur, and they brought their art to North America. The Celtic boundary stone at Ardmore, Oklahoma, is inscribed with the language of Gadelic, similar to modern Irish Gaelic.

Many legends are told of white Indians in Kentucky thought to be descendants of a Welchman named Prince Madoc. Skeletons found buried in brass-plated armor around the turn of the century at Sand Island bear symbols of the mermaid and harp that comprised the Welch coat of arms. Nearby, a tombstone fragment bore the date 1186. Prince Madoc is reported to have landed in Mobile Bay in 1170 and then returned to Wales to fetch fellow countrymen to help found a new nation in America.

European explorers spoke of a mysterious tribe of Indians that spoke Welch and descended from Madoc. An English surveying party encountered a camp of Mandan Indians in present day Missouri. One Indian joined in conversation, and the English were surprised that 50 percent of the Mandan language was Welch. Lewis and Clark spent a winter with the Mandans in North Dakota and observed their European influence.

THE PHOENICIAN CONNECTION

Following the influx of Celtic settlers into North America came the Phoenician traders of Cadiz, Spain, who spoke the Punic tongue but wrote in a peculiar style of lettering called Iberian script. Some Phoenicians remained in North America and together with Egyptian miners became part of the Wabanake tribe of New England. Inscriptions on a triangular tablet found at the Mystery Hill ruins were dedications to the Phoenician god, Baal, and were written in Iberian Punic script. Punic refers to the Phoenicians who had ties to Carthage.

By the eighth century B.C., a group of Syrian colonists had settled in the Valley of Guadalquivir River of Andalusia in southwest Spain. They traded for metals mined in the region by the natives, who were primarily Basques. Around 500 B.C., Celts invaded the region, and thereafter the Phoenicians were not heard about in this area. However, their language in southwest Spain became a variant of the Phoenician tongue.

Tarshish was the city founded by these new settlers in Spain, and the Bible says Tarshish ships were the largest seagoing vessels known to the Semitic world. According to Phoenician sources, the Phoenician merchants of Tarshish were known for their wealth. Fell believes the Tarshish merchants may have been responsible for the trans-Atlantic migration of the Celts to North America. He thinks the American Celts were deliberately brought here by the Phoenicians.

Only a few Tartessian inscriptions have been found in New England. The first inscription was found on a rock on the seashore of Mount Hope Bay near Bristol, Rhode Island. The script, first described by Ezra Stiles, who later became president of Yale College, reads, "Voyagers from Tarshish this stone reads." Fell believes these voyagers were not explorers but merchants trading with the New England Celts. It is estimated to be from the era 700 to 600 B.C., but the inscription cannot be accurately dated.

The visitors from Tarshish established colonies in eastern North America. The settlers were probably native Iberians, Celts and Basques from the Guadalquiver Valley in Andulasia. The colonists spoke the Tartessian language, and documents unearthed in chieftan burial mounds illustrate some of their chieftains were literate in this Phoenician (Punic) tongue. The first Phoenician tablet found in an American archaeological site was discovered in 1838 at the base of Mammoth Mound in Moundsville, West Virginia.

During the Bronze Age, Iberian chiefs and kings were buried in mounds of varying size. The body was placed in a stone-lined chamber sixty feet below the summit of the mound. In the eastern and middle United States, the mounds had timbers not stone. These American sites have yielded a considerable number of copper tablets in the shape of animal hides.

Ancient American artwork suggests a Phoenician influence. Pottery suddenly appeared in northeastern American sites, suggesting it was introduced by settlers or visitors from Iberia during the Bronze Age. Phoenicians were known for a characteristic high-crowned hat they often wore, and figurines with a similar hat have been excavated from burial mounds estimated to be from the eighth to sixth century B.C.

The New England Antiquities Research Society owns 450 inscribed stones, collected in the 1940s from Susquehanna Valley in Pennsylvania. The variety of scripts identify them as Basque, Celtic, and Punic. An inscription on the Bourne Stone records the annexation of the land of present-day Massachusetts to Hanno, a Punic king who may have been the same person as an historical Carthaginian king of that name.

The Ogam inscriptions on Monhegan Island, ten miles off the coast of Maine, attest to the periodic arrival of ships from Phoenicia to the New England coast. The script infers that international commerce was well established during the late Bronze Age, and the island was a trading station used by Phoenician captains. It appears the Phoenician merchants capitalized on the North Atlantic resources. To Cadiz (in Spain), they brought the copper of North America and the tin of Cornwall to provide the raw material for a booming bronze industry in Europe and the Middle East. The Celts of New England played a role in this international trade by supplying fur and hides, which the Phoenicians re-exported to the eastern Mediterranean.

An ancient manuscript written by a Greek historian named Plutarch (born around 50 A.D.) discusses an ancient Carthaginian document found in the ruins of a city. It describes the voyage across the Atlantic and accurately depicts the landmarks en route, including Nova Scotia and New England. He called America, *Epeiros,* "the continent that rims the western ocean." The Carthaginians named the great north land *Asga Samal.* Greeks called the Phoenician traders "the Purple People" famous for their purple cloth. They manufactured the cloth by a secret dyeing process that used the pigment of a sea snail called the murex.

The Phoenicians of Carthage were the greatest sailors of that era. They discovered a source of tin in Britain, and established a complete monopoly of sea trade by blockading the Straits of Gibraltar. Ancient Carthaginian coins have been found on coastal sites of North America and along navigable rivers. All the coins have similar characteristics. They belonged to the earliest issue of Carthage coins, between the fourth and third centuries B.C. Skilled Greek artists used symbols for the coins such as the goddess Tanith, the spouse of Baal, seen on Carthaginian tombstones in North Africa. This same design of coin was also discovered in southern England.

The Phoenicians also influenced the Native Americans. Many supposed Indian petroglyphs of the western states were ancient inscriptions. A prayer for rain in the Punic language was discovered on a petroglyph at Massacre Lake, Nevada. Petroglyphs in Colorado matched the coin artwork of the goddess Tanith.

The Pima Indian tribes of the Southwest may also have been influenced by these ancient Phoenician traders, according to Fell. They speak a Semitic tongue believed to be derived from Iberian Punic colonists, twenty-five hundred years ago. They also preserved with great fidelity the ancient scriptures of the colonists. Fell believes the Pima Indians descended from a Celtic-Iberian tribe who had converted to the use of Punic language by Phoenician colonists in Spain, and whose members migrated to America. Shoshone Indians have many words similar to the modern Basque tongue.

The greatest war in classical times was fought between the two great powers of the western Mediterranean: Rome and Carthage. These Punic wars left Rome exhausted and Carthage in total ruin. Carthage controlled the tin necessary for major metal weapons, but Rome controlled the pine forests necessary for building ships. Each Carthaginian ship was a quinquireme, a large ship requiring five rowers to each oar. Each ship had fifty oars. The total crew numbered four hundred. Carthage lost a great number of ships in the wars and lacking pine to build ships, they ceased to be a major naval power after 241 B.C.. Between 300 and 241 B.C., Carthage experienced an unexplained increase of gold holdings, which Fell believes came from the Americas. They also picked up shipments of pine logs from the Algonquian tribes of northeastern America.

EGYPT AND LIBYA

Egyptians in America before Christ sounds unbelievable, but they too left clues hard to repudiate. In 1874, a calendar known as the Davenport Calendar was discovered in a burial mound near Davenport, Iowa with inscriptions written in three languages. Egyptian hieroglyphics topped the calendar, Iberian Punic script was found in an upper arc, and Libyan inscriptions were found on the lower arc of the stele. Iberian and Libyan texts each report that the stone carries an inscription revealing the secret of regulating the calendar. The Egyptian text reads, "To a pillar a mirror in such manner that when the sun rests on New Year's Day it will cast a reflection on the stone called 'the watcher.' New Years Day occurs when the sun is in conjunction with the zodiacal constellation Aries, in the house of the Ram, the balance of night and day being about to reverse. At this time (spring Equinox) hold the Festival of the New Year." The Davenport Calendar is similar to an inscription on a tomb in Thebes, Egypt, concerning the ceremony of the Djed Column on New Year's Day. About 700 B.C., the Djed Festival of Osiris was celebrated in Iowa.

The New Year's Pillar, called the Djed, is illustrated on the stele. It is comprised of a bundle of reeds surmounted by four or five rings to represent the backbone of Osiris. The Egyptian text on the calendar explained that the stele is the work of Wnty (star watcher), a priest of Osiris in the Libyan region. It was a genuine artifact, as neither Libyan nor Iberian scripts had been deciphered at the time of the discovery. Fell speculates the settlers had presumably sailed up the Mississippi River to colonize the Davenport area. They came on ships commanded by a Libyan skipper of the Egyptian navy during the 22nd Dynasty, called the Libyan Dynasty. Stone carvings of African animals such as the elephant have also been excavated in the fields near Davenport.

The ancient Egyptian visitors who came to North America

imparted their hieroglyphic writing to the natives living in eastern Canada and the United States. Eugene Vetromile wrote a book in 1861 about the Wabanaki Indians whom he had ministered to as a priest. One page is titled "The Lord's Prayer in Micmac hieroglyphics." The hieroglyphic signs were similar to Egyptian hieroglyphics found in the simpler cursive called hieratic. Meanings of their hieroglyphic signs in Egyptian matched the meaning assigned to them in the English transcript of the Micmac text. The Micmac are a tribe of Algonquian Indians found in Acadia, Canada; other tribes in Maine, called the Wabanaki, are closely related to the Micmac.

Another manuscript, written by father Maillard (died 1762), was discovered in the Widener Library. Maillard's book contained 450 pages written in Micmac hieroglyphics. Hundreds of cliff hieroglyphic signs in the book were identical to ancient Egyptian hieroglyphics. The book also contained much of the Catholic Order of the Mass. Father Millard had borrowed and adapted a system of writing that was in use among the Micmac.

When the French arrived at Acadia, the Indians were writing on bark, trees, and stones, using sharp stones and arrows. They sent their writings to other Indian tribes who were literate in these symbols of hieroglyphics. The Micmac claimed they could express any idea with every modification by these signs. French missionaries used these signs to help instruct the natives about Christianity. Hundreds of Egyptian root words have been identified in the languages of the Wabanaki and Micmac tribes.

Greek roots, too, are prevalent in the Micmac language. Dr. Silas Rand implies it derived from the Greek spoken in North Africa during the Ptolemaic times around 300-100 B.C.

As mentioned earlier, in 1200 B.C. the Sea People who belonged to a half-dozen tribes from the north, including Antolia (Turkey) and Philistia (Lebanon) attempted a major invasion of Egypt. After Ramses defeated them, the Sea People retreated westward into Libya and vanished from history for two hundred years. A group called Shardana of Libya, one segment of the Sea People, regrouped and overthrew Egypt. They ruled Egypt for two centuries, called the Libyan Dynasty. Under the leadership of Shishong (mentioned on an American artifact), Egypt became a great maritime power. In 750 B.C. the Libyans, expelled by the Egyptians, became the Phoenicians who established colonies around the Mediterranean, including Carthage.

Greeks had settled in Libya prior to the Phoenicians in the famous city of Cyrene. Under the intellectual leadership of the Greeks at Cyrene, Libya became a major source of learned men for the court of Ptolemy in Alexandria. This followed the era of Alexander the Great.

When the Libyans arrived in North America is a mystery, as is their port of entry. A Libyan inscription found on the Rio Grande cliffs in Texas reads, "A crew of Shishong the king took shelter in this place of concealment." Several kings by this name did rule Libya and Egypt between 1000 and 800 B.C., a time when North African sailors began exploring the New World.

In 700 B.C., Libyans were writing in the Mimbres Valley of New Mexico. Evidence suggests the Libyans had sailed across the Pacific Ocean to America. The Polynesian people, like the Libyans, descended from the Anatolian Sea People. Early Polynesian and Libyan inscriptions are both similar in alphabet and language. The pharaohs employed Libyan seamen for the Egyptian fleet before the Libyan chiefs seized control of Egypt. It is also believed that Libyans explorered southern California while sailing for the Pharaoh Ptolemy III around 232 B.C. Written fragments of the Libyan language are found in Quebec, California, and at sites in Nevada. They are also found on cliff faces along the Arkansas and Cimarron Rivers, suggesting the Libyans entered the Mississippi from the Gulf of Mexico.

The Zuni language of the southwest relates to no other American native language. Fell believes the Zuni tongue largely derived from North African dialects of Coptic, Middle Egyptian, and the Nubians of the Nile Valley, as the basic vocabulary of Zuni is North African. The Libyan language is mostly Egyptian with Anatolian roots introduced by the Sea People. Matching pairs of words from the Zuni tongue of New Mexico and North Africa are numerous. Fell concludes that Libyan is the parent language of Zuni.

Ruins of an ancient civilization that mysteriously vanished are sprinkled throughout the arid Southwest. The builders, the Pueblo people, suddenly abandoned their villages and disappeared. Fell believes the explanation of the enigmas of these people can be found engraved on the bedrock. When the North Africans arived in the Americas twenty-two hundred years ago, they brought along their culture and way of life. Cliff dwellings at Mesa Verde National Park, Colorado, and at Montezuma Castle National Park, Arizona, are similar to the cliff dwellings of North African people such as the Habbi. The adobe buildings of North Africa were typically rectangular and located near cultivated fields, often-irrigated fields, which was the case of the Berbers in the Atlas Mountains of Morocco. The Anasazi Indians of New Mexico and Colorado incorporated timber beams in their stone kivas, which were characteristic of North African design. Fell implies that the vanished Southwest tribes might be descendants of the North African voyagers who mysteriously disappeared.

In Chaco Canyon, New Mexico, the Anasazi built great cities and roads throughout the area more than a thousand years ago. They began building in the early 900s A.D. and by the year 1000 A.D., they had constructed seventy-five small cities within the canyon. More than four hundred miles of roads connected these cities, the farthest reaching forty-two miles to the north. Scholars believe their decline coincided with a prolonged drought in the San Juan Basin between 1150 and 1180 A.D. Many anthropologists believe the Anasazi Indians were ancestors of the Navajo, Ute, and Zuni tribes. As mentioned, the Zuni tongue is thought to have been derived from North Africa.

The Libyans had discovered America divided the ocean, and with this knowledge they landed on both sides of the continent. Two thousand years ago, America became a haven for refuges of learned men from the Mediterranean who established schools and maintained friendly relations with the Indians as California and Nevada became colonized. Archaeological evidence shows that math, astronomy, navigation, and geography were taught in the schools. Scattered petroglyphs of stylized ships, sometimes with Arabic and Libyan writing, are widespread in the remote areas of Nevada. Petroglyphs were used for schooling children. They showed the earth as a globe encircled by the equator and tropics.

Around 239 B.C., Eratosthenus, the Libyan scientist, claimed the earth was a globe and estimated the earth to be 25,000 miles in circumference. He determined the principles of latitude and longitude, and this knowledge was characteristic in the petroglyphs found in southern California. America's first maritime academy was located near East Walker River, in Lyon County, Nevada, as well as another site near Virginia City, Nevada. The sites provided instruction in navigation and geography, written in Kufic Arabic and

Libyan. The training allowed mariners to sail the Pacific routes. One petroglyph has a map of the outline of North America, and judging from the Libyan lettering, dates about 200 B.C. Another petroglyph depicts the Hawaiian Islands.

Early voyagers possessed the magnetic compass since 300 B.C. They also understood how to use the stars for navigation. A disc unearthed in Tennessee, called the Tennessee Disc, was a simplified compass disk lettered in Ogam, which employed Libyan terms for the cardinal navigation points.

Many western petroglyph sites suggest they were used to teach students math. Petroglyphs discovered at Keyhole Canyon, Nevada, revealed numerical values using the ancient Iberian system of numbers, which were identified by the engraved Libyan word "S-R-O" meaning "enumeration." Multiplication grids were found at the Whiskey Flat, Nevada, site. After the third century A.D. ancient Hindu numerals were brought to America by the voyagers of Nevada. In the fifth century A.D., math was revolutionized in North America with the introduction of the newly invented Sanskrit system of decimal notations brought back by the Nevada mariners. A mathematical petroglyph discovered at Massacre Lake of northwest Nevada depicted the annual report on maize written in Libyan script (Arabic language) with the numerals expressed in Sanskrit script.

The Nevada residents were well acquainted with the mathematics taught at the Mediterranean Arab universities. The most sophisticated system was found within a checkerboard pattern discovered at the Whiskey Flat site. Each square contained five associated grids that yielded a sequence of numbers, called the Fibonacci series by mathematicians. When plotted geometrically, they yielded a logarithmic spiral. This series was taught at the Arab universities. Fibonacci, an Italian monk, disguised himself as a Moslem in the late 1100s, and learned the principle and subsequently brought it back to Italy. Another petroglyph in Washoe County, Nevada gives instruction on how to find the area of a circle. It was written in Arabic Kufi script.

Until recently, no one had a clue what these strange petroglyphs on the high plateau of Nevada meant. Archaeologists called these markings the "Great Basin Curvilinear." They were later found to be writings of ancient Punic, Greek, and Libyan Arabic of North Africa, which used alphabets indicative of their tongue. The Nevada sites were isolated and consequently in a state of excellent preservation. Thousands of these petroglyphs were discovered and recorded, culminating in a publication titled *Prehistoric Rock Art of Nevada and Eastern California.* In 1976, Dr. Fell and other scholars realized what the inscriptions were, and began to decipher them.

The ancient scientists and philosophers of America remained for twelve centuries in the Nevada area. They vanished without a trace, leaving a legacy of rock art inscriptions. These North African seafarers had brought to America a knowledge of navigation, astronomy, and mathematics. Twenty-two centuries ago, under the guise of an Egyptian pharaoh, they sailed down the Red Sea, crossed the Indian and Pacific Oceans, and discovered the west coast of America.

ANCIENT COINS OF AMERICA

After the fourth century B.C., the early visitors to America brought with them the dated proof that modern historians demand: coins. With the advent of a new type of iron plow in 1797, farmers began to plow up Roman coins. Americans discovered coins while sinking well shafts and digging foundations. About the same time, plows unearthed similar coins in England, France, Germany, and Scandinavia. American archaeologists had difficulty explaining away these Roman coins and concluded that they were coins accidently lost in modern times. If this were true, Fell asserts, then "all coins of all periods would be represented in the American finds." Other countries where ancient coins have been discovered take the finds seriously, while American archaeologists totally ignore them. Most of the coins have been discovered near navigable rivers; the ancient ships were purposely constructed with a shallow draft and flat keel to navigate the inland waterways. Coins have been discovered from Carthage, Rome, Byzantine, and the Arabian countries and must have been brought to American soil during their respective epochs of shipping activity.

Roman coins from the era of 337 to 383 A.D. were found in a one square meter area on the beach of Beverly, Massachusetts by a metal detector. Evidence suggests they came from a Roman ship wrecked off the Massachusetts coast that had been carrying a money chest in 375 A.D. The currents carried the coins toward the beach. Studies have shown of all the ancient coins found in America, about 25 percent are found on the beach, 25 percent in plowed farmland, 20 percent in horticulture, 15 percent while digging foundations, 5 percent in stream beds, and 5 percent while digging wells. The geographical distribution of ancient coin finds in America correlates with the navigable coastal and river waterways.

Many petroglyphs extending along the Oregon Trail depict ancient coins. The Wyoming Castle Garden Petroglyphs, which are predominantly circular, suggests this may have been the site of the first American bank. Many circular petroglyph designs depict Roman Republican coins minted for Spanish and Portuguese subjects of Rome. They were used following the conquest of Spain by Rome. The inscription reads "MNDR," which is the Gaelic biblical word, "Monadair" used in the New Testament meaning "money changers." Its root word "MND" is the same word as the Latin word "moneta", meaning "money." Ironically, the nearby town's name is Moneta. Fell believes the petroglyph is the equivalent of a banker's shingle. Celtic was the language spoken at the "Moneta Bank" petroglyph site, and Fell believes the time was 20 B.C. The actual name of the bank is given in Greek, reflecting the transfer of power from Carthage to Rome. Greeks had taken an interest in American banking. Customers of the bank were Gaelic-speaking Celtic-Iberian trappers who settled in the community with their Native American wives. The petroglyhs familiarized fur trappers and others with the relative value of coins. One design depicts two weasels equaling a bronze penny. America had become a busy trading arena, two thousand years ago, with maritime activity on both coasts. The major exports were fur and skins.

Another Iberian bank was discovered in western Arkansas and even yielded a Carthaginian coin. Other coins of Carthage have been discovered in America, with one bearing the arms of Carthage, and believed to have been first minted in 325 B.C. A coin inscription depicted in a Nevada petroglyph near Paradise Valley has a monogram of the Greek letters Kappa and Upsilon, which stands for Kura, the abbreviated form of the city, Cyrene.

Roman coins discovered in America have the same context as those found in European countries that were not part of the Empire. They are believed to have come from Roman traders or relic traders of countries that used the Roman coins. A coin of Antonius Pius

(138 to 161 A.D.) was discovered five feet below the soil at Fayetteville, Tennessee. Another coin of the same vintage was discovered in Columbus, Georgia. Coins of Septimus Severus (193 to 211 A.D.) were found at Grafton, Massachusetts, and a coin of Maximianus Herculius (284 to 305 A.D.) was plowed up in Maxton, North Carolina. A Roman goblet of Pompeiian style was found eighteen inches below the surface on a farm in Clarkville, Virginia. Also a ceramic perfume vial and oil lamp, probably of Pompeiian manufacture before 29 A.D., were found on the Coosa River in Alabama. Many Roman coins have been found in mounds, but detailed records were not kept. Coins of Constantine the Great (306 to 337 A.D.) were discovered in mounds located in Texas and Massachusetts.

Archaeological findings in the west show a Byzantine influence. The Byzantine Empire was the Eastern Roman Empire from 395 to 1453 A.D. Petroglyph designs in Colorado are patterned after Byzantine copper coins. These copper coins probably circulated in the Libyan settlements of the Southwest. At Cripple Creek, Colorado, a memorial stele of a North African Greek from the Byzantine period offers the grave inscription, "Herein is the last resting place of Palladis, the servant of God" and is written in Coptic Greek. The Byzantine Greeks' influence in Colorado is shown too by the petroglyph of a portrait of Christ and of saints. The petroglyph was found with Byzantine Greek abbreviated lettering similar to the art found in North African, Coptic, and Byzantine churches. Nevada Greek and North African Greek also have similar epigraphic peculiarities. Early Christian art found in Nevada draws its inspiration from Byzantine coinage, and Byzantine coins have been found in Churchill, Nevada.

The earliest ship depicted in America to date is found on a Colorado petroglyph in Baca County. It is a first century Iberian ship with the marking "OSVNB" on the hull. Fell believes it may have been copied from a coin of Osunoba.

Academic scholars are now accepting the fact that Leif Eriksson preceded Columbus to America. Engraved shell discs found in burial mounds in the eastern part of the United States resemble the Viking coins that were current at the time of Eriksson's voyage in 1000 A.D. In 1930, an unusual sword and battle axe were discovered at Beardmore, Ontario where a prospector's dynamite explosion unveiled the ancient artifacts. They were identified as Norse, being dated 1025 A.D. This was the period of Leif Eriksson's first voyage to Vinland beginning in 1000 A.D., the year Iceland converted to Christianity. Icelander stories claim the Icelanders settled Greenland in 985 A.D. The founder's son, Leif Eriksson, fifteen years later voyaged to a land lying to the southwest, which he called Vinland. Here he established a settlement, but within a season or two abandoned it because of hostile relations with the natives.

Fell writes the Norsemen first brought paganism to America and then later Christianity. They built the oldest surviving church on American soil, the old Romanesque Tower at Newport, Rhode Island. Norse artifacts recorded the tower's origin.

THE ANCIENT AMERICAN JEW

Some early historians believed the Native Americans originated from the ten lost tribes of Israel. Many similarities occur between the Indians and Hebrews: marriage within the tribe, marriage by purchase, animal sacrifice, the lunar and ritual calendars, purification rites, fasting, food taboos, flood legends, and the act of circumcision. According to the Old Testament, in 731 B.C., ten of the twelve tribes that comprised the ancient Hebrew kingdom were conquered and taken away by the King of Assyria. Some of these tribes were said to have migrated to southwest Asia and finally made their way to America and fathered the Native American civilization.

The Church of Jesus Christ of Latter-day Saints (Mormons) teaches there were two migrations to America, as revealed to Joseph Smith by the angel Moroni and recorded in the *Book of Mormon*. The book describes how America was settled by a tribe of Israelites called Jaredites who came to America following the confusion of languages at the Tower of Babel. They came by boat and landed on the Gulf Coast of Mexico and founded a number of centers such as Monte Alban and LaVenta in Central America. In the second century they were destroyed by a series of catastrophes.

A second migration came to America around 600 B.C., led by a man named Lehi. These people came directly from Jerusalem and upon their arrival divided into two groups, the Nephites and Lamanites. The Nephites are said to have built the great pre-Columbian sites of Central America and the Andes, such as Tikal and Teotihuacan. The Lamanites became a nomadic agricultural people and one of the ancestors of the North American Indian tribes. The Mormons assert that the Mexican Maya god Quetzalcoatl-Kukulan and Christ were the same entity, and they believe Jesus visited America and taught a number of Indian tribes following his resurrection. However, some of these sites are much older than the Book of Mormon allows.

In 1977, a controversy arose over the origin of this material in the *Book of Mormon,* which claimed to be a hoax. Stored in the church's Salt Lake City archive is the original manuscript of the *Book of Mormon* written by Joseph Smith. There are twelve pages written by an unknown author, whose handwriting matched that of Solomon Spalding, attested to by three handwriting analysts. Spalding was a congregational minister who died in 1816. These pages were taken from his unpublished manuscript on the origin of the Indians, fourteen years before the *Book of Mormon* was published. Other similarities existed between Joseph Smith's scripture and the missing Spalding manuscript. Supposedly, the missing manuscript was given to Joseph Smith.

David Hatcher Childress writes in *Lost Cities of North and Central America* that the Jews apparently had a two- to three thousand-year history of sailing to the Americas. Dr. Cyclone Covey, a history professor at Wake Forest University, wrote in his book *Calalus* about a Portuguese community in Florida, asserting the Jews had sailed from the port of Porto Cale, Portugal, and founded a city in Florida. They named it Cale, now known as Ocala in north central Florida.

Porto Cale became a Jewish Roman outpost in 725 A.D. Other Jews, Covey states, also escaped Roman persecution and sailed from Porto Cale to establish a city named Rhoda where Tucson now lies. A few years prior to this, a reported five thousand people and seven bishops fled Spain to escape the Moors. They sailed from Porto Cale for Antilla but landed on the west coast of Florida. Some believe this group founded the city Cale.

Fell describes other evidence that suggests Jews were in America long before Columbus. At Las Lunas near Albuquerque, New Mexico, an abbreviated version of the Ten Commandments written in a form of Phoenician or early Hebrew was discovered. Childress writes the Jews departed Porto Cale and came to Las

Lunas, naming it Calalus. Kentucky and Tennessee became a haven for persecuted Hebrews after various revolts against Syrian, Greek, and Roman oppression. Some Hebrews were already here in 69 A.D. when the first revolt of Jerusalem occurred against the Romans. An inscription found on the Bat Creek Stone in Tennessee reads, "A comet for the Hebrews" and refers to Haley's Comet, which hung over Jerusalem like a flaming sword in the year 69 A.D. Scattered Hebrew shekels dating from the second revolt in 132 A.D. have been found in parts of Kentucky and Arkansas. Hebrew religious cere-monies have been found among Yuchi Indian tribes in the southeast.

Evidence now suggests that Christopher Columbus was a Spanish Jew. August 3, 1492, was the day Jews were banished from Spain, and to beat the deadline, Columbus and his crew reported on board at 11:00 p.m. on August 2. An estimated 3 million Jews were expelled from Spain prior to the August 3 deadline. It is believed that Columbus assumed the identity of a young Italian wool mer-chant from Genoa with a similar name, whom Columbus had met before the merchant died at sea. All the chronicles of the trip were recorded in Spanish by Columbus. It is now believed, Columbus possessed several maps that showed portions of North and South America. The famous Piri Re'is map claims to be based on the map used by Columbus.

Washington Irving writes in *Life and Voyage of Christopher Columbus* about the summer of 1494 when Columbus was anchored off the coast of Cuba. While on shore, one of the crew came across thirty well-armed Indians. Among them were three white men wear-ing white tunics that reached to their knees. One of the three white men stepped forward to speak, which frightened the crew member into runing away.

In 1511, Columbus discovered abandoned gold mines on the island of Hispaniola, which is today's Haiti. He thought he had dis-covered Solomon's gold mine, Ophir, which Columbus's son Bartome confirmed.

THE AMERICAN INDIAN

Scholars and Indians differ in opinion about the origin of the Native American. The academicians, writes Jeffrey Goodman in *American Genesis*, take a very conservative view of the origin of the

Indian and underestimate their antiquity. Most scholars believe the Indian forefathers were Mongoloids who crossed the Bering Strait to reach America. The academicians believe the Indians could not have entered North America until well after the last Ice Age, which ended 10,000 years ago, because the ice sheets that covered North America first needed to melt.

However, a "monkey wrench" was thrown into their theory with the discovery of a spearhead found between the ribs of a *Bison antiguus,* an animal that had been extinct for 10,000 years. This proved that man lived in North America during the Ice Age. The discovery was made in Folsom, New Mexico, and shortly afterward eight Paleo-Indian points used to kill a mammoth 12,000 years ago, were discovered near Naco, Arizona.

Achaeologists and geologists had to modify the Bering Strait theory because of all the ice 10,000 years ago. Not believing the Indians could have paddled fifty-six miles, they explained it away by saying a land bridge existed between Alaska and Asia. Because the land was locked up by the ice, the sea level was three hundred feet lower than the shallows of today's Bering Strait, which are 140 feet deep. Geologists believed the bridge was exposed from 23,000 years ago to 8000 years, and this allowed the Indians and Ice Age animals to move freely across the bridge.

Another dilemma arose that negated this theory. The areas of Siberia, Beringia, and Central Alaska were unglaciated. However, the Cordileran Ice Cap covered the Canadian Rockies from eastern Alaska to Vancouver, and the Laurentide Ice Cap covered much of the northern United States and most of Canada. The two ice caps merged at the foot of the Canadian Rockies, thus blocking entry into the western United States. However, 12,000 years ago a brief warm period caused a glacial retreat, which some believe may have created an ice-free corridor. Recent radiocarbon dating now shows this 375-mile-long, ice-free corridor was open eight thousand years ago, four thousand years too late to fit the Bering Strait bridge theory on the route of the Indians. The land bridge appeared well after man first lived in the New World.

No concrete evidence supports the Bering Strait bridge theory. No artifacts nor archaeological support have been found on the land areas adjoining the sunken Bering Strait bridge. Not all Native Americans look alike; physical attributes among tribes vary greatly. Some have hawk noses, unlike the Mongoloids. Their languages also vary greatly. The academic scenario does not correspond to the Indian myths. None of the ancient Indian legends describe the Bering route or the long, arduous journey across the ice and snow of the north.

Some tribes describe their arrival in the Americas by way of an ocean voyage from land that sank in the ocean. The Arizona Pueblo Indians tell that during the "fourth world" they came from the west and crossed the sea in boats, sailing from one island to the next until they reached the California coast. Legends from the Dakota, Sioux, Mandans, Delaware, and Iroquois refer to their arrival from an island in the Atlantic Ocean, toward the sunrise. The Okanagan Indians tell of coming from a lost island in the ocean. Some tribes say they were created in the Americas, emerging from within the earth. As Goodman appropriately states, "All groups seem to be united against a common foe, academics."

The Hopis relate that not all tribes had the same origin. Different clans have come from different times, some clans being much older than others. Only the Hopi priests know the exact details of origin, and they have been initiated into certain secret societies. However, evidence is now coming forward suggesting that the American Indian may be the earliest true man. This does not surprise the Indians as their legends have said this all along.

In 1975, ancient American history underwent another shocking paradigm shift. A fire pit, ten feet wide and six inches deep, was discovered on Santa Rosa Island, a California island off the coast of Santa Barbara. Here man had roasted a dwarf woolly mammoth, which roamed the island long ago. Radiocarbon dating of four chunks of charcoal dated the find over 40,000 years, the earliest date radiocarbon dating can ascertain.

Since then, a new technique for dating has been developed called racemization that can go back at least a million years. It is based on the principle that the amino acids of a plant or animal have a geometric property that, in crystal form, causes them to rotate polarized light waves to the left. When the organism dies, the amino acid, at a controlled rate, racemizes or changes this geometry to a mirror image configuration in which the light is rotated to the left. The time for reversal in the direction of left rotation is long, and the degree of rotation determines the age. This technique dates much further back than radiocarbon dating.

Racemization was used to date two human skulls unearthed

near Laguana Beach outside San Diego, California. One skull was dated at 44,000 years old and the other at 48,000 years old. Another skull unearthed in Sunnyvale, California was dated at 70,000 years old. The Bering Strait land bridge theory was now totally disproved; man first arrived in America much earlier than 12,000 years ago.

Other ancient artifacts have been dated at 40,000 years old at a site near American Falls, Idaho; 38,000 years at Lewisville, Texas; and 15,000 years at Meadowcraft Rockshelter in Pennsylvania.

The oldest skull of modern man in the Old World has been dated at 35,000 years, the Cro-Magnon man. Goodman believes Cro-Magnon came from the New World, and that the New World colonized the Old World.

ATLANTIS AND LEMURIA

We now return to the oldest civilizations to leave their legacies in America, Atlantis and Lemuria. Atlantis left its clues in Florida and the Lemurians left their mark in California.

Science News (138:6, 1990) reported on mysterious circular canals in Florida. One large canal located in the savannah and flood plain around Lake Okeechobee was six feet deep, with a diameter of 1,450 feet. Forty of these man-made circles were discovered all over central Florida. Scientists estimated they were constructed around 450 B.C., but perhaps much earlier.

Dr. Carl Clausen discovered a skull in a Florida sinkhole dated 10,000 B.C. that had brain matter still preserved in it. In 1959, a 10,000-year-old skull was discovered near Little Salt Springs, Florida, and contained an intact brain. They also found bones of a prehistoric bison, a mastodon, a mammoth, a giant ground sloth, and a giant land tortoise at the site. Wooden pins driven into the limestone carbon dated to 9,572 years old, and an oak boomerang dated to 9,080 years old.

Evidence suggests a highly developed civilization was destroyed in a cataclysm at the close of the last Ice Age around 10,000 B.C. Underwater ruins, as mentioned in the Atlantis chapter, have been found in the Bahama Banks, especially around Bimimi. Researchers also found segments of a wall composed of blocks weighing twenty-five tons each and measuring eighteen feet by twenty feet by ten feet. The wall appears to have encircled the islands of North and South Bimini to form a dike. Sections of three-foot and five-foot columns were discovered near the wall, as were a stone archway and a pyramid with a flat top and base measuring 140 feet by 180 feet.

During the last Ice Age the present Caribbean sea floor was above sea level, so during that time the wall, pyramids, and temples could have been built. As the northern glaciers melted, the sea level rose. The gigantic, submerged walls apparently served as a dike, an attempt to protect the land from the rising sea. Approximately 18,000 years ago, estimates put the sea level at five hundred to six hundred feet below its present level.

At one time, much of central California was a large inland sea. A map discovered by Henry Biggs in 1625 shows California as an island. Later detailed Spanish maps show a gigantic inland sea with an inlet at San Francisco Bay.

Over the past 40,000 years, five aboriginal cultures have occupied the Santa Barbara channel islands. White-skinned Indian communities living on Catalina Island have been reported in old ship logs. Across the channel from the Santa Rosa Island fire pit, skeletons of giants thought to be over 30,000 years old were uncovered at Lompoc Rancho. Nearby in the LaBrea tar pit, rhinos, camels, mammoths, cave bears, and saber-toothed tigers were found. Mainland tribes tell legends of the islanders being great wizards. A mysterious temple complex served as the center of Indian worship of the channel islands for the sun god, Chingichnich. The native legends claim that California and Mount Shasta were part of an advanced civilization whose legacy was a race of people. Anticipating a catastrophe on their land in the Pacific (Lemuria), some people migrated to California and Mount Shasta.

The Piute Indians have legends of a city beneath Death Valley they call Shin-au-av. Several different people claim to have come across this underground city, with one accidently wandering into a tunnel and another finding an entrance to a mile-long labyrinth beneath the valley floor. A prospector named White visited the site three times, once with his wife and once with a partner. They discovered humanoid mummies dressed in leather, along with stacked gold bars. When he tried to show archaeologists, he was unable to re-locate the tunnel entrance.

Vitrified ruins have been discovered in Death Valley between the Gila and San Juan Rivers. The burned-out city was vitrified by fire hot enough to liquefy rock. Other vitrified ruins have been discovered in southern California, Arizona, and Colorado.

A Nevada newspaper, the *Hot Citizen*, reported on eight-foot to nine-foot giant skeletons uncovered in several of thirty-two caves, discovered in an 180-square mile area of Death Valley. Within the caves lay the remains of dinosaurs, saber-toothed tigers, and elephants, "as if they were on display," said the article.

Many sightings of a "mystery people" have circulated in the Mount Shasta area. Childress writes about two people who claimed they contacted these people, both in somewhat similar circumstances. Abraham Mansfield was approached at Mount Shastas by a group of Indians who said they were direct descendants of Lemurian colonists. They guided Mansfield to a remote, sacred area that led to an Etruscan gold mine. It contained a set of records called the "Plates of Time" written in strange characters and containing the ancient knowledge of the Lemurians. The Indians said they were responsible for locating in each generation "a keeper of the ancient Lemurian treasure." They had chosen Mansfield for the honor, and he proceeded to write several books about the Lemurians and founded the Lemurian Foundation in Redding, California.

Mansfield tells about a friend who became lost while hunting at Mount Shasta in 1931. A seven-foot-tall stranger approached him and offered to take him to a cave where he would be protected from the cold. The cave went beneath the surface for one mile and was lined with gold, as were the rooms that adjoined it. The Lemurian said the gold-lined tunnel extended for miles, and that other Lemurians lived deep within the mountain. Mansfield's friend was also shown Etruscan jewelry and told about the "Plate of Time."

The Lemurian Fellowship inhabits the interior of Mount Shasta, and they claim the mountain was the secret headquarters of the Lemurian Brotherhood. Just prior to the sinking of the Lemurian continent 24,000 years ago, the "Thirteenth School of Mu" relocated somewhere on the Tibetan Plateau in the Kun Lun Mountains region of western Tibet. The school became the nucleus of the Great White Brotherhood.

The first of seven secret brotherhoods was started in Mount Shasta. Each head of the seven brotherhoods supposedly meets in a council known as the Council of Seven. The archangel Melchizedak is said to be the eighth member of the Council of Seven. According to Nestorian Christianity, Melchizedek was the Christ of biblical prophecy. However, Nestorian Theology was banned from the Holy Roman Empire in 431 A.D. After the destruction of Atlantis around 8000 B.C., Melchizedek planned through the Great White Brotherhood, to uplift humanity through the gradual rise of civilization. The plan includes the creation of a new Golden Age, where the New Jerusalem would be created following a cataclysmic pole shift predicted to occur on May 5, 2000, when a planetary alignment occurs. Europe will be located at the North Pole, and North America will shift south. According to the Lemurian Fellowship, this will be a literal time for the Kingdom of God on Earth.

As we are entering the next millemium, one has to reflect on these ancient civilizations and the knowledge they have shared. Some have undergone great destructive catalclysms, while other civilizations were seeded from their legacy. Prophecies from the ancients predict major planetary changes to occur as we now enter the age of Aquarius, and many in today's society are planning for such changes. Have we learned anything from our ancient past to prevent us from experiencing what our forefathers suffered? Or, are these planetary changes a necessary step in humanity's evolution? This next millennium will provide the answer.

Other Sacred Science Chrinicles

Keepers of the Secrets, Volume II of the *Sacred Science Chronicles,* gives the reader a unique perspective of mystical societies throughout civilization. It summarizes the history and spiritual philosophy of the shamans, Druids, Essenes, Gnostics, Hermetics, Kabbalists, alchemists, magicians, witches, Sufis, Rosicrucians, and Freemasons. The book provides insight on how these societies have influenced the world through the centuries.

These mystical societies shared many spiritual truths that contradicted orthodox beliefs. As a result, the church and state tried to suppress most of these societies, forcing them to become secret as humanity was not ready for many of these truths.

The Science of Soul: Proof of a Spiritual World is Volume III of *The Sacred Science Chronicles.* It will be available at the end of 1999.

To update your set of *Sacred Science Chronicles,* please contact your local bookstore of Sacred Science Publications.

REFERENCES

Listed below the reference material are the subheadings of the chapter with the reference numbers indicated

CHAPTER ONE: LEMURIA

(1) Blavatsky, H.P., *The Secret Doctrine, The Synthesis of Science, Religion, and Philosophy,* The Theosophical Publishing Company, 1888, 1977.

(2) Cerve, Wishar S., *The Lost Continent of the Pacific,* Grand Lodge of Amorc, Inc, 1931.

(3) Churchward, James, *The Lost Continent of Mu,* Ives Washburn, New York, 1931.

(4) Churchward, James, *The Children of Mu,* Ives Washburn, New York, 1931.

(5) Churchward, James, *The Saced Symbols of Mu,* Ives Washburn, New York, 1933.

> Ancient Writings (2) (3) (5)
> Land of Mu (2) (3) (4)
> The People (2) (3) (4)
> Spiritual Philosophy (2) (3) (4)
> Remnants of Lemuria (3) (4)
> Colonization (1) (2) (3) (4)

CHAPTER TWO: ATLANTIS

(1) Berlitz, Charles, *The Mystery of Atlantis,* Avon, New York, 1969

(2) Donnelly, Ignatius, *Atlantis,* Harper & Row Publishers, San Francisco, 1971.

(3) Hope, Murray, *Atlantis, Myth or Reality!,* Penguin Books, London, 1991.

(4) Muck, Otto, *The Secrets of Atlantis,* Times Books, New York, 1978.

(5) Spence, Lewis, *The History of Atlantis,* Adventures Unlimited Press, Kempton, Illinois, 1996 (first published 1926).

> Introduction (1) (2) (3) (5)
> Plato's Atlantis (2) (3) (4) (5)
> Legendary Evidence (1) (2) (3) (4) (5)
> Geological Evidence (1) (2) (3) (4)
> The Races of Atlantis (3) (4) (5)
> The Kings and Gods of Atlantis (2) (3) (4) (5)
> Other Mysteries of Atlantis (1) (3)

CHAPTER THREE: SUMER

(1) Contenau, Georges, *Everyday Life in Babylon and Assyria,* Edward Arnold Publishing, Ltd., London, 1954.

(2) Cottrell, Leonard, *The Quest for Sumer,* G. P. Putnam's Sons, New York, 1965.

(3) Kramer, Samuel N., *The Sumerians: Their History, Culture, and Character,* The University of Chicago Presss, 1963.

(4) Kramer, Samuel N., *History Begins at Sumer,* Thames & Hudson, London, 1956.

(5) Nesbit, William M., *Sumerian Records from Drehem,* AMS Press Inc., New York, 1966.

(6) Woolley, Leonard C., *The Sumerians,* Norton & Company, New York, 1965.
> Introduction (2) (3) (4)
> History (1) (2) (3) (5) (6)
> The People Of Sumer (2) (3) (6)
> Sumer's Economy (3) (4) (6)
> The Government (2) (3) (4) (6)
> Science and Art (2) (3) (4) (6)
> Religions and Gods (2) (3) (4) (6)

CHAPTER FOUR: THE ANCIENT GODS

(1) Sitchin, Zecharia, *The Twelfth Planet,* Avon Books, New York, 1976.
(2) Sitchin, Zecharia, *The Stairway to Heaven,* Avon Books, New York, 1980.
(3) Sitchin, Zecharia, *The Wars of God and Men,* Avon Books, 1985.
> Introduction (3)
> The Creation of Earth (1) (2)
> Colonization of Earth (1) (3)
> The Creation of Man (1) (3)
> Early Man (1) (2) (3)
> A Nuclear Catastrophe (3)
> The Interactions of Gods (1) (3)
> Egypt and the Sumerian Gods (1) (3)

CHAPTER FIVE: EGYPT

(1) Capt, Raymond E., *The Great Pyramid Decoded,* Artisan Sales, 1971.
(2) Hancock, Graham and Robert Bauval, *The Message of the Sphinx, A Quest for the Hidden Legacy of Mankind,* Three Rivers Press, New York, 1996.
(3) Lemesurier, Peter, *The Great Pyramid Decoded,* Element, Rockport, Massachusetts, 1977.
(4) Montet, Pierre, *History of Civilization, Eternal Egypt,* Praeger Publishers, New York, 1969.
(5) Pochan, A., *The Mysteries of the Great Pyramid,* Avon Books, New York, 1971.
(6) Smith, Worth, *Miracle of the Ages,* Book of Gold, Tarrytown, New York, 1948.
(7) Waddell, W. G. (Translator), *The Aegyptiaca of Manetho: Manetho's History of Egypt,* Harvard University Press, London, 1940.
(8) West, John Anthony, *Serpent in the Sky, The High Wisdom of Ancient Egypt,* Quest Books, Wheaton, Illinois, 1993 (first published in 1978).
> Early History (2) (4) (7) (8)
> The Sphinx (2) (8)
> The Pyramids (1) (2) (5) (6) (8)
> Sacred Science (1) (2) (3) (8)

CHAPTER SIX: THE PHARAOHS AND GODS

(1) Hancock, Graham and Bauval, Robert, *The Message of the Sphinx A Quest for the Hidden Legacy of Mankind,* Three Rivers Press, New York, 1996.

(2) Meeks, Dimitri and Christine Favaro Meeks, *Daily Life of the Egyptian Gods,* Cornell University Press, Ithaca and London, 1996.

(3) Montet, Pierre, *History of Civilization, Eternal Egypt,* Praeger Publishers, New York, 1969.

(4) Pochan, A., *The Mysteries of the Great Pyramids,* Avon Books, New York, 1971.

(5) Rawlinson, George, *History of Ancient Egypt, Vol. I,* Dodd, Mead, & Co., New York, 1897.

(6) Sitchin, Zecharia, *The Stairway to Heaven,* Avon Books, New York, 1980.

(7) Waddell, W. G., *The Aegyptiaca of Manetho: Manetho's History of Egypt,* Harvard University Press, London, 1940.

(8) West, John Anthony, *Serpent in the Sky, The High Wisdom of Ancient Egypt,* Quest Books, Wheaton, Illinois, 1993.
>   Pharaohs (1) (3) (7)
>   Moses (7)
>   The Gods (1) (2) (3) (5) (6) (8)
>   The Afterlife (2) (3) (4) (6) (8)
>   Initiation and the Name (1) (4) (8)

CHAPTER SEVEN: LOST CIVILIZATIONS OF CENTRAL AMERICA

(1) Arguelles, Jose, *The Mayan Factor: Path Beyond Technology,* Bear & Company, Santa Fe, New Mexico, 1987.

(2) Brundage, Burr Cartwright, *The Fifth Sun, Aztec Gods, Aztec World,* University of Texas Press, Austin, 1979.

(3) Carrasco, David, *Quetzalcoatl and the Irony of Empire, Myths and Prophecies in the Aztec Tradition,* The University of Chicago Press, Chicago, 1992.

(4) Gallenkamp, Charles, *The Riddle and Rediscovery of a Lost Civilization, Maya,* Penguin Books, New York, 1985.

(5) Graulich, Michel, *Myths of Ancient Mexico,* University of Oklahoma Press, Norman, 1997.

(6) Morley, Sylvanus Griswold (revised by George Brainerd), *The Ancient Maya,* Stanford University Press, Stanford, California, 1946.

(7) Tompkins, Peter, *Mysteries of Mexican Pyramids,* Harper & Row, New York, 1976.

(8) Sharer, Robert J., *The Ancient Maya (Fifth Edition),* Stanford University Press, Stanford, California, 1994.

(9) Sitchin, Zecharia, *The Lost Realms,* Avon Books, New York, 1990.

(10) Waters, Frank, *Mexico Mystique, The Coming Sixth World of Consciousness,* Sage Books, Chicago, 1975.
>   Introduction (8) (10)
>   The Atlantean Legacy (7)
>   The Olmecs (7) (9)
>   The Maya (4) (6) (7) (8)
>   The Toltecs (1) (3) (5) (9) (10)
>   The Aztecs (2) (9) (10)
>   The Pyramids (7) (10)

CHAPTER EIGHT: THE LEGENDS AND GODS OF MESOAMERICA

(1) Arquelles, Jose, *The Mayan Factor: Path Beyond Technology,* Bear & Company, Santa Fe, New Mexico, 1987.

(2) Brundage, Burr Cartwright, *The Fifth Sun, Aztec Gods, Aztec World,* University of Texas Press, Austin, 1979.

(3) Carrasco, David, *Quetzalcoatl and the Irony of Europe, Myths and Prophecies,* The University of Chicago Press, Chicago, 1992.

(4) Freidel, David, Schele, Linda, and Joy Parker, Maya Cosmos, *Three Thousand Years on the Shamans Path,* William Morrow and Company, 1993.

(5) Gallenkamp, Charles, *The Riddle and Rediscovery of a Lost Civilization, Maya,* Penguin Books, New York, 1985.

(6) Graulich, Michel, *Myths of Ancient Mexico,* University of Oklahoma Press, Norman, 1997.

(7) Markman, Roberta and Peter T. Markman, *The Flayed God, The Mesoamerican Mythological Tradition,* Harper, San Francisco, 1992.

(8) Morley, Sylvanus Griswold (Revised by George Brainerd), *The Ancient Maya,* Stanford University Press, Stanford, California, 1946.

(9) Sharer, Robert J., *The Ancient Maya (Fifth Edition),* Stanford University Press, Stanford, California, 1994.

(10) Sitchin, Zecharia, *The Lost Realms,* Avon Books, 1990.

(11) Tedlock, Dennis, *Popul Vuh,* Touchstone Book, New York, 1996.

(12) Tompkins, Peter, *Mysteries of Mexican Pyramids,* Harper & Row, New York, 1976.

(13) Waters, Frank, *The Coming Sixth World of Consciousness,* Sage Books, Chicago, 1975.

> Cosmology of Mesoamerica (3) (4) (6) (7) (10)
> Quetzalcoatl (2) (3) (7) (10) (13)
> The Mayan Calendar (1) (5) (8) (10) (12)
> The Mayan Factor (1)
> The Spiritual Influence (5) (6) (7) (8) (9) (12)
> Human Sacrifice (3) (8) (10)

CHAPTER NINE: MYSTERIES IN THE ANDES

(1) Cobo, Father Bernabe (Translated by Roland Hamilton), *Inca Religion and Custom,* University of Texas Press, Austin, 1990.

(2) Davies, Nigel, *The Incas,* University Press of Colorado, Niwot, 1995.

(3) Hancock, Graham, *Fingerprints of the Gods,* Crown Publishers, Inc., New York, 1995.

(4) Means, Philip Ainsworth, *Ancient Civilizations of the Andes,* Gordian Press, Inc., New York, 1964.

(5) Sitchin, Zecharia, *The Lost Realms,* Avon Books, New York, 1990.

(6) Sullivan, William, *The Secret of the Incas: Myth, Astronomy, and the War Against Time,* Crown Publishing, New York, 1996.

(7) Von Daniken, Erik, *Chariots of the Gods,* Bantom Books, 1968.
  Introduction (3) (5) (6)
  Lake Titicaca (2) (3) (4) (5)
  Cuzco, The Sacred City (3) (5) (7)
  Viracocha and Andean Spirituality (1) (3) (6)
  The Nazca Figures (3) (7)

CHAPTER TEN: ANCIENT MEDITERRANEAN AND EUROPEAN CIVILIZATIONS

(1) Aubert, Maria Eugenia, *The Phoenicians and the West,* Cambridge University Press, New York, 1987.
(2) Ceram, C. W., *Narrow Pass, Black Mountain, The Discovery of the Hittite Empire,* Victor Gollancz, Limited, London, 1955.
(3) Childress, David Hatcher, *Lost Cities of Atlantis, Ancient Europe, and the Mediterranean,* Adventures Unlimited Press, Stelle, Illinois, 1996.
(4) Edwards, Frank, *Strange Worlds,* Bantom Books, New York City, 1964.
(5) Ellul, Joseph, *Malta's Prediluvian Culture,* Printwell, Malta, 1988.
(6) Gurney, O. R., *The Hittites,* Penquin Books, 1952.
(7) Hancock, Graham, *Fingerprints of the Gods,* Crown Publishing, Inc., New York, 1995.
(8) Harden, Donald, *The Phoenicians,* Thames and Hudson, London, 1962.
(9) Herm, Gerhard, *The Phoenicians,* William Morrow and Company, Inc., New York, 1975.
(10) Lehmann, Johannes, *The Hittites, People of a Thousand Gods,* The Viking Press, New York, 1975.
(11) MacQueen, J. G., *The Hittites and their Contemporaries in Asia Minor,* Westview Press, Boulder, CO, 1975.
(12) Mavor, James W., *Voyage to Atlantis, The Discovery of a Legendary Land,* Park Street Press, Rochester, Vermont, 1969.
(13) Noorberger, Rene, *Secrets of the Lost Races,* Barnes & Noble Publishers, New York, 1977.
(14) Scrutton, Robert, *Secrets of Lost Atland,* Neville Spearman, Jersey, 1978.
(15) Sitchin, Zecharia, *The Wars of Gods and Men,* Avon Books, New York, 1985.
(16) Sitchin, Zecharia, *The Twelfth Planet,* Avon Books, New York, 1976.
(17) Sitchin, Zecharia, *The Lost Realms,* Avon Books, New York, 1990.
(18) Wisham, E. M., *Atlantis in Andulucia,* Rider Publishing, London. Reprinted as *Atlantis in Spain,* Adventures Unlimited, Stelle, Illinois.
  Introduction (3)
  The Hittites (2) (3) (4) (6) (10) (11) (15) (16) (17)
  The Minoan Empire (3) (9) (12) (16)
  Phoenicians (1) (3) (7) (8) (9)
  The Ancient Mediterranean (3) (5)
  Ancient European Civilizations (3) (13) (14) (18)

CHAPTER ELEVEN: ANCIENT NORTH AMERICA
(1) Childress, David Hatcher, *Lost Cities of North and Central America,* Adventures Unlimited Press, Stelle, Illinois, 1992.
(2) Fell, Barry, *Ancient Settlers in the New World,* Wildwood House, London, 1976.
(3) Fell, Barry, *Saga America,*Time Books, New York, 1980.
(4) Goodman, Jeffrey, *American Genesis,* Summitt Books, New York, 1981.
(5) Joseph, Frank, *Atlantis in Wisconsin,* Glade Press, Inc., St. Paul, Minnesota, 1995.

Introduction (2) (4)
Copper in America (1) (5)
Celtic America (2) (3) (4)
The Mounds of America (1)
The Phoenician Connection (2) (3)
Egypt and Libya (1) (2) (3)
Ancient Coins in America (3)
The Ancient American Jew (1) (3) (4)
The American Indian (4)
Atlantis and Lemuria (1)

INDEX

σ   273